Bernard Shaw's Ready-Reckoner

BERNARD SHAW'S
READY-RECKONER

A Guide to Civilization

Edited and with an Introduction by

N. H. LEIGH-TAYLOR

Random House   New York

Preface to *Fabian Essays*, first published 1889, Second Edition 1908, Third Edition 1920, Fourth Edition 1931, Jubilee Edition 1948.

Widower's Houses, The Philanderer, Mrs. Warren's Profession, Copyright 1898 by George Bernard Shaw, Copyright 1898 by Herbert S. Stone & Co., Copyright 1905 by Brentano's.

Candida, Copyright 1898 by George Bernard Shaw, Renewal Copyright 1926 by George Bernard Shaw.

You Never Can Tell, Copyright 1898 by Herbert S. Stone & Co., Copyright 1926 by Bernard Shaw.

Preface to *Pygmalion*, Copyright 1900 by Herbert S. Stone & Co., Renewal Copyright 1928 by George Bernard Shaw.

Man and Superman and *The Revolutionist's Handbook and Pocket Companion*, Copyright 1903 by G. Bernard Shaw.

The Irrational Knot and Preface to *The Irrational Knot*, Copyright 1905 by G. Bernard Shaw.

How He Lied to Her Husband, Major Barbara, and Preface to *Major Barbara*, first published 1907. Revised and reprinted for . . . Standard Edition 1932. All rights fully protected and reserved.

Getting Married and Preface to *Getting Married*, Copyright 1909 by Brentano's, Copyright 1911 by G. Bernard Shaw.

Misalliance and Preface to *Misalliance*, first published 1910. Revised and reprinted for . . . Standard Edition 1932. All rights fully protected and reserved.

Androcles and the Lion, Preface and Epilogue to *Androcles and the Lion*, Copyright 1913 by George Bernard Shaw. Renewal Copyright by George Bernard Shaw.

Heartbreak House, Copyright 1919 by George Bernard Shaw.

Peace Conference Hints, Copyright 1919 by George Bernard Shaw.

Back to Methuselah, Copyright 1921 by George Bernard Shaw.

The Intelligent Woman's Guide to Socialism and Capitalism, Copyright 1928 by Brentano's, Inc.

The Apple Cart and Preface to *The Apple Cart*, Copyright 1930, 1931 by George Bernard Shaw.

Overruled and Preface to *Overruled*, Copyright 1930 by George Bernard Shaw, Copyright © 1958 The Public Trustee as Executor of the Estate of George Bernard Shaw.

Sham Education and *Crude Criminology*, first published 1931 in the Limited Collected Edition. Revised and reprinted for . . . Standard Edition 1932, reprinted 1950.

"The Transition to Social Democracy," "The Economic Basis of Socialism," "The Impossibilities of Anarchism," "Socialism & Superior Brains," "Socialism for Millionaires," and "The Common Sense of Muncipal Trading," first published in the Limited Collected Edition 1932. Revised and reprinted for . . . Standard Edition 1932.

The Future of Political Science in America, Copyright 1933 by George Bernard Shaw.

Too True To Be Good and Preface to *Too True To Be Good*, *On the Rocks* and Preface to *On the Rocks*, Copyright 1934 by George Bernard Shaw.

Village Wooing, Copyright 1934 by George Bernard Shaw, Copyright © 1958 The Public Trustee of the Estate of George Bernard Shaw.

Preface to *The Simpleton of the Unexpected Isles, The Millionaires* and Preface to *The Millionaires*, Copyright 1936 by George Bernard Shaw.

Everybody's Political What's What?, Copyright 1944 by George Bernard Shaw.

Sixteen Self Sketches, Copyright 1949 by George Bernard Shaw.

Buoyant Billions, Farfetched Fables and Preface to *Farfetched Fables*, Copyright 1948, 1949 by George Bernard Shaw, Copyright 1950, 1951 by The Estate of George Bernard Shaw.

Love Among the Artists, Copyright in Berne Convention Countries. All rights reserved. Issued in 1962 by The Viking Press.

To the Memory of
P. F. Leigh-Taylor
Parent and Shavian

CONTENTS

the Gods • Worldliness of the Majority • The Impostor
in Strange Robes • Same Salvation for All • The Average
Clergyman • "Gawd" with a Long Face • The Philistine
Church • "Really, Barbara . . ." • The Church Captured
by the Rich • Sermons Will Not Kill Poverty & Slavery
• "My Religion? . . ." • Torpedo Morality • The Reli-
gious Bodies: Auxiliary Police • Cheap Conversion • The
Way to Get Rescue Money • Why the Christian System
Failed • The Church Corrupted by Its Own Property •
Russia Rediscovers the Church System • Russia Teaches
Christian Communism

CRIME AND PUNISHMENT   37

Competition in Evil Between Prison & Slum • What Price
the Exchange? • The Economy Aspect • Soft Cases that
We Turn into Hard Ones • Most Prisoners no Worse than
Ourselves • Honesty Varies with the Strain Put on It • The
Trade in Good Looks • Our Plague of Unrestrained Crime •
Criminal Characteristics in Polite Society • The Model Em-
ployer • Man Must Justify His Existence • Torture as
Justice • Contracting-Out of the Moral Code

DEMOCRACY   49

"Democracy reads well . . ." • Democracy: The Vision &
The Reality • Anarchism's Supreme Achievement • Slaves
Will Be Slaves • The Constitution: A Great Protest • The
Government: A Gabble Shop • Democracy's Pretenses •
Democracy: Unashamed Plutocracy • Limits of the Indis-
pensable Man • "Air, Promise Crammed" • The Mounte-
bank Catches the Votes • Democracy: Anarchy • Democ-
racy versus Time • Democracy's Extravagant Hopes •
Democracy & the Madness of God • Political Proselytizing
• The Two Inseparable Problems • Democracy a Nuisance
• The State: Robber & Slavedriver • The People against
the Classes

Contents

Profit • Commercial Auditing Absurd in Municipal Business • Incentive: Commercial & Municipal • Public Need & Purchasing Power • Private Enterprise Not Enterprising Enough • Commercial Man's Grievance • The Ordinary Citizen: His Sense of Property • Unfair Competition? • Municipal Enterprise Struggles

A Special Occasion Difference • The Question We Never Tire of • Sex Relation Impersonal • Two Storeys to Men & Women • Majority Ignorance • Secrecy No Solution • Sexual Instruction: Nasty Stories & Whispered Traditions • Sex Candor Curiously Disconcerting • The Duel of Sex • Jealousy Independent of Sex • Honorable Advances: An Extraordinary Irrelevance • Scientific Natural History Needed • Sexual Attraction Misused • Absolute Right to Sexual Experience • The Woman of Fifty • "Oh, these sex episodes! . . ." • Daydreams about Women • Sexual Intercourse Not Delinquency • Sex: A Prelude to Intellectual Ecstasy • The Promiscuity Legend • Disproportionately Savage Punishments • Lopsided Sex Laws • Monogamy Will Take Care of Itself • Sedulously Inculcated False Notion • "Don't Tell Me: I Don't Want To Know"

Love the First Need • "Ah, if we were only . . ." • "Love gets people into . . ." • "How is a man . . ." • A Queer Thing • Love: Three Quarters Curiosity • A Man Cant Keep It Up • Love: Slavery • Love the Inexplicable • Love in Imagination • Love: A Tiresome Subject • Love: Illusions, Infatuations, Impulses • The Brain Says No, Life Says Yes • The Test of Domestic Familiarity • A Man's Heart • "Remember: a man's power . . ." • An Unregretted Deficiency • Love's Growing Pains • Love: Tedious & Terrifying • "Yes, my dear . . ." • A Common Mistake • "The fickleness of women . . ." • Passion:

Contents   (*xiii*

INTRODUCTION

This book is neither another "interpretation" of Bernard Shaw nor a compilation of the "wit and wisdom" kind, but a presentation in condensed form of his ideas on important social questions. It consists entirely of extracts from novels, tracts, plays, prefaces, articles, and textbooks written between the years 1880 and 1949. His age at the beginning of this period was twenty-three, at the end, ninety-three. To the inevitable question, "Have we not had enough of Shaw's books?" the following answer must be given.

A first justification for this assembly of Shaw's exhortations to mankind to develop better habits and aspirations is derived from his own *Everybody's Political What's What?*, toward the end of which the following paragraph appears: "The pressing need for breaking off this unfinishable book has now become imperative. It consists largely of things often said before by myself and others. They will have to be said again and again, oftener than a nail has to be hit by a hammer, before they get effectively knocked into Mr Everyman's consciousness." Mr Everyman, conditioned by the present trend toward capsulization of the thoughts of the great, may stand aghast at the prospect of plowing through the prodigious mass of Shaw's work, but will perhaps find this distillation a relatively painless means of acquainting or reacquainting himself with the essence of Shaw's social views. Let it not be supposed, however, that the ideas propounded by Shaw are any easier to take merely by reason of their having been squeezed into one volume rather than twenty.

An equally valid reason for floating such a work as this into the contemporary sea of social opinion is that the old notion that truth will triumph in any free exchange of ideas cannot be taken for granted. Truth may triumph in bits and pieces, but our newspapers and popular journals demonstrate beyond a doubt that it is too often crushed by lies, delusion, myth, and hypocrisy. Another difficulty regarding truth in the social sciences is that, unlike mathematical truth, it may not be the same thing to different people or in different times and places. For most if not all of us, such a dilemma is solved by studying the thought of those extraordinary mortals who seem to be endowed with superior vision, but they too have their personal dilemmas, complicating the matter of truth-seeking still further.

The core of Shaw's predicament appears in its most concentrated form in the Don Juan in Hell sequence of *Man and Superman,* an eloquent exposition of futility and the doom of man. Like Schweitzer,[1] Shaw was appalled when he looked at the world of men, but discouragement and renunciation were paths neither of them found it possible to take. While Schweitzer packed himself off to Africa to become dedicated to healing the sick and to writing appeals to mankind to develop more reverence for life, Shaw stuck it out at the center of civilization and mounted upon his gloomy knowledge of man's frailties a campaign for the remaking of society that placed him in the front rank of agitator-reformers. His greatness thus lies not so much in the tremendous fecundity of his mind nor in the matchless brilliance of his prose, the qualities on which his popular reputation rests and which he regarded as natural endowments for which he could not take the credit, but in his tenacious struggle to keep himself above despair and spell out the direction in which man's hopes lay.

[1] Albert Schweitzer, *Out of My Life and Thought, An Autobiography,* Translated by C. T. Campion, (see p. 186), New York: the New American Library, (Mentor) 1960.

Whether or not his lifelong occupation, "world-bettering," a term he used in his play *Buoyant Billions,* was a delusive pursuit, must be left to the psychologists to wrestle with, and to time for a conclusive answer. We can partially solve the question by applying to Shaw the test he himself said must be put to every artist-thinker: Did he have a proper message for his Age? Since the Man with a Message is, according to the evidence of history, all too often born before his time, it must also be asked if he was a true prophet.

Shaw's standing as seer cannot be determined by reading what others have written about him, but only by looking at what *he* wrote. Simple as this prescription sounds, it is necessary to remember that examining the original works of soothsayers is frequently if not most of the time frowned upon by "official interpreters." The withholding of the Bible from Catholics, the suppression of "subversive" literature, and the censoring of "obscene" matter are familiar examples of the fear produced by boat-rocking truths in what is now called The Establishment. A close look at Shaw's pronouncements and predictions concerning the civilization that his genius forced him to dissect shows clearly enough why The Establishment, or The Machine, or Vested Interest, or whatever you want to name it, is quite content to see him consigned to history as a funny old cranky Irishman.

One of the almost endless list of points on which Shaw penetrated the mud of superstition, habit, and ignorance to the bedrock of fact was in connection with Trade Unionism, which he called a department of free enterprise and not at all a true organization of the working class. He warned that the time would come when the outcry against robber barons would change to a call for regulation of the unions. The Taft-Hartley Act and other legislation aimed at control of organized labor in the United States, and similar measures in other free enterprise nations, testify to the truth of this prophecy.

Consider his observations on the duel between private and public enterprise in *The Common Sense of Municipal Trading.* They are even more pertinent today than when he wrote the tract in 1904, especially in the United States, where book after book, notably Lincoln Steffens' *The Shame of the Cities*, exposes the continuing corruption and waste that is central to the folly of trying to conduct public business while at the same time catering to the clamor of private money interests which insist on their "democratic" right to a reasonable profit.[2] The ultimate insanity of this perpetual war between personal privilege and the common welfare is that at each new scandal about profiteering on a government contract (whether city, state or Federal), some foolishly righteous citizen can be relied on to denounce the money-grabbers and to say not one word about the fundamental American belief in the sacredness of the profit motive, which requires the free-enterprisers to get whatever they can at the expense of whatever victim is handy. These tedious denunciations of venality are a dime a thousand in the American scandal industry, a prosperous one in itself, but does anybody, except the Socialists or the Communists (whose voices are very small in domestic affairs), dare to suggest that the profit game had better be scrapped as thoroughly impractical, and replaced by methods of government and public service not based on keeping secret from the right hand what the left is doing. Shaw proposed this, as many others did and do, the special merit of it in his case being that he declined the safe honor of practicing art for art's sake, at which he could have achieved sufficient eminence, and always responded in fullest measure to the inner light that drove him to speak out clearly and courageously against sham wherever he found it. (In "Mainly About Myself," the Preface to Volume One of *Plays, Pleasant & Unpleasant*, Shaw offers insight into the passions that activated him as a responsible citizen.)

[2] At the Federal level, the game of "dualism" is well documented in Kenneth G. Crawford's *The Pressure Boys* (New York: Julian Messner, 1939). An interesting fact is that Shaw was castigated by many Americans, including his authorized biographer Archibald Henderson, for flagrant misrepresentation in writing about a "country he had never visited." That his comments on the United States were painfully on target can be ascertained by looking into such American works as Thorstein Veblen's *The Theory of the Leisure Class*, Theodore Dreiser's *America is Worth Saving*, and the more recent studies of the sociologist C. Wright Mills.

Remembering his agonies of shyness as a young man and his fear of physical assault, the record of Shaw's public life becomes even more impressive. We have only to think of our own timidities, of how the great majority of us shrink from voicing even a conventional opinion, much less a dissident or rebellious one, in a public setting, to realize Shaw's achievement. (In middle age, when his career as an artist was going full blast, he still managed to put in several years' service with the London municipal government, a task that must have taxed his sensibilities and patience to the limit.) We may fall back on the theory that if a man's vanity, and his desire for the adulation and applause of the crowd, are powerful enough, he will become a celebrity regardless of the obstacles in his path. The theory may be good for general purposes, but in the case of Shaw it is inadequate, for he achieved his fame not in one of the many quite ordinary and safe ways in which it is possible to become a distinguished personage, but as a defier of society. And his defiance was not simply the neurotic shotgun anger of the undisciplined and directionless anarchist, but from the very start of his writing, and later his public speaking, it was the careful criticism of an astute and irresistibly humane man answering the call of his conscience. This fact shines through all the arrogant clownishness and bland conceit with which he tried to camouflage his very real sensitivity.

The five novels he wrote during his twenties (his apprenticeship as an author, he calls them), though stiff as to style—[3] Shaw himself readily conceded this—are first-rate social documents deeply concerned with human folly and dilemma. (It is obvious in these early works, incidentally, why Shaw could not have become a pure tracteer in the fashion of a De Leon or a Lenin, but had to allow his brain to range over the entire spectrum of human affairs, a fact which provoked cries of "sell-out" and deviationism from some quarters of the dogmatic left.) In contrast, the first work of Upton Sinclair, destined to emerge as Shaw's great peer

[3] The "stiffness" of Shaw's language in the novels was not so much an individual trait as a reflection of the literary style of the age. A famous American novel of the period, Henry Adams' *Democracy*, is written in a style almost identical with that of Shaw.

in propagandizing for socialism, was literary trifling: manufacturing adventure stories for the going market. It is true that Sinclair's hackwork was done while he was in his teens, and that at the age of twenty-five he set the world agog with *The Jungle,* which placed him immediately in the front rank as a protest writer. Thus he imposed himself on the world at a much earlier age than Shaw, and gained a reputation equal to Shaw's as a writer who looked at civilization with the utmost seriousness and determination to change it for the better. But though Shaw was a comparatively late starter in point of public recognition, he wasted no time in committing himself to the risky role of rebel. His own view of such commitment was that anyone who passed the age of thirty without becoming a socialist was either an ignoramus or a scoundrel, and he lived up to his own preachment, carrying it to the length of delivering socialist lectures on the streets of London, a means by which, he wrote, he conquered his shyness. Consider, on this point, the case of Theodore Dreiser, whose novels were much like the youthful works of Shaw in abundance of detail and heaviness of style. It was not until his declining years that Dreiser made a public avowal of communism as the coming basis of civilization, and was villified for his mature convictions, a perfectly logical event in this country, where socialism is regarded at best as a childish dream of visionaries and at worst as a creeping cancer that threatens to destroy the "greatness" of America.

Shaw was criticized as something less than a great revolutionary on the ground that he had never gone to jail for his beliefs, the presumption being that a true Marxist is not complete nor authoritative until he has served a prison term as a dangerous subversive. This simplification of the specifications for revolutionary heroism may hold true for certain times and places, but what can its advocates say of the fact that the arch-communists Engels and Marx, during all their active years in England, never once were put in jail? Shaw openly proclaimed that Marx "made a man of him," and continued to call himself a communist throughout his long life, though Engels and other Marxists regarded the Fabian socialists, of which Shaw was a brilliant spokesman, as "silly." He did everything, short of throwing bombs or carrying a loaded rifle, that could have been expected of him as an anti-capitalist. But the British capitalists would not rise to the bait, first because they were accustomed to London as a haven for revolutionaries of all sorts who were allowed to write and talk as much as they pleased so long as they did not become violent, and second because they were so firm in their faith in the imperishability of British ways and capitalism that they could not bring themselves to take the agitators seriously. Besides, as Shaw often pointed out, there were always the soldiers and the police to put down any real insurrection, in which case, he asserted, you would be likely to find him under the bed, for he was no front-line fist-and-bullet actionist, but essentially a man of the pen. On this score, too, he has been found wanting as a complete revolutionary by some critics of the left.

The brilliant young communist writer Christopher Caudwell, who died in 1936 at age twenty-nine while fighting with the British Battalion of the International Brigade in Spain, wrote perhaps the most damning denunciation of Shaw, calling him a bourgeois superman and a pseudo-socialist, an "intellectual attempting to dominate hostile reality by 'pure' thought."[4] In point of simple fact, Caudwell had the advantage of Shaw in that he was an intellectual who actually went off to a real war to fight fascism; in this he was the ideal proletarian hero—a man of thought and a man of action. The fact that he died in vain, that the side on which he fought was crushed by the big guns and money of fascism, does not invalidate the question that he raised in his attack on Shaw, a question that is central to the biggest issue of our time: Will the world of tomorrow be a capitalist world or a communist one, and will it be arrived at by the gradualism that has brought about Britain's present mongrel form of socialism-capitalism or by laying on with bayonet and dynamite? At the moment the issue is clouded by much talk of coexistence, and by serious attempts to make coexistence work, but the military might of both camps makes it obvious that an epic struggle continues

[4] *Studies and Further Studies in a Dying Culture,* New York: Dodd, Mead, 1958. Another work in the same vein is Alick West's *George Bernard Shaw,* "A Good Man Fallen Among Fabians," New York: International Publishers, 1950.

between the champions of socialism and those of capitalism. The natural inclination of most of us is to look the other way and pretend the problem is not there, which is easy enough when no bombs are dropping on our own houses and we are living in relative peace. But every day, somewhere on the globe, men are giving up their lives in the capitalist-communist conflict. The surviving relatives of these victims know well enough that there is no ground for the wishful belief that the conflict will be resolved by any sudden access of sense, common or uncommon. Besides, the intensity of the propaganda war on both sides makes short work of any illusion that it is a lightweight affair. Also, the propaganda is now conducted on a world-wide scale, so that no one alive may escape its implications. It forces us all to the painful extremity of having to ask ourselves: Can I manage to ride through this struggle somehow, playing both ends against the middle, so that I will come out unscathed on the far side, wherever and whatever the far side may be?

It was on this matter of tactics, the means by which capitalist society should be transformed into a socialist society, that the orthodox Marxist materialists based their principal grievance against Shaw, for they believed in a clear-cut class war necessitating the forceful seizure of power by the proletariat, whereas Shaw kept insisting that the classes overlapped each other, and that capitalist-style dreamers and idlers and parasites could be found among the lower classes as well as the upper. For this reason, he contended that it was ridiculous to expect to find, or even instil, the needed revolutionary enthusiasm in the working class. What was most desperately needed, he wrote, was a socialist conscience in the populace at large as a prelude to the establishment of socialism, and he and his fellow Fabians strove mightily to create that conscience in the British public. The good-and-bad quasi-socialism of present-day Britain is considered largely the result of their efforts, and the opinion has been expressed that this half-baked welfare state is proof of the futility of gradualism. Well before his death in 1950 at the age of ninety-four, Shaw had modified his hopes for the nonviolent, educative process of reforming society, and apparently conceded that no true communism could be established except by the ruthless imposition of its principles on the populace, followed up by equally ruthless stamping out, by firm re-education or by extermination where necessary, of every last shred of capitalist thought and practice. This was quite in keeping with his long-standing conviction that liberty under capitalism was a delusion; that the only true individual liberty for man was that which would issue from equal sharing of labor and leisure by the entire citizenry. These views are incorporated in his article "The Dictatorship of the Proletariat" published in the October, 1921, issue of the London journal *Labor Monthly.*

Shaw's kind words for Lenin and Stalin, along with his obdurate approval of the Russian experiment, made him a hero in the Soviet Union, and his former denunciations of "old-fashioned Marxist theories" and Lenin's description of him as "a good man fallen among Fabians" were swept into the dustbin of history. He was triumphantly received in Russia in 1931, and declared in a radio address to the Soviet people that the West, still playing with socialism, "will have to follow your steps whether we like it or no." In 1950, shortly before his death, he was still saying that the future belonged to communism, and that a war on communism "is ignorant blazing nonsense."[5]

Other advocates of socialism outside the Soviet Union could not swallow Shaw's wholehearted sanction of the new "red" society. Even Upton Sinclair, described as the most widely read socialist writer in the world, and whose works Shaw had called the true history of the United States, boggled at the Russian brand of socialism. Some socialists equated the Red Menace with fascism, and continue to this day to hold that view.

One of the serious implications of these divergent interpretations of the great Russian experiment issues from the question as to whether the "share and share alike" society is a dangerous delusion. (Shaw was an adamant advocate of absolute economic

[5] Interview in *Reynold's News,* August 6, 1950.

equality, saying there was no way of determining that one man's service to society was worth more than another's; so was Edward Bellamy in his pre-turn-of-the-century novels *Looking Backward* and *Equality*. But Russia has not yet established such a leveling of the national income.) One need only listen to popular oratory or read any newspaper editorial page to discover the familiar sentiment that the communist dream of an equalitarian society is not only pure delusion but psychopathic derangement. "Communists are madmen" is one of the first comments one hears in any discussion of the subject among people who get their opinions from the popular press (which must now include radio and television, where the very same kind of "news" and "opinion" are dispensed). Such thinking in terms of scare slogans, if it can be called thinking at all, has been amply dissected in such works as Stuart Chase's *The Tyranny of Words*, S. I. Hayakawa's *Language in Thought and Action*, and the book that inspired both Chase and Hayakawa to write theirs: *Science & Sanity*, by the Polish-American Alfred Korzybski. But though these men brought the logic of science to the realm of language and significs, and demonstrated with irrefutable clarity that the larger portion of what is daily given out as rational political comment is pure drivel, the American people continue to behave as if the old ways are quite good enough for them, and to submit by the tens of millions, without consciousness of irrationality, to hundred- and thousand-dollar-a-plate tweedledum-and-tweedledee democracy and to that great modern madness the election campaign, in which bidders for public office strive to outdo each other in a gibberish contest that drives the sensitive and informed citizen to distraction. The books on semantics mentioned above were well received in the United States, which brings us to one of Shaw's chronic complaints: No matter how often he and others repeated the truth, it needed always to be stated again and again, for the voice of reason seemed to have small power to influence the popular mind. Being a Fabian, he came to this conclusion reluctantly, for it meant that mankind would somehow have to be bludgeoned into helping itself if it could not do it by the relatively painless, or at least bloodless, process of education. This was no startling discovery, crushing as it might be to the one who must realize it against his fondest hopes. Plato's *Republic* and Sir Thomas More's *Utopia* both failed to move the world by the simple and eloquent power of reason.

Nor is it surprising to find the question of sanity raised whenever some stubborn individual persists in propagating an idea opposed to tradition. This was the case with Socrates and Christ, and seems to be the case with every poor mortal selected by destiny to be a hero of man's highest aspirations. There seems to be little doubt that "insanity" and what we call "progress" go hand in hand. Quite often, the insanity is disguised under some such epithet as villainy, heresy, anarchy or subversion, scare words under the power of which we all quake regardless of our pretensions to impartiality. Since the advent of Freud it has become fashionable to pin the label "neurotic" on those we wish to set apart as malcontents and misfits. Freud himself rejected communism, and one of his noted disciples, Robert Lindner,[6] regarded Soviet society as psychopathic and its system as a religious cult quite as distasteful as the "opium of the masses" that Marx denounced. Still another of Freud's followers, Erich Fromm,[7] placed Marx above Freud in importance to the world's progress. Fromm, however, did not join the Communist Party, but has thrown in his lot with one of the American socialist groups opposed to Russia. With such conflict of feeling or belief among celebrated thinkers, what are we average people to do about reaching decisions that historical pressure now seems to indicate we can no longer evade?

The social documentarian Robert S. Lynd has dealt with this question in the following way: "Even so-called 'scientific' description of social phenomena is inevitably selective, the field being strained . . . through the awareness of the observer as sensitized by his past experience." He goes on to say: "If research were mere photography science would stand still, swamped in the mass of undifferentiated and unoriented detail. Science depends on sensitized, coherent points of view oriented around reality."[8] This is

[6] *Must You Conform?*, New York: Grove Press, 1956.
[7] *Beyond the Chains of Illusion*, New York: Simon & Schuster, 1962.
[8] *Middletown In Transition*, Robert S. Lynd and Helen Merrell Lynd, New York: Harcourt, Brace, 1937. Preface, pp. xv, xvii.

no more than the "frame of reference" and the "co-ordinate factor" of Einstein's relativity concept, and its significance here is that those of us who have been misled by false interpretations and demagogic glamorization of an "open mind," as well as those who dread having to make decisions (all of us do), may avoid taking a stand forever on the ground that "everything is relative." The world is full of these avoidists, who take refuge in some form of mindless mysticism, or join humanist or utopian societies, or stand staunchly on their dignity as democrats or liberals or republicans, or whatever belief offers escape from the necessity of real thinking. Now Shaw observed the mass of detail in the social structure and knew at once that what he would most need to give expression to his genius was a firmly closed mind. In one of his letters to Ellen Terry he wrote: "In this world you must know *all* the points of view, and take One, and stick to it." He chose socialism as his co-ordinate factor, and stuck to it valiantly and spectacularly through the seventy years he was to live after reaching his decision. Shaw has been joined in his selection of viewpoint by some of the most distinguished men of our time, among them the "red" Dean of Canterbury, Hewlett Johnson, the artist Pablo Picasso, and the philosopher-playwright Jean-Paul Sartre. The socialist convictions of other great mortals, Albert Einstein and Helen Keller, for example, have been ignored by ruling interests only too glad to be able to play up some relatively undangerous aspect of the feared dissident.

It was Shaw's unswerving concept of socialism as man's only possible answer to the tyranny of natural fact, and to the lessons of history, that provoked astonishment, dismay, or anger among the myth-worshippers who confused sentiment and popular morality with hard truth, and therefore could not fathom his apparent inconsistencies which were in reality merely his steadfast, single-purposed attack upon their jumble of illogicalities. Thus, when he denounced "property" marriage and family life under capitalism as a morbid disgrace, advocated easy divorce *sans* scandal as the only means of averting the ruin of ill-mated persons, and recommended the legitimatizing of children born out of wedlock to ensure their economic security,[9] they thought he was proposing free-love and the break-up of home life. His own respectable marriage, which lasted almost half a century, caused still more ignorant comment, as if he had become a traitor to his own theories. When he became rich, the thoughtless ones made jokes about the "wealthy communist," ignoring his repeated warning that the poor as well as the rich could be saved only by socialist reconstruction, and that if he threw away his money to be gathered up by the poor, it would not be the starving destitute who got it but the able-bodied, well-fed ones. (His private philanthropies, which included contributions to the London *Daily Worker*, are now too well known to need repeating here.) Again, popular legend would have it that as a socialist, and therefore a crackpot "idealist," he must necessarily be a pacifist. He was, and so are we all, theoretically, but how idealist pacifism is set back on its heels is well demonstrated in the case of Einstein, a socialist and devout conscientious objector who was drawn into the vortex of World War II and subsequently obliged to explain, and apologize for, his connection with the development of the nuclear bomb. In a letter to the Japanese people he used precisely the same argument Shaw had used earlier: The public-spirited citizen caught in the madness of war must choose not pacifist do-nothingism but simply the least evil course. Einstein wrote that to bring the war to an end by dropping the A-bomb on Japan was a necessary crime, small in comparison to the barbarity of allowing the massacre to drag on indefinitely. Shaw had used essentially this reasoning in taking sides during the Boer War and World War I.

It was on the question of religion, however, that Shaw most upset the non-thinkers, to whom God meant property rights supported by church-going, hymn-singing, and common prayers.[10] That Shaw, as a "Godless" Marxist, would denounce such religion as Cross-

[9] Shaw's proposals regarding divorce and provision for children of unmarried parents, made over half a century ago, have just (February, 1964) been adopted as the basis of a new family law in the Soviet Union.

[10] One of Shaw's most impressive diatribes against historic religion is contained in Scene IV of *Saint Joan*, in which Cauchon, Warwick, and the Chaplain discuss Joan's heresy in terms of their own interests and, therefore, prejudices.

tianity, and write a play (*The Shewing-Up of Blanco Posnet*) which would earn the disfavor of the censor for its apparent irreverence respecting God Almighty, was to be expected. But it was the most outrageous inconsistency for him to say that mankind could not get along without a religion, and that moreover that religion should be communism. There had to be a recognition of right and wrong in our world, he said, and the only way in which such a sense could be inculcated was by religious instruction, as an adjunct to reading, writing, arithmetic, and the other necessities of civilized life. In his considered view (see the Preface to *Androcles and The Lion*), Christianity—which to him meant communism—had been slain with Christ and did not reappear until it became the foundation of the new Soviet society.

Such an idea must naturally appear preposterous to anyone who has been indoctrinated with the belief that Christianity and communism are antithetical. In his several writings on education—see for example the long essay *Sham Education* and certain portions of *The Intelligent Woman's Guide to Socialism and Capitalism* and of *Everybody's Political What's What?*—Shaw held that such indoctrination was calculatedly impressed on the young in capitalist countries, always had been, and always would be, so long as private property forced the Church to its will. There are some observers in the Western democracies who will tolerantly allow that the aims of communism are admirable, and perhaps even Christian, but that it simply will not work. They are of the "human nature" school of thought which declares that man's basic character will not permit him to function in an equalitarian state. They point to the evidence of crime and corruption in Russia and the other communist lands. Their final argument may be summed up as: "You see, Old Marx and Old Shaw and the rest of them dreamed their grand dream, but that's all it is—a dream. The human race is not good enough for it."

If ever there was a socialist who did *not* expect that the human race, as he found it, would welcome socialism and be capable of adopting it with as much ease as it sat down to breakfast, that socialist was Shaw. His entire career testifies to the fact that he kept one eye cocked on the possibility that the human race might have to be scrapped in favor of something better. His later plays deal endlessly with this theme. Such excursions into the question of man's ultimate destiny earned him the epithet "bourgeois superman," but it is ridiculous to call him either a pessimist or an unrealistic utopian on the basis of these later writings. He would not have been the Shaw who has enriched the world if he had not told us of his visions and premonitions concerning the future of man. But no matter in what direction his fertile imagination drove him, he never lost sight of his basic commitment to the problem of social economics. His *The Dictatorship of the Proletariat* concludes with these words: ". . . I should very much like to see Communism tried for a while before we give up civilization as a purely pathological phenomenon. At any rate, it can hardly produce worse results than Capitalism." He did not see socialism as an automatic paradise, but simply as the best arrangement by which man could replace money relations with real social relations, and begin the fight to conquer his own weaknesses. Again he was prophetic, for now in the Soviet press are appearing discussions of the future socialist man who will grow out of the society in which his material needs and useful employment have been guaranteed on a permanent basis.

Shaw's perpetual nagging at the problem of giving ourselves a chance to develop into something better, on the most realistic basis possible and not in any idle utopian terms, was an integral part of his role as agitator-prophet. He could no more have avoided dealing with this question than Marx could have avoided sitting in the British Museum (as Shaw did) year in and year out on his quest for facts that would reveal the economic basis of history. This drive for totalness, or for venturing beyond the safety fence of traditional thought, is the hallmark of the genius breed, and explains also why Freud, a timid man, had to persist in his embarrassingly intimate contacts with his patients. Knowing this, it is easier to understand both Shaw's multiple facets as artist-philosopher and the agonies of protest that arose from his tradition-bound critics.

Shaw's plays, a familiar complaint goes, lack realism. They are too talky and peopled with synthetic, unreal types. Such criticism can be equated with the attacks on Wagner who was accused of being incapable of "writing a tune," much less real music, or with the sneers leveled at Shaw's contemporary, Arnold Schoenberg, whose atonal music allegedly contained "no melody, no harmony, no rhythm." The breakdown of familiar forms achieved by Picasso aroused similar fury, but the protests were in vain, for the new drama as well as the new music and new art were due, and nothing could stop them. Had Shaw pursued what was understood as realism by the average critic of his day he would have been no more than another Ibsen, or a Pirandello, or an O'Neill—in other words, Shakespeare redone. Such realism culminates in the *Ulysses* of James Joyce, in Existentialism, in Henry Millerism, and in the works of the modern absurdist playwrights. (It is well to note that in his astonishing versatility Shaw anticipated the absurdists with the play considered by many to be his masterpiece, *Heartbreak House.*) Shaw was quite capable of the most precise kind of popular reality, as witness his portrait of an alcoholic lady of the theater in *The Irrational Knot,* Bill Walker in *Major Barbara,* Freddy Eynsford-Hill in *Pygmalion,* but in order to function at his own level as an historic synthesizer, and not at a dictated commercial level, he had to overlay his dramatic work with the special Shaw ingredient: Propaganda, a purpose skilfully advanced by what may be called a Shaw invention—the self-knowing character (Mr. Doolittle in *Pygmalion* is a conspicuous example of this amusing and useful device). He knew that ordinary realism of the mirror-to-life variety was a blind alley. This was the basis of his criticism of Shakespeare who, he said, had no message for his time. It was not enough for the artist to see life truly; he must add some judgment of what he saw, if he was capable of it. If he was not capable of dispensing constructive judgments, he was a mere art-for-art's-saker, despised by Shaw.

If propaganda was so necessary a part of his function as a playwright-thinker, why then did he not write pure proletarian plays, or at least "plays of the people" in the vein of his fellow communist-sympathizers, O'Casey and Brecht? As well ask Aristophanes or Molière why they did not write like Sophocles and Racine. Shaw saw his task in much the same spirit that infected his predecessor as the great man of European letters, Heinrich Heine, the sardonic rebel who called God "the Aristophanes of the Heavens." Shaw absolutely refused to take his assignment on earth as a punishment, or to dissolve in tears over the tragedy of it all. He would show God or the Life Force that he could not only take it like a man but fight back as well. And if the Ruler of the Universe was a Jokester (a thought not uncommon among serious thinkers), then he would employ the same weapon—laughter, because no other human device could possibly cope with the day-to-day trials of existence nor so effectively explode the conceits and pretensions and villainies of humanity. Anyone who has tried to plow his way through the dreary doctrinaire expositions of socialism that are available everywhere must be forever grateful that Shaw was determined to avoid being lost in the pages of the little protest journals which are always glad to print sober, scholarly articles that induce sleep rather than revolutionary fervor.

Yet Shaw was equally determined that he should not be misunderstood as a mere "funny Irishman," like Oscar Wilde, and in consequence was a lifelong tracteer, beginning with the *Fabian Essays*, continuing with the Prefaces to his plays and an endless stream of articles and letters to the press, and ending with *Everybody's Political What's What?*. It was with these didactic writings that he compensated for the necessary propaganda deficiencies of his plays (which might have died a-borning had they been overloaded with "message"). With exhaustive histories, monographs, and textbooks expanding on the themes of the plays he erected what must without a doubt be the most monumental pitched battle in history by a single individual doggedly demanding a saner world. It is quite possible that this spectacular conversation of ego-force will result in his going down in history as the clearest head of the twentieth century. If this distinction does not come to him, the chances seem good that he will earn some such title as Great Confessor to the Age of the Communist-Capitalist showdown, having done for the social unconscious what Freud did for the individual unconscious.

If Shaw, in achieving what he achieved, was simply "working out his inner conflicts," which our psychoanalyst friends suggest is the fount of all achievement, then with his personal life, public and private, he wrote a universal blueprint for overcoming the "disease" of human existence, and there may be hope for the race. As a young man, Shaw was thought to be a bohemian—what is now called a beatnik—but he quickly disabused those who came to know him of any idea but that he was destined to become one of the world's great "squares"—rude, puckish, and on occasion insulting (for propaganda reasons) in his public behavior, but determinedly sober and responsible in his life work, and kind and almost totally respectable in his private affairs. One must use the word "almost" advisedly, for Shaw, apparently considering himself safe for life from the horrors of sex with his marriage at age forty-two to a wealthy Irishwoman who reputedly abhorred the carnal relation, came perilously close fourteen years later to a re-enactment of his humiliating experience before his marriage with the tempestuous and passionate widow Jennie Patterson. At fifty-six he fell embarrassingly in love with the celebrated actress Mrs. Patrick Campbell, but she, according to the evidence, thwarted what might have turned into a sad end to his honorable and philosophic retreat from sex. Far from being puritanically ignorant of sex, Shaw had had his share of it,[11] and he tried to examine it as mercilessly as he examined everything else. We are without information as to whether he had to resort to self-relief after his marriage, but whatever the truth may be on that point, he had some eminently sane things to say about sex, not the least significant of which is that it can be a bit of a nuisance, to put it mildly. No sane person with the requisite experience and the ability to interpret truthfully that experience will disagree. Gandhi shared this view with Shaw, and writes in his autobiography of renouncing sex at age thirty-seven because it had become an impediment to his growth. The marriage of Carlyle was also reputed to be a sexless one. Whether or not the curtailing or renunciation of sex activity is a mischievous denial

[11] See C. G. L. Du Cann, *The Loves of George Bernard Shaw*, New York: Funk & Wagnalls, 1963.

or a step toward "higher" expression of human potential must be left to each individual to decide for himself as best he can. On the bright side of the question are the well-known results of sublimation, which, according to psychologists, has produced some of man's finest achievements. What cannot be doubted is that Shaw added significantly to the stock of useful information on the subject, as he did on the larger question of a better life through self-discipline.

The ridicule of what were called Shaw's "fads," his abstention from tobacco, alcohol, stimulants, or drugs of any kind, plus his refusal to eat the flesh of his fellow creatures, is a measure not of his eccentric habits but rather of the guilt and insanity of those who would not or could not see these practices as the result of his determination to avoid desecrating the God-given temple of his body and mind. Making, as usual, social propaganda of his ascetic health, Shaw pointed to the stupefying waste of human energy in the raising of millions of animals to be slaughtered for food, and in the production of alcohol and tobacco for the poisoning of minds and bodies. He himself fell short of perfection in his vegetarianism, eating the "incipient flesh" of eggs and during a serious illness in later life yielding to the advice of doctors that he be dosed with fish oil. Though he was disturbed by these blemishes on his record as a clean liver, they must be as less than a grain of sand to those millions for whom the giving up of their cocktails and chops and tranquilizers is not only impossible, but preposterous. Perhaps, as Shaw surmises, the Life Force has a better breed up Its sleeve.

Shaw's way of life naturally provoked the supposition that he was not only a superbrain, but *all* brain with no heart. Nothing could be a grosser distortion. In spite of his rigorous schedule of work, and the isolation that it entailed, he remained a compassionate man whose sympathies were aroused by the sufferings of others, and who refused to be diverted by pettiness. Thus, when it would have been expedient to look the other way, as others with less courage were doing, he came to the aid of Oscar Wilde, whom he did not think much of as a man or an artist. He championed the Chicago Anarchists and went to the defense of a German actor being tried for appearing in a Jewish play. He took time to edit, as a friend, the monumental work of Lawrence of Arabia, *The Seven Pillars of Wisdom*. When the WPA Federal Theatre Project in the United States asked for permission to produce his plays, he granted performing rights on such generous terms (because he approved of government-sponsored art programs) that those who had heard only of his tough business policy were confounded. Such gestures, and many more that are detailed in the various books about him (mostly those written since his death), reveal a man of practically saintly largeness of heart, who gave of himself not as an hysterically guilt-ridden philanthropist, but with a genuine passion for making as many moves as possible that would count on the right side of the Recording Angel's ledger. As a thinker and a doer, beneath all the scintillating satire and the purposeful braggadocio, his life was one of valorous service to his fellow man.

When all the "interpretations" of Shaw have been examined, when we have quite done with estimating his measure as philosopher, scientist, psychologist, historian, revolutionary, cynic-optimist, clown, critic, sexologist, moralist, educator, stylist, mystic, communist, dramatist, citizen, and public servant, we find that he was constant in the only virtue that means anything in our vale of tears and laughter—courage. It was, of course, a special kind of courage, the kind needed in the most dangerous profession on earth —the propagation of New Idea.

The various editions of Shaw's works from which the extracts in the *Ready-Reckoner* were taken did not scrupulously respect his attempts to reform printed English. Thus, *dont* appears sometimes in its commoner form, *don't*, *oneanother* occasionally is found separated into two words, and *Mr* and *Mrs* in certain places have the period restored. Since the *Ready-Reckoner's* concern is with Shaw's sociological ideas and not his interest in language reform, no attempt has been made to repair these inconsistencies in spelling and punctuation.

N. H. L-T.
Los Angeles
September, 1964

Poverty

Modern poverty is not the poverty that was blest in the Sermon on the Mount: the objection to it is not that it makes people unhappy, but that it degrades them; and the fact that they can be quite as happy in their degradation as their betters are in their exaltation makes it worse. (IWGSC-42)*

---

*Symbols appearing after quotes throughout the text designate the sources as listed at the back of the book. For example, (IWGSC-42), above, indicates page 42 of *The Intelligent Woman's Guide to Socialism and Capitalism*.

The Worst of Dangers. Security, the chief pretence of civilization, cannot exist where the worst of dangers, the danger of poverty, hangs over everyone's head, and where the alleged protection of our persons from violence is only an accidental result of the existence of a police force whose real business is to force the poor man to see his children starve whilst idle people overfeed pet dogs with the money that might feed and clothe them. (P-MB-209)

The Worst of Crimes. "All the other crimes are virtues beside it: all the other dishonors are chivalry itself by comparison. Poverty blights whole cities; spreads horrible pestilences; strikes dead the very souls of all who come within sight, sound, or smell of it. What you call crime is nothing: a murder here and a theft there, a blow now and a curse then: what do they matter? they are only the accidents and the illnesses of life: there are not fifty genuine professional criminals in London. But there are millions of poor people, abject people, dirty people, ill fed, ill clothed people. They poison us morally and physically: they kill the happiness of society: they force us to do away with our own liberties and to organize unnatural cruelties for fear they should rise against us and drag us down into their abyss. Only fools fear crime: we all fear poverty." (*Undershaft*, MB-329)

Blessed Are the Poor? The thoughtless wickedness with which we scatter sentences of imprisonment, torture in the solitary cell and on the plank bed, and flogging, on moral invalids and energetic rebels, is as nothing compared to the stupid levity with which we tolerate poverty as if it were either a wholesome tonic for lazy people or else a virtue to be embraced as St. Francis embraced it. If a man is indolent, let him be poor. If he is drunken, let him be poor. If he is not a gentleman, let him be poor. If he is addicted to the fine arts or to pure science instead of to trade and finance, let him be poor. If he chooses to spend his urban eighteen shillings a week or his agricultural thirteen shillings a week on his beer and his family instead of saving it up for his old age, let him be poor. Let nothing be done for "the undeserving": let him be poor. Serve him right! Also—somewhat inconsistently—blessed are the poor! (P-MB-210-211)

The Salt of the Earth? Whenever your sympathies are strongly stirred on behalf of some cruelly ill used person or persons of whom you know nothing except that they are ill used, your generous indignation attributes all sorts of virtues to them, and all sorts of vices to those who oppress them. But the blunt truth is that ill used people are worse than well used people: indeed this is at bottom the only good reason why we should not allow anyone to be ill used. If I thought you would be made a better woman by ill treatment I should do my best to have you ill treated. We should refuse to tolerate poverty as a social institution not because the poor are the salt of the earth, but because "the poor in a lump are bad." And the poor know this better than anyone else. When the Socialist movement in London took its tone from lovers of art and literature who had read George Borrow until they had come to regard tramps as saints, and passionate High Church clergymen (Anglo-Catholics) who adored supertramps like

St. Francis, it was apt to assume that all that was needed was to teach Socialism to the masses (vaguely imagined as a huge crowd of tramplike saints) and leave the rest to the natural effect of sowing the good seed in kindly virgin soil. But the proletarian soil was neither virgin nor exceptionally kindly. The masses are not in the least like tramps; and they have no romantic illusions about oneanother, whatever illusions each of them may cherish about herself. When John Stuart Mill was a Parliamentary candidate in Westminster, his opponents tried to defeat him by recalling an occasion on which he had said flatly that the British workman was neither entirely truthful, entirely sober, entirely honest, nor imbued with a proper sense of the wickedness of gambling: in short, that he was by no means the paragon he was always assumed to be by parliamentary candidates when they addressed his class as "Gentlemen," and begged for his vote. Mill probably owed his success on that occasion to the fact that instead of denying his opinion he uncompromisingly reaffirmed it. The wage workers are as fond of flattery as other people, and will swallow any quantity of it from candidates provided it be thoroughly understood that it is only flattery, and that the candidates know better; but they have no use for gushingly idealistic ladies and gentlemen who are fools enough to think that the poor are cruelly misunderstood angels. (IWGSC-219-220)

Infectious Degradation. Such poverty as we have today in all our great cities degrades the poor, and infects with its degradation the whole neighborhood in which they live. And whatever can degrade a neighborhood can degrade a country and a continent and finally the whole civilized world, which is only a large neighborhood. Its bad effects cannot be escaped by the rich. When poverty produces outbreaks of virulent infectious disease, as it always does sooner or later, the rich catch the disease and see their children die of it. When it produces crime and violence the rich go in fear of both, and are put to a good deal of expense to protect their persons and property. When it produces bad manners and bad language the children of the rich pick them up no matter how carefully they are secluded; and such seclusion as they get does them more harm than good. If poor and pretty young women find, as they do, that they can make more money by vice than by honest work, they will poison the blood of rich young men who, when they marry, will infect their wives and children, and cause them all sorts of bodily troubles, sometimes ending in disfigurement and blindness and death, and always doing them more or less mischief. The old notion that people can "keep themselves to themselves" and not be touched by what is happening to their neighbors, or even to the people who live a hundred miles off, is a most dangerous mistake. The saying that we are members one of another is not a mere pious formula to be repeated in church without any meaning: it is a literal truth; for though the rich end of the town can avoid living with the poor end, it cannot avoid dying with it when the plague comes. People will be able to keep themselves to themselves as much as they please when they have made an end of poverty; but until then they will not be able to shut out the sights and sounds and smells of poverty from their daily walks, nor to feel sure from day to day that its most violent and fatal evils will not reach them through their strongest police guards. (IWGSC-42-43)

Wealth: Pearl Necklaces & Pekingese Dogs. Think of the whole country as a big household, and the whole nation as a big family, which is what they really are. What do we see? Half-fed, badly clothed, abominably housed children all over the place; and the money that should go to feed and clothe and house them properly being spent in millions on bottles of scent, pearl necklaces, pet dogs, racing motor cars, January strawberries that taste like corks, and all sorts of extravagances. One sister of the national family has a single pair of leaking boots that keep her sniffing all through the winter, and no handkerchief to wipe her nose with. Another has forty pairs of high heeled shoes and dozens of handkerchiefs. A little brother is trying to grow up on a penn'orth of food a day, and is breaking his mother's heart and wearing out her patience by asking continually for more, whilst a big brother, spending five or six pounds on his dinner at a fashionable hotel, followed by supper at a night club, is in the doctor's hands because he is eating and drinking too much.

Now this is shockingly bad political economy. When thoughtless people are asked to explain it they say "Oh, the woman with the forty shoes and the man drinking at the night club got their money from their father who made a fortune by speculating in rubber; and the girl with the broken boots, and the troublesome boy whose mother has just clouted his head, are only riff-raff from the slums." That is true; but it does not alter the fact that the nation that spends money on champagne before it has provided enough milk for its babies, or gives dainty meals to Sealyham terriers and Alsatian wolf-hounds and Pekingese dogs whilst the infant mortality rate shews that its children are dying by thousands from insufficient nourishment, is a badly managed, silly, vain, stupid, ignorant nation, and will go to the bad in the long run no matter how hard it tries to conceal its real condition from itself by counting the pearl necklaces and Pekingese dogs as wealth, and thinking itself three times as rich as before when all the pet dogs have litters of six puppies a couple. The only way in which a nation can make itself wealthy and prosperous is by good housekeeping: that is, by providing for its wants in the order of their importance, and allowing no money to be wasted on whims and luxuries until necessities have been thoroughly served. (IWGSC-50-51)

Overpopulation. But indeed the more you degrade the workers, robbing them of all artistic enjoyment, and all chance of respect and admiration from their fellows, the more you throw them back, reckless, on the one pleasure and the one human tie left to them—the gratification of their instinct for producing fresh supplies of men. You will applaud this instinct as divine until at last the excessive supply becomes a nuisance: there comes a plague of men; and you suddenly discover that the instinct is diabolic, and set up a cry of "overpopulation." But your slaves are beyond caring for your cries: they breed like rabbits; and their poverty breeds filth, ugliness, dishonesty, disease, obscenity, drunkenness, and murder. In the midst of the riches which their labor piles up for you, their misery rises up too and stifles you. You withdraw in disgust to the other end of the town from them; you appoint special carriages on your railways and special seats in your churches and theatres for them; you set your life apart from theirs by every class barrier you can devise; and yet they swarm about you still: your face gets stamped with your habitual loathing and suspicion of them: your ears get so filled with the language of the vilest of them that you break into it when you lose your self-control: they poison your life as remorselessly as you have sacrificed theirs heartlessly. You begin to believe intensely in the devil. Then comes the terror of their revolting; the drilling and arming of bodies of them to keep down the rest; the prison, the hospital, paroxysms of frantic coercion, followed by paroxysms of frantic charity. And in the meantime, the population continues to increase. (EBS-21-22)

The Cynicism of the Poor. Walk through the poorer quarters of our cities on Sunday when the men are not working, but resting and chewing the cud of their reflections. You will find one expression common to every mature face: the expression of cynicism. . . . They have found that every man has his price; and they have been foolishly or corruptly taught to mistrust or despise him for that necessary and salutary condition of social existence. When they learn that General Booth,* too, has his price, they do not admire him because it is a high one, and admit the need of organizing society so that he shall get it in an honorable way: they conclude that his character is unsound and that all religious men are hypocrites and allies of their sweaters and oppressors. They know that the large subscriptions which help to support the (Salvation) Army are endowments, not of religion, but of the wicked doctrine of docility in poverty and humility under oppression; and they are rent by the most agonizing of all the doubts of the soul, the doubt whether their true salvation must not come from their most abhorrent passions, from murder, envy, greed, stubbornness, rage, and terrorism, rather than from public spirit, reasonableness, humanity, generosity, tenderness, delicacy, pity and kindness. The

* Founder of the Salvation Army.

confirmation of that doubt, at which our newspapers have been working so hard for years past, is the morality of militarism; and the justification of militarism is that circumstances may at any time make it the true morality of the moment. It is by producing such moments that we produce violent and sanguinary revolutions, such as the one now in progress in Russia and the one which Capitalism in England and America is daily and diligently provoking. (P-MB-230-231)

Cancers in the Commonwealth. What do you give a man an income for? Obviously to keep him alive. Since it is evident that the first condition on which he can be kept alive without enslaving somebody else is that he shall produce an equivalent for what it costs to keep him alive, we might quite rationally compel him to abstain from idling by whatever means we employ to compel him to abstain from murder, arson, forgery, or any other crime. The one supremely foolish thing to do with him is to do nothing: that is, to be as idle, lazy, and heartless in dealing with him as he is in dealing with us. Even if we provided work for him instead of basing, as we do, our whole industrial system on successive competitive waves of overwork with their ensuing troughs of unemployment, we should still sternly deny him the alternative of not doing it; for the result must be that he will become poor and make his children poor if he has any; and poor people are cancers in the commonwealth, costing far more than if they were handsomely pensioned off as incurables. (P-AL-57)

A National Crime. Besides, as long as poverty remains possible we shall never be sure that it will not overtake ourselves. If we dig a pit for others we may fall into it: if we leave a precipice unfenced our children may fall over it when they are playing. We see the most innocent and respectable families falling into the unfenced pit of poverty every day; and how do we know that it will not be our turn next?

It is perhaps the greatest folly of which a nation can be guilty to attempt to use poverty as a sort of punishment for offences that it does not send people to prison for. It is easy to say of a lazy man "Oh, let him be poor: it serves him right for being lazy: it will teach him a lesson." In saying so we are ourselves too lazy to think a little before laying down the law. We cannot afford to have poor people anyhow, whether they be lazy or busy, drunken or sober, virtuous or vicious, thrifty or careless, wise or foolish. If they deserve to suffer let them be made to suffer in some other way; for mere poverty will not hurt them half as much as it will hurt their innocent neighbors. It is a public nuisance as well as a private misfortune. Its toleration is a national crime. (IWGSC-43-44)

Saving as Suicide & Murder. Saving, investment, life assurance, all of them most prudent and excellent operations for people who have had as much of present nourishment as they need, and still have something to spare, are, for heads of families in a state of privation, slow forms of suicide and murder; and those who preach them indiscriminately should be indicted for incitement to crime. When a bishop offends in this way, people who really understand the situation feel their blood rising almost to guillotining point. Yet, after all, the bishop does not force people to take his inconsiderate advice. But the municipality does. The London County Council, for instance, goes to many an unfortunate wretch grimly struggling with poverty in a little shop, underfed, underclothed, underhoused, and consequently desperately in want of more money to spend on himself and his family. Taking him by the scruff of the neck, it says to him, "Come: you must invest in the general prosperity of this magnificent metropolis, of which you are—or ought to be—proud to be a citizen. You must no longer cross the Thames in a wretched penny ferry boat; you must build a colossal Tower Bridge, with splendid approaches; or you must pass underneath in tubular triumphs of modern engineering. You must no longer walk through slums from the Strand to Oxford Street: you must make a new and lordly avenue flanked with imposing buildings. And you must cheer yourself up with parks and bands, and run delightful steamboats on the river for your recreation summer evenings." Is it any wonder that the unhappy victim of this comprehensive civic patriotism turns savagely on his Progressive benefactors and asks them whether they suppose his name is Carnegie or Pierpont Morgan or Rothschild that he should be forced into the schemes of millionaires? And the irony of the proposals is the more biting as he well knows that if the improvements happen to affect his own business beneficially, his landlord will take the first opportunity to appropriate the increment by putting up his rent. (CSMT-233-234)

Income & Conscience. UNDERSHAFT (*gravely*) Poverty, my friend, is not a thing to be proud of.

SHIRLEY (*angrily*) Who made your millions for you? Me and my like. Whats kep us poor? Keepin you rich. I wouldnt have your conscience, not for all your income.

UNDERSHAFT I wouldnt have your income, not for all your conscience, Mr Shirley. (MB-279)

Income & Justice. When we come to the courts of law the hopeless incompatibility of inequality of income with justice is so plain that you must have been struck by it if you ever notice such things. The very first condition of legal justice is that it shall be no respecter of persons; that it should hold the balance impartially between the laborer's wife and the millionairess; and that no person shall be deprived of life or liberty except by the verdict of a jury of her peers, meaning her equals. Now no laborer is ever tried by a jury of his peers: he is tried by a jury of ratepayers who have a very strong class prejudice against him because they have larger incomes, and consider themselves better men on that account. Even a rich man tried by a common jury has to reckon with their envy as well as their subservience to wealth. Thus it is a common saying with us that there is one law for the rich and another for the poor. (IWGSC-56)

Shall the Poor Be Rich? Granted that people should not on any account be allowed to be poor, we have still to consider whether they should be allowed to be rich. When poverty is gone, shall we tolerate luxury and extravagance? This is a poser, because it is much easier to say what poverty is than what luxury is. When a woman is hungry, or ragged, or has not at least one properly furnished room all to herself to sleep in, then she is clearly suffering from poverty. When the infant mortality in one district is much greater than in another; when the average age of death for fully grown persons in it falls far short of the scriptural three-score-and-ten; when the average weight of the children who survive is below that reached by well-fed and well-cared-for children, then you can say confidently that the people in that district are suffering from poverty. But suffering from riches is not so easily measured. That rich people do suffer a great deal is plain enough to anyone who has an intimate knowledge of their lives. They are so unhealthy that they are always running after cures and surgical operations of one sort or another. When they are not really ill they imagine they are. They are worried by their property, by their servants, by their poor relations, by their investments, by the need for keeping up their social position, and, when they have several children, by the impossibility of leaving these children enough to enable them to live as they have been brought up to live; for we must not forget that if a married couple with fifty thousand a year have five children, they can leave only ten thousand a year to each after bringing them up to live at the rate of fifty thousand, and launching them into the sort of society that lives at that rate, the result being that unless these children can make rich marriages they live beyond their incomes (not knowing how to live more cheaply) and are presently head over ears in debt. They hand on their costly habits and rich friends and debts to their children with very little else; so that the trouble becomes worse and worse from generation to generation; and this is how we meet everywhere with ladies and gentlemen who have no means of keeping up their position, and are therefore much more miserable than the common poor.

Perhaps you know some well-off families who do not seem to suffer from their riches. They do not overeat themselves; they find occupations to keep themselves in health; they do not worry about their position; they put their money into safe investments and are content with a low rate of interest; and they bring up their children to live simply and do useful work. But this means that they do not live like rich people at all, and might therefore just as well have ordinary incomes. The general run of rich people do not know what to do with themselves; and at the end of it is that they have to join a round of social duties and pleasures mostly manufactured by West End shopkeepers, and so tedious that at the end of a fashionable season the rich are more worn out than their servants and trades-men. They may have no taste for sport; but they are forced by their social position to go to the great race meetings and ride to hounds. They may have no taste for music; but they have to go to the Opera and to the fashionable concerts. They may not dress as they please nor do what they please. Because they are rich they must do what all the other rich people are doing, there being nothing else for them to do except work, which would immediately reduce them to the condition of ordinary people. So, as they cannot do what they like, they must contrive to like what they do, and imagine that they are having a splendid time of it when they are in fact being bored by their amusements, humbugged by their doctors, pillaged by their tradesmen, and forced to console themselves unamiably for being snubbed by richer people by snubbing poorer people. (IWGSC-45-46)

Almsgiving & the Deserving Poor. There is no getting over the fact that the moment an attempt is made to organize alms-giving by entrusting the funds to a permanent body of experts, it is invariably discovered that beggars are perfectly genuine persons: that is to say, not "deserving poor," but people who have discov-ered that it is possible to live by simply impudently asking for what they want until they get it, which is the essence of beggary. The permanent body of experts, illogically instructed to apply their funds to the cases of the deserving poor only, soon become a mere police body for the frustrating of true beggars, and consequently of true almsgiving. Finally, their experience in a pursuit to which they were originally led by natural benevolence lands them in an almost maniacal individualism and an abhorrence of ordinary "charity" as one of the worst of social crimes. This may not be an amiable attitude; but no reasonable person can fail to be impressed by the certainty with which it seems to be produced by a practical acquaintance with the social reactions of mendicity and benevolence. (SFM-109)

Conscience Money. . . . Most of the money given by rich people in "charity" is made up of conscience money, "ransom," political bribery, and bids for titles. The traffic in hospital subscriptions in the name of Royalty fulfills exactly the same function in modern society as Texel's traffic in indulgence in the name of the Pope did before the Reformation. One buys moral credit by signing a cheque, which is easier than turning a prayer wheel. I am aware, further, that we often give to public objects money that we should devote to raising wages among our own employees or substituting three eight-hour shifts for two twelve-hour ones. But when a millionaire does not care whether his money does good or not, provided he finds his conscience eased and his social status improved by giving it away, it is useless for me to argue with him. I mention him only as a warning to the better sort of donors that the mere disbursement of large sums of money must be counted as a distinctly suspicious circumstance in estimating personal character. Money is worth nothing to the man who has more than enough; and the wisdom with which it is spent is the sole social justification for leaving him in possession of it. (SFM-120-121)

Good Samaritans: Bad Symptoms. It is perhaps natural that ignorant poor women should imagine that inequality is the fault of the rich women. What is more surprising is that many rich women, though they ought to know better than anybody that a woman can no more help being born rich than born poor, feel guilty and ashamed of their wealth, and plunge into almsgiving to relieve their sickly consciences. They often conceive Socialism as a charitable enterprise for the benefit of the poor. Nothing could be further from the truth. Socialism abhors poverty, and would abolish the poor. A hearty dislike and disapproval of poor people as such is the first qualification of a good Equalizer. Under Socialism people would be prosecuted for being poor as they are now for being naked. Socialism loathes almsgiving, not only sentimentally because it fills the paupers with humility, the patrons with evil pride, and both with hatred, but because in a country justly and providently managed there could be neither excuse for it on the pauper's part nor occasion for it on the patron's. Those who like playing the good Samaritan should remember that you cannot have good Samaritans without thieves. Saviors and rescuers may be splendid figures in hagiography and romance; but as they could not exist without sinners and victims they are bad symptoms. (IWGSC-95-96)

The Seven Deadly Sins. "Food, clothing, firing, rent, taxes, respectability and children. Nothing can lift those seven millstones from Man's neck but money; and the spirit cannot soar until the millstones are lifted. I lifted them from your spirit. I enabled Barbara to become Major Barbara; and I saved her from the crime of poverty." (*Undershaft*, MB-329)

Virtues that Feed on Suffering. The virtues that feed on suffering are very questionable virtues. There are people who positively wallow in hospitals and charitable societies and Relief Funds and the like, yet who, if the need for their charitable exercise were removed, could spend their energy to great advantage in improving their own manners and learning to mind their own business. There will always be plenty of need in the world for kindness; but it should not be wasted on preventible starvation and disease. Keeping such horrors in existence for the sake of exercising our sympathies is like setting our houses on fire to exercise the vigor and daring of our fire brigades. It is the people who hate poverty, not those who sympathize with it, who will put an end to it. Almsgiving, though it cannot be stopped at present, as without it we should have hunger riots, and possibly revolution, is an evil. At present we give the unemployed a dole to support them, not for love of them, but because if we left them to starve they would begin by breaking our windows and end by looting our shops and burning our houses. (IWGSC-96)

Poverty: The Chief Evil To Be Attacked. The universal regard for money is the one hopeful fact in our civilization, the one sound spot in our social conscience. Money is the most important thing in the world. It represents health, strength, honor, generosity and beauty as conspicuously and undeniably as the want of it represents illness, weakness, disgrace, meanness and ugliness. Not the least of its virtues is that it destroys base people as certainly as it fortifies and dignifies noble people. It is only when it is cheapened to worthlessness for some, and made impossibly dear to others, that it becomes a curse. In short, it is a curse only in such foolish social conditions that life itself is a curse. For the two things are inseparable: money is the counter that enables life to be distributed socially: it *is* life as truly as sovereigns* and bank notes are money. The first duty of every citizen is to insist on having money on reasonable terms; and this demand is not complied with by giving four men three shillings each for ten or twelve hours' drudgery and one man a thousand pounds for nothing. The crying need of the nation is not for better morals, cheaper bread, temperance, liberty, culture, redemption of fallen sisters and erring brothers, nor the grace, love and fellowship of the Trinity, but simply for enough money. And the evil to be attacked is not sin, suffering, greed, priestcraft, kingcraft, demagogy, monopoly, ignorance, drink, war, pestilence, nor any other of the scapegoats which reformers sacrifice, but simply poverty. (P-MB-215)

The Real Degradation. "It is not killing and dying that degrades us, but base living, and accepting the wages and profits of degradation. Better ten dead men than one live slave or his master." (*Don Juan*, MS-110)

* A gold coin equalling a pound.

Christianity

In a living society every day is a day of judgement; and its recognition as such is not the end of all things but the beginning of a real civilization. (P-SUI-15)

CHRIST'S

Christianity Independent of Any Individual Preacher.   Christianity is a step in moral evolution which is independent of any individual preacher. If Jesus had never existed (and that he ever existed in any other sense than that in which Shakespear's Hamlet existed has been vigorously questioned) Tolstoy would have fought and taught and quarrelled with the Greek Church all the same. Their creed has been fragmentarily practised to a considerable extent in spite of the fact that the laws of all countires treat it, in effect, as criminal. Many of its advocates have been militant atheists. But for some reason the imagination of white mankind has picked out Jesus of Nazareth as *the* Christ, and attributed all the Christian doctrines to him; and as it is the doctrine and not the man that matters, and, as besides, one symbol is as good as another provided everyone attaches the same meaning to it, I raise, for the moment, no question as to how far the gospels are original, and how far they consist of Greek and Chinese interpolations. The record that Jesus said certain things is not invalidated by a demonstration that Confucius said them before him. Those who claim a literal divine paternity for him cannot be silenced by the discovery that the same claim was made for Alexander and Augustus. And I am not just now concerned with the credibility of the gospels as records of fact; for I am not acting as a detective, but turning our modern lights on to certain ideas and doctrines in them which disentangle themselves from the rest because they are flatly contrary to human practice, common sense, and common belief, and yet have, in the teeth of dogged incredulity and recalcitrance, produced an irresistible impression that Christ, though rejected by his posterity as an unpractical dreamer, and executed by his contemporaries as a dangerous anarchist and blasphemous madman, was greater than his judges. (P-AL-5-6)

Which Fairy Stories The Truest?   "Are your Christian fairy stories any truer than our stories about Jupiter and Diana, in which, I may tell you, I believe no more than the Emperor does, or any educated man in Rome?" (*The Captain,* AL-136)

The Miracles.   If it could be proved today that not one of the miracles of Jesus actually occurred, that proof would not invalidate a single one of his didactic utterances; and conversely, if it could be proved that not only did the miracles actually occur, but that he had wrought a thousand other miracles a thousand times more wonderful, not a jot of weight would be added to his doctrine. And yet the intellectual energy of sceptics and divines has been wasted for generations in arguing about the miracles on the assumption that Christianity is at stake in the controversy as to whether the stories of Matthew are false or true. According to Matthew himself, Jesus must have known this only too well; for wherever he went he was assailed with a clamor for miracles, though his doctrine created bewilderment.

So much for the miracles! Matthew tells us further, that Jesus declared that his doctrines would be attacked by Church and State, and that the common multitude were the salt of the earth and the light of the world. His disciples, in their relations with the political and ecclesiastical organizations, would be as sheep among wolves. (P-AL-26)

Credibility of the Gospels. It will be noted by the older among my readers, who are sure to be obsessed more or less by elderly wrangles as to whether the gospels are credible as matter-of-fact narratives, that I have hardly raised this question, and have accepted the credible and incredible with equal complacency. I have done this because credibility is a subjective condition, as the evolution of religious belief clearly shews. Belief is not dependent on evidence and reason. There is as much evidence that the miracles occurred as that the Battle of Waterloo occurred, or that a large body of Russian troops passed through England in 1914 to take part in the war on the Western front. The reasons for believing in the murder of Pompey are the same as the reasons for believing in the raising of Lazarus. Both have been believed and doubted by men of equal intelligence. Miracles, in the sense of phenomena we cannot explain, surround us on every hand; life itself is the miracles of miracles. Miracles in the sense of events that violate the normal course of our experience are vouched for every day: the flourishing Church of Christ Scientist is founded on a multitude of such miracles. Nobody believes all the miracles; everybody believes some of them. I cannot tell why men who will not believe that Jesus ever existed yet believe firmly that Shakespear was Bacon. I cannot tell why people who believe that angels appeared and fought on our side at the battle of Mons, and who believe that miracles occur quite frequently at Lourdes, nevertheless boggle at the miracle of the liquefaction of the ·blood of St. Januarius, and reject it as a trick of priestcraft. I cannot tell why people who will not believe Matthew's story of three kings bringing costly gifts to the cradle of Jesus, believe Luke's story of the shepherds and the stable. I cannot tell why people, brought up to believe the Bible in the old literal way as an infallible record and revelation, and rejecting that view later on, begin by rejecting the Old Testament, and give up the belief in a brimstone hell before they give up (if they ever do) the belief in a heaven of harps, crowns, and thrones. I cannot tell why people who will not believe in baptism on any terms believe in vaccination with the cruel fanaticism of inquisitors. I am convinced that if a dozen sceptics were to draw up in parallel columns a list of the events narrated in the gospels which they consider credible and incredible respectively, their lists would be different in several particulars. Belief is literally a matter of taste. (P-AL-44-45)

Credibility & Truth. When men believed that the earth was flat, they were not credulous: they were using their common sense, and, if asked to prove that the earth was flat, would have said simply, "Look at it." Those who refuse to believe that it is round are exercising a wholesome scepticism. The modern man who believes that the earth is round is grossly credulous. Flat Earth men drive him to fury by confuting him with the greatest ease when he tries to argue about it. Confront him with a theory that the earth is cylindrical, or annular, or hour-glass shaped, and he is lost. The thing he believes may be true, but that is not why he believes it: he believes it because in some mysterious way it appeals to his imagination. If you ask him why he believes that the sun is ninety-odd million miles off, either he will have to confess that he doesn't know, or he will say that Newton proved it. But he has not read the treatise in which Newton proved it, and doesnt even know that it was written in Latin. . . .

It is therefore idle to begin disputing with the reader as to what he should believe in the gospels and what he should disbelieve. He will believe what he can, and disbelieve what he must. . . . Every reader takes from the Bible what he can get. (P-AL-46-48)

The Danger Is Not Disbelief, But Belief. You may deny the divinity of Jesus; you may doubt whether he ever existed; you may reject Christianity for Judaism, Mahometanism, Shintoism, or Fire Worship; and the iconolaters, placidly contemptuous, will only classify you as a freethinker or a heathen. But if you venture to wonder how Christ would have looked if he had shaved and had his hair cut, or what size in shoes he took, or whether he swore when he stood on a nail in the carpenter's shop, or could not button his robe when he was in a hurry, or whether he laughed over the repartees by which he baffled the priests when they tried to trap him into sedition and blasphemy, or even if you tell any part of his story in the vivid terms of modern colloquial slang, you will produce an extraordinary dismay and horror among the iconolaters. You will have made the picture come out of its frame, the statue descend from its pedestal, the story become real, with all the incalculable consequences that may flow from this terrifying miracle. It is at such moments that you realize that the iconolaters have never for a moment conceived Christ as a real person who meant what he said, as a fact, as a force like electricity, only needing the invention of suitable political machinery to be applied to the affairs of mankind with revolutionary effect.

Thus it is not disbelief that is dangerous in our society: it is belief. The moment it strikes you (as it may any day) that Christ is not the lifeless harmless image he has hitherto been to you, but a rallying centre for revolutionary influences which all established States and Churches fight, you must look to yourselves; for you have brought the image to life; and the mob may not be able to bear that horror. (P-AL-48-49)

The Confirmed Doctrines of Jesus. Now those who, like myself, see the Barabbasque social organization as a failure, and are convinced that the Life Force (or whatever you choose to call it) cannot be finally beaten by any failure, and will even supersede humanity by evolving a higher species if we cannot master the problems raised by the multiplication or our own numbers, have always known that Jesus had a real message, and have felt the fascination of his character and doctrine. Not that we should nowadays dream of claiming any supernatural authority for him, much less the technical authority which attaches to an educated modern philosopher and jurist. But when, having entirely got rid of Salvationist Christianity, and even contracted a prejudice against Jesus on the score of his involuntary connection with it, we engage on a purely scientific study of economics, criminology, and biology, and find that our practical conclusions are virtually those of Jesus, we are distinctly pleased and encouraged to find that we were doing him an injustice, and that the nimbus that surrounds his head in the pictures may be interpreted some day as a light of science rather than a declaration of sentiment or a label of idolatry.

The doctrines in which Jesus is thus confirmed are, roughly, the following:

1. The kingdom of heaven is within you. You are the son of God; and God is the son of man. God is a spirit, to be worshipped in spirit and in truth, and not an elderly gentleman to be bribed and begged from. We are members one of another; so that you cannot injure or help your neighbor without injuring or helping yourself. God is your father: you are here to do God's work; and you and your father are one.

2. Get rid of property by throwing it into the common stock. Disassociate your work entirely from money payments. If you let a child starve you are letting God starve. Get rid of all anxiety about tomorrow's dinner and clothes, because you cannot serve two masters: God and Mammon.

3. Get rid of judges and punishment and revenge. Love your neighbor as yourself, he being a part of yourself. And love your enemies: they are your neighbors.

4. Get rid of your family entanglements. Every mother you meet is as much your mother as the woman who bore you. Every man you meet is as much your brother as the man she bore after you. Dont waste your time at family funerals grieving for your relatives: attend to life, not to death: there are as good fish in the sea as ever came out of it, and better. In the kingdom of heaven, which, as aforesaid, is within you, there is no marriage nor giving in marriage, because you cannot devote your life to two divinities: God and the person you are married to.

Now these are very interesting propositions; and they become more interesting every day, as experience and science drive us more and more to consider them favorably. In considering them, we shall waste our time unless we give them a reasonable construction. We must assume that the man who saw his way through such a mass of popular passion and illusion as stands between us and a sense of the value of such teaching was quite aware of all the objections that occur to an average stockbroker in the first five minutes. It is true that the world is governed to a considerable

extent by the considerations that occur to stockbrokers in the first
five minutes; but as the result is that the world is so badly governed
that those who know the truth can hardly bear to live in it, an
objection from an average stockbroker constitutes in itself a *prima
facie* case for any social reform. (P-AL-49-51)

History Bears out the Case against Jesus. Jesus was from the
point of view of the High Priest a heretic and an imposter. From
the point of view of the merchants he was a rioteer and a Communist. From the Roman Imperialist point of view he was a traitor.
From the commonsense point of view he was a dangerous madman.
From the snobbish point of view, always a very influential one,
he was a penniless vagrant. From the police point of view he was
an obstructor of thoroughfares, a beggar, an associate of prostitutes,
an apologist of sinners, and a disparager of judges; and his daily
companions were tramps whom he had seduced into vagabondage
from their regular trades. From the point of view of the pious he
was a Sabbath breaker, a denier of the efficacy of circumcision and
the advocate of a strange rite of baptism, a gluttonous man and a
winebibber. He was abhorrent to the medical profession as an un-
qualified practitioner who healed people by quackery and charged
nothing for the treatment. He was not anti-Christ: nobody had
heard of such a power of darkness then; but he was startlingly
anti-Moses. He was against the priests, against the judiciary, against
the military, against the city (he declared that it was impossible for a rich man to enter the kingdom of heaven), against all
the interests, classes, principalities and powers, inviting everybody
to abandon all these and follow him. By every argument, legal,
political, religious, customary, and polite, he was the most
complete enemy of the society of his time ever brought to the bar.
He was guilty on every count of the indictment, and on many more
that his accusers had not the wit to frame. If he was innocent then
the whole world was guilty. To acquit him was to throw over civilization and all its institutions. History has borne out the case against
him; for no State has ever constituted itself on his principles or
made it possible to live according to his commandments:
those States who have taken his name have taken it as an alias

to enable them to persecute his followers more plausibly. (P-OR-190-191)

Jesus as Economist. To hang me for cutting a dock laborer's throat after making much of me for leaving him to starve when I do not happen to have a ship for him to unload is idiotic; for as he does far less mischief with his throat cut than when he is starving, a rational society would esteem the cutthroat more highly than the capitalist. The thing has become so obvious, and the evil so unendurable, that if our attempt at civilization is not to perish like all the previous ones, we shall have to organize our society in such a way as to be able to say to every person in the land, "take no thought, saying What shall we eat? or What shall we drink? or Wherewithal shall we be clothed?" We shall then no longer have a race of men whose hearts are in their pockets and safes and at their bankers. As Jesus said, where your treasure is, there will your heart be also. That is why he recommended that money should cease to be a treasure, and that we should take steps to make ourselves utterly reckless of it, setting our minds free for higher uses. . . . Decidely, whether you think Jesus was God or not, you must admit that he was a first-rate political economist. (P-AL-60-61)

Modernization of Christianity. We must . . . bear in mind that whereas, in the time of Jesus, and in the ages which grew darker and darker after his death until the darkness, after a brief false dawn in the Reformation and the Renascence, culminated in the commercial night of the nineteenth century, it was believed that you could not make men good by Act of Parliament, we now know that you cannot make them good in any other way, and that a man who is better than his fellows is a nuisance. The rich man must sell up not only himself but his whole class; and that can be done only through the Chancellor of the Exchequer. The disciple cannot have his bread without money until there is bread for everybody without money; and that requires an elaborate municipal organization of the food supply, rate supported. Being members one of another means One Man One Vote, and One Woman One Vote, and universal suffrage and equal incomes and all sorts of modern political measures. . . .

In short, Christiantiy, good or bad, right or wrong, must perforce be left out of the question in human affairs until it is made practicably applicable to them by complicated political devices; and to pretend that a field preacher under the governorship of Pontius Pilate, or even Pontius Pilate himself in council with all the wisdom of Rome, could have worked out applications of Christianity or any other system of morals for the twentieth century, is to shelve the subject much more effectually than Nero and all its other persecutors ever succeeded in doing. Personal righteousness, and the view that you cannot make people moral by Act of Parliament, is, in fact, the favorite defensive resort of the people who, consciously or subconsciously, are quite determined not to have their property meddled with by Jesus or any other reformer. (P-AL-52-53)

We Cannot Resist Jesus. When the Protestants translated the Bible into the vernacular and let it loose among the people, they did an extremely dangerous thing, as the mischief which followed proves; but they incidentally let loose the sayings of Jesus in open competition with the sayings of Paul and Koheleth and David and Solomon and the authors of Job and the Pentateuch; and, as we have seen, Jesus seems to be the winning name. The glaring contradiction between his teaching and the practice of all the States and all the Churches is no longer hidden. And it may be that though nineteen centuries have passed since Jesus was born (the date of his birth is now quaintly given as 7 B.C., though some contend for 100 B.C.), and though his church has not yet been founded nor his political system tried, the bankruptcy of all the other systems when audited by our vital statistics, which give us a final test for all political systems, is driving us hard into accepting him, not as a scapegoat, but as one who was much less of a fool in practical matters than we have hitherto all thought him. (P-AL-85-86)

OURS

Christianity Slain. Christianity as a specific doctrine was slain with Jesus, suddenly and utterly. He was hardly cold in his grave, or high in his heaven (as you please), before the apostles dragged the tradition of him down to the level of the thing it has remained ever since. (P-AL-73)

Religion: A Frame of Reference. As it is, Christianity has split into sects, persuasions, and Nonconformities in all directions. The Statesman's Yearbook has given up trying to list them. They range from Pillars of Fire, Jehovah's Witnesses, Plymouth Brothers, and Glasites, to Presbyterians, Methodists, Congregationalists, Baptists, Friends (Quakers), and Unitarians. Within the Established Church itself there are Ritualists, Anglo-Catholics who call their services Masses and never mention the Reformation, Laodicean Broad Churchmen, and Low Church Protestants. The Friends abhor ritual and dictated prayers, and repudiate cathedral services and Masses as playacting, whilst the Anglo-Catholics cannot think religiously without them. Presbyterians and Congregationalists differ from the clergy of the Established Church on the political issue of episcopal or lay Church government. The Unitarians reject the Trinity and deny deity to Jesus. Calvinists deny universal atonement, preached by our missionaries, who are practically all Independents.

Common to these irreconcilable faiths is the pretension that each is the true Catholic Church, and should hand over all whom it cannot convert to the State (the Secular Arm) to be exterminated for the crime of heresy by the cruellest possible methods, even to burning alive. This does not mean that all rulers who order such extermination are horribly cruel. "Bloody Mary" believed that heretics must be liquidated; but she was not responsible for the political circumstances that the secular criminal law was atrociously cruel, and that no other agency could effect the liquidation. Calvin agreed that Servetus must be killed; but he objected humanely to his being burned. Charles II, humane (indeed, as some think, too humane in his kindness to his dozen dogs and half dozen mistresses), could not question the necessity for punishing the Regicides with death; but he loathed the butchering of them in the hideous manner ordained centuries earlier for the punishment of William Wallace, and stopped it as soon as he dared. It was still unrepealed during my own lifetime; and has only just (1948) been repealed in Scotland.

So far I have not been imprisoned, as poorer men have been in my time, for blasphemy or apostasy. I am not technically an apostate, as I have never been confirmed; and my godparents are dead. But having torn some of the Thirtynine Articles to rags, I should have been pilloried and had my ears cropped had I lived in the days of the British Inquisition called the Star Chamber. Nowadays Nonconformity and Agnosticism are far too powerful electorally for such persecution. But the Blasphemy Laws are still available and in use against obscure sceptics, whilst I suffer nothing worse than incessant attempts to convert me. All the religions and their sects, Christian or Moslem, Buddhist or Shinto, Jain or Jew, call me to repentance, and ask me for subscriptions. I am not so bigoted as to dismiss their experiences as the inventions of liars and the fancies of noodles. They are evidence like

any other human evidence; and they force me to the conclusion
that every grade of human intelligence can be civilized by providing
it with a frame of reference peculiar to its mental capacity, and
called a religion. (P-FF-74-75)

Pity the Gods. If we could only realize that though the Life
Force supplies us with its own purpose, it has no other brains to
work with than those it has painfully and imperfectly evolved in
our heads, the peoples of the earth would learn some pity for their
gods; and we should have a religion that would not be contradicted
at every turn by the thing that is giving the lie to the thing that
ought to be. (P-IK-xxv-xxvi)

Worldliness of the Majority. The first common mistake to
get rid of is that mankind consists of a great mass of religious people
and a few eccentric atheists. It consists of a huge mass of worldly
people, and a small percentage of persons deeply interested in religion and concerned about their own souls and other peoples';
and this section consists mostly of those who are passionately
affirming the established religion and those who are passionately
attacking it, the genuine philosophers being very few. (P-AL-10)

The Imposter in Strange Robes. At present, if a woman
opens a consulting room in Bond Street, and sits there in strange
robes professing to tell the future by cards or crystals or revelations
made to her by spirits, she is prosecuted as a criminal for imposture.
But if a man puts on strange robes and opens a church in which
he professes to absolve us from the guilt of our misdeeds, to hold
the keys of heaven and hell, to guarantee that what he looses or
binds on earth shall be loosed and bound in heaven, to alleviate
the lot of souls in purgatory, to speak with the voice of God, and
to dictate what is sin and what is not to all the world (pretensions which, if you look at them objectively, are far more extravagant and dangerous than those of the poor sorceress with her cards
and tea leaves and crystals), the police treat him with great respect; and nobody dreams of prosecuting him as an outrageous
impostor. (IWGSC-429)

Same Salvation for All. "There are neither good men nor scoundrels; there are just children of one Father; and the sooner they stop calling one another names the better. You neednt talk to me: I know them. Ive had scores of them through my hands: scoundrels, criminals, infidels, philanthropists, missionaries, county councillors, all sorts. Theyre all just the same sort of sinner; and there's the same salvation ready for them all." (*Barbara,* MB-262)

The Average Clergyman. The average clergyman is an official who makes his living by christening babies, marrying adults, conducting a ritual, and making the best he can (when he has any conscience about it) of a certain routine of school superintendence, district visiting, and organization of almsgiving, which does not necessarily touch Christianity at any point except the point of the tongue. (E-AL-148).

"Gawd" with a Long Face. "When you really believe in God you can make fun of him. When you are only pretending you pull long faces and call Him GAWD." (*Mrs. Thirdborn,* BB-37)

The Philistine Church. The Church, like the society of which it is an organ, is balanced and steadied by the great central Philistine mass above whom theology looms as a highly spoken of and doubtless most important thing, like Greek tragedy, or classical music, or the higher mathematics, but who are very glad when church is over and they can go home to lunch or dinner, having in fact, for all practical purposes, no reasoned convictions at all, and being equally ready to persecute a poor Freethinker for saying that St. James was not infallible, and to send one of the Peculiar People to prison for being so very peculiar as to take St. James seriously. (E-AL-148-149)

"Really, Barbara, you go on as if religion were a pleasant subject. Do have some sense of propriety." (*Lady Britomart,* MB-263)

The Church Captured by the Rich. Just as Parliament and the Courts are captured by the rich, so is the Church. The average parson does not teach honesty and equality in the village school: he teaches deference to the merely rich, and calls that loyalty and religion. He is the ally of the squire, who, as magistrate, administers the laws made in the interests of the rich by the parliament of rich men, and calls that justice. The villagers, having no experience of any other sort of religion or law, soon lose all respect for both, and become merely cynical. They may touch their hats and curtsey respectfully; but they whisper to oneanother that the squire, no matter how kind his wife may be at Christmas by way of ransom, is a despoiler and oppressor of the poor, and the parson a hypocrite. In revolutions, it is the respectful peasants who burn the country houses and parsonages, and rush to the cathedrals to deface the statues, shatter the stained windows, and wreck the organ.

. . . you may know parsons who are not like that. At least I do. There are always men and women who will stand out against injustice, no matter how prosperous or well-spoken-of it may be. But the result is that they are ill-spoken-of themselves in the most influential quarters. Our society must be judged, not by its few rebels, but by its millions of obedient subjects. (IWGSC-63)

Sermons Will Not Kill Poverty & Slavery. "I hate poverty and slavery worse than any other crimes whatsoever. And let me tell you this. Poverty and slavery have stood up for centuries to your sermons and leading articles: they will not stand up to my machine guns. Dont preach at them: dont reason with them. Kill them." (*Undershaft*, MB-331)

"My religion? Well, my dear, I am a Millionaire. That is my religion." (*Undershaft*, MB-279)

Torpedo Morality. "I am not one of those men who keep their morals and their business in water-tight compartments. All the spare money my trade rivals spend on hospitals, cathedrals, and other receptacles for conscience money, I devote to experiments and researches in improved methods of destroying life and

property. I have always done so; and I always shall. Therefore
your Christmas card moralities of peace on earth and goodwill
among men are of no use to me. Your Christianity, which enjoins
you to resist not evil, and to turn the other cheek, would make
me a bankrupt. My morality—my religion—must have a place
for cannons and torpedoes in it." (*Undershaft*, MB-261-262)

The Religious Bodies: Auxiliary Police. Churches are suf-
fered to exist only on condition that they preach submission to
the State as at present capitalistically organized. The Church of
England itself is compelled to add to the thirty-six articles in
which it formulates its religious tenets, three more in which it
apologetically protests that the moment any of these articles
comes in conflict with the State it is to be entirely renounced,
abjured, violated, abrogated and abhorred, the policeman being a
much more important person than any of the Persons of the
Trinity. And this is why no tolerated Church nor Salvation Army
can ever win the entire confidence of the poor. It must be on the
side of the police and the military, no matter what it believes or
disbelieves; and as the police and the military are the instruments
by which the rich rob and oppress the poor (on legal and moral
principles made for the purpose), it is not possible to be on the
side of the poor and of the police at the same time. Indeed the
religious bodies, as the almoners of the rich, become a sort of
auxiliary police, taking off the insurrectionary edge of poverty with
coals and blankets, bread and treacle, and soothing and cheering
the victims with hopes of immense and inexpensive happiness in
another world when the process of working them to premature
death in the service of the rich is complete in this. (P-MB-231)

Cheap Conversion. "It is cheap work converting starving
men with a Bible in one hand and a slice of bread in the other."
(*Undershaft*, MB-330)

The Way To Get Rescue Money. "Them Salvation lasses
is dear good girls; but the better you are, the worse they likes to

think you were before they rescued you. Why shouldnt they av a bit o credit, poor loves? theyre worn to rags by their work. And where would they get the money to rescue us if we was to let on we're no worse than other people? You know what ladies and gentlemen are." (*Rummy*, MB-268)

Why the Christian System Failed. The . . . Christian System failed, not because it was wrong in its psychology, its fundamental postulate of equality, or its anticipation of Lenin's principle that the rulers must be as poor as the ruled so that they can raise themselves only by raising their people, but because the old priests' ignorance of economics and political science blinded them to the mischief latent in the selfishness of private property in the physical earth. Before the Church knew where it was (it has not quite located itself yet) it found itself so prodigiously rich that the Pope was a secular Italian prince with armies and frontiers, enjoying not only the rent of Church lands, but selling salvation on such a scale that when Torquemada began burning Jews instead of allowing them to ransom their bodies by payments to the Roman treasury, and leaving their souls to God, a first-rate quarrel between the Church and the Spanish Inquisition was the result. (P-TTTBG-22)

The Church Corrupted by Its Own Property. Whilst the Church was being so corrupted by its own property, and by the influence on it of the lay proprietors, that it lost all its moral prestige, the warriors and robbers of the Empire had been learning from experience that a pirate ship needs a hierarchy of officers and an iron discipline even more than the police boats, and that the work of robbing the poor all the time involves a very elaborate system of government to insure that the poor shall, like bees, continue to produce not only their own subsistence but the surplus that can be robbed from them without bringing on them the doom of the goose that lays the golden eggs. Naked coercion is so expensive that it became necessary to practise on the imaginations of the poor to the extent of making them believe that it is a pious duty to be robbed, and that their moment of life in this world is only a prelude to an eternity in which the poor will be blest and happy, and the rich horribly tortured. (P-TTTBG-22-23)

Russia Rediscovers the Church System. A tremendous importance is given to a clear understanding of the Catholic system at this moment by the staggering fact that the biggest State in the modern world, having made a clean sweep of its Church by denouncing its religion as dope, depriving its priests and bishops of any greater authority than a quack can pick up at a fair, encouraging its most seriously minded children to form a League of the Godless, shooting its pious Tsar, turning its cathedrals into historical museums illustrating the infamies of ecclesiastical history and expressly entitling them anti-religious: in short, addressing itself solemnly and implacably to a root-and-branch extermination of everything that we associate with priesthood, has, under pressure of circumstances, unconsciously and spontaneously established as its system of government an as-close-as-possible reproduction of the hierarchy of the Catholic Church. The nomenclature is changed, of course: the Church is called the Communist Party; and the Holy Office and its familiars are known as the Komintern and the Gay Pay Oo. . . . But essentially the system is that of the old Christian Catholic Church, even to its fundamental vow of Communism and the death penalty on Ananias and Sapphira for violating it.

If our newspapers knew what is really happening in the world, or could discriminate between the news value of a bicycle accident in Clapham and that of a capsize of civilization, their columns would be literally full of this epoch-making event. And the first question they would address to Russia would be "Why, seeing that the Christian system has been such a hopeless failure, do you go back to it, and invite us to go back to it?" (P-TTTBG-20-22)

Russia Teaches Christian Communism. In Russia it is now established that capital was made for Man, and not Man for

Capitalism. The children are taught the Christian morality of Communism instead of the Mammonist morality of Capitalism. The palaces and pleasure seats of the plutocrats are used for the recreation of workers instead of for the enervation of extravagant wasters. Idle ladies and gentlemen are treated with salutary contempt, whilst the worker's blouse is duly honored. The treasures of art, respected and preserved with a conscientiousness which puts to shame our own lootings in China, and our iconoclasms and vandalisms at home, are accessible to everyone. The Greek Church is tolerated (the Bolsheviks forebore to cut off their Archbishop's head as we cut off Archbishop Laud's); but it is not, as the Church of England is, allowed without contradiction to tell little children lies about the Bible under pretence of giving them religious instruction, nor to teach them to reverence the merely rich as their betters. That sort of doctrine is officially and properly disavowed as dope. (IWGSC-374)

Crime & Punishment

What we are confronted with now is a growing perception that if we desire a certain type of civilization and culture we must exterminate the sort of people who do not fit into it. (P-OR-181)

Competition in Evil Between Prison & Slum. When we get down to the poorest and most oppressed of our population we find the conditions of their life so wretched that it would be impossible to conduct a prison humanely without making the lot of the criminal more eligible than that of many free citizens. If the prison does not underbid the slum in human misery, the slum will empty and the prison will fill. This does in fact take place to a small extent at present, because slum life at its worst is so atrocious that its victims, when they are intelligent enough to study alternatives instead of taking their lot blindly, conclude that prison is the most comfortable place to spend the winter in, and qualify themselves accordingly by committing an offence for which they will get six months. But this consideration affects only those people whose condition is not defended by any responsible publicist: the remedy is admittedly not to make the prison worse but the slum better. Unfortunately the admitted claims of the poor on life are pitifully modest. The moment the treatment of the criminal is decent and merciful enough to give him a chance of moral recovery, or, in incorrigible cases, to avoid making bad worse, the official descriptions of his lot become so rosy that a clamor arises against thieves and murderers being better off than honest and kindly men; for the official reports tell us only of the care that is taken of the prisoner and the advantages he enjoys, or can earn by good conduct, never of his sufferings; and the public is not imaginative or thoughtful enough to supply the deficiency. (CC-175)

What Price the Exchange? What sane man, I ask the clamorers, would accept an offer of free board, lodging, clothing, waiters in attendance at a touch of the bell, medical treatment, spiritual advice, scientific ventilation and sanitation, technical instruction, liberal education, and the use of a carefully selected library, with regular exercise daily and sacred music at frequent intervals, even at the very best of the Ritz Hotels, if the conditions were that he should never leave the hotel, never speak, never sing, never laugh, never see a newspaper, and write only one sternly censored letter and have one miserable interview at long intervals through the bars of a cage under the eye of a warder? And when the prison is not the Ritz Hotel, when the lodging, the food, the bed, are all deliberately made so uncomfortable as to be instruments of torture, when the clothes are rags promiscuously worn by all your fellow-prisoners in turn with yourself, when the exercise is that of a turnspit, when the ventilation and sanitation are noisome, when the instruction is a sham, the education a fraud, when the doctor is a bully to whom your ailments are all malingerings, and the chaplain a moral snob with no time for anything but the distribution of unreadable books, when the waiters are bound by penalties not to speak to you except to give you an order or a rebuke, and then to address you as you would not dream of addressing your dog, when the manager holds over your head a continual threat of starvation and confinement in a punishment cell (as if your own cell were not punishment enough), then what man in his senses would voluntarily exchange even the most harassed freedom for such a life, much less wallow luxuriously in it, as the Punch burglar always does on paper the moment anyone suggests the slightest alleviation of the pains of imprisonment. (CC-176)

The Economy Aspect. The Prison Commissioners know that if prisons were made reasonably happy places, and thrown open to volunteers like the army, they might speedily be overcrowded. And this, with its implied threat of an enormous increase of taxation, seems a conclusive objection.

But if its effect would be to convert a large mass of more or less dishonest, unproductive or half productive, unsatisfactory, feckless, nervous, anxious, wretched people into good citizens, it is absurd to object to it as costly. It would be unbearably costly, of course, if the life and labor of its subjects were as stupidly wasted as they are in our prisons; but any scheme into which the conditions of our present system are read will stand condemned at once. Whether the labor of the subject be organized by the State, as in Government dockyards, post offices, municipal industries and services and so forth, or by private employers obtaining labor service from the authorities, organized and used productively it must be; and anyone who maintains that such organization and production costs the nation more than wasting the labor power of able-bodied men and women either by imprisonment or by throwing criminals on the streets to prey on society and on themselves, is maintaining a monstrous capitalistic paradox. Obviously it will not cost the nation anything at all: it will enrich it and protect it. The real commercial objection to it is that it would reduce the supply of sweatable labor available for unscrupulous private employers. But so much the better if it does. Sweating may make profits for private persons here and there; but their neighbors have to pay through the nose for these profits in poor rates, police rates, public health rates (mostly disease rates), and all the rest of the gigantic expenditure, all pure waste and mischief, which falls on the ratepayer and taxpayer in his constant struggle with the fruits of the poverty which he is nevertheless invited to maintain for the sake of making two or three of his neighbors unwholesomely and unjustly rich. (CC-208-209)

Soft Cases that We Turn into Hard Ones. Now let us look
at the other end of the scale, where the soft cases are. Here we
are confronted with the staggering fact that many of our prisoners
have not been convicted of any offence at all. They are awaiting
their trial, and are too poor and friendless to find bail; whilst others
have been convicted of mere breaches of bye-laws of which they
were ignorant, and which they could not have guessed by their
sense of right and wrong; for many bye-laws have no ethical character whatever. For example, a boy sells a newspaper on the prem-
ises of a railway company, and thereby infringes a bye-law the
object of which is to protect the commercial monopoly of the news-
agents who have paid the company for the right to have a book-
stall on the platform. The boy's brother jostles a passenger who is
burdened with hand luggage; and says "Carry your bag, sir?" These
perfectly innocent lads are sent to prison, though the warders
themselves admit that a sentence of imprisonment is so ruinous
to a boy's morals that they would rather see their own sons dead
than in prison. (CC-201)

Most Prisoners no Worse than Ourselves. We may take
it ... that the thief who is in prison is not necessarily more dishonest than his fellows at large, but mostly only one who, through
ignorance or stupidity, steals in a way that is not customary.
He snatches a loaf from the baker's counter and is promptly
run into gaol. Another man snatches bread from the tables of
hundreds of widows and orphans and simple credulous souls who
do not know the ways of company promoters; and, as likely as
not, he is run into Parliament. You may say that the remedy for
this is not to spare the lesser offender but to punish the greater;
but there you miss my present point, which is, that as the great
majority of prisoners are not a bit more dishonest naturally than
thousands of people who are not only at liberty, but highly pam-
pered, it is no use telling me that society will fall into anarchic
dissolution if these unlucky prisoners are treated with common
humanity. On the contrary, when we see the outrageous extent
to which the most shamelessly selfish rogues and rascals can be

granted not only impunity but encouragement and magnificent re-
muneration, we are tempted to ask ourselves have we any right
to restrain anyone at all from doing his worst to us. The first prison
I ever saw had inscribed on it *CEASE TO DO EVIL: LEARN
TO DO WELL;* but as the inscription was on the outside, the
prisoners could not read it. It should have been addressed to the
self-righteous free spectator in the street, and should have run
*ALL HAVE SINNED, AND FALLEN SHORT OF THE
GLORY OF GOD.* (CC-203)

Honesty Varies with the Strain Put on It. We must get
out of the habit of painting human character in soot and white-
wash. It is not true that men can be divided into absolutely honest
persons and absolutely dishonest ones. Our honesty varies with the
strain put on it: this is proved by the fact that every additional
penny of income tax brings in less than the preceding penny. The
purchaser of a horse or motor-car has to beware much more carefully than the purchaser of an article worth five shillings. If you
take Landru* at one extreme, and at the other the prisoner whose
crime is sleeping out: that is to say, whose crime is no crime at
all, you can place every sane human being, from the monarch to
the tramp, somewhere on the scale between them. Not one of
them has a blank page in the books of the Recording Angel. From
the people who tell white lies about their ages, social positions,
and incomes, to those who grind the faces of the poor, or marry
whilst suffering from contagious disease, or buy valuable properties from inexperienced owners for a tenth of their value, or sell
worthless shares for the whole of a widow's savings, or obtain vast
sums on false pretenses held forth by lying advertisements, to say
nothing of bullying and beating in their homes, and drinking and
debauching in their bachelorhood, you could at any moment find
dozens of people who have never been imprisoned and never will
be, and are yet worse citizens than any but the very worst of our
convicts. Much of the difference between the bond and the free
is a difference in circumstances only: If a man is not hungry, and

* The French murderer.

his children are ailing only because they are too well fed, nobody can tell whether he would steal a loaf if his children were
crying for bread and he himself had not tasted a mouthful for
twenty-four hours. Therefore, if you are in an attitude of moral
superiority to our convicts: if you are one of the Serve Them Right
and Give Them Hell brigade, you may justly be invited, in your
own vernacular, either to Come Off It, or else Go Inside and take
the measure you are meeting out to others no worse than yourself.
(CC-203-204)

The Trade in Good Looks. "Do you think we were such
fools as to let other people trade in our good looks by employing
us as shopgirls, or barmaids, or waitresses, when we could trade in
them ourselves and get all the profits instead of starvation wages?"
(*Mrs. Warren*, MWP-203)

Our Plague of Unrestrained Crime. If it be true, as it certainly is, that it is conscience and not the fear of punishment that
makes civilized life possible, and that Dr. Johnson's
          How small, of all that human hearts endure,
          That part that laws or kings can cause or cure!
is as applicable to crime as to human activity in general, it is none
the less true that commercial civilization presents an appalling
spectacle of pillage and parasitism, of corruption in the press and
in the pulpit, of lying advertisements which make people buy rank
poisons in the belief that they are health restorers, of traps to
catch the provision made for the widow and the fatherless and
divert it to the pockets of company promoting rogues, of villainous
oppression of the poor and cruelty to the defenceless; and it is
arguable that most of this could, like burglary and forgery, be kept
within bearable bounds if its perpertrators were dealt with as bur-
glars and forgers are dealt with today. It is, let us not forget, equally
arguable that if we can afford to leave so much villainy unpunished
we can afford to leave all villainy unpunished. Unfortunately, we
cannot afford it: our toleration is threatening our civilization. The
prosperity that consists in the wicked flourishing like a green bay

tree, and the humble and contrite hearts being thoroughly despised, is a commercial delusion. (CC-183)

Criminal Characteristics in Polite Society. The gentleman beats the criminal hollow in the magnitude of his operations and the number of people employed in them. For the depredations of the criminal are negligibly small compared to the military holocausts and ravaged areas, the civic slums, the hospitals, the cemeteries crowded with the prematurely dead, and the labor markets in which men and women are exposed for sale for all purposes, honorable and dishonorable. These are the products of criminal ideas imposed on the entire population. The common thief and burglar, miserably sweated by the receiver to whom he has to sell his plunder, steals a few spoons or diamonds at a monstrous risk, and gets less than a tenth of their value from a rascal who runs no risk worth considering; and the poor wretch is content with the trumpery debauch his hard-earned percentage brings him. The gentleman steals a whole country, or a perpetual income for himself and his descendants, and is never satisfied until he has more conquests and more riches to boast of. What is more, the illicit thief does not defend his conduct ethically. He may cry "To hell with the parsons and with honesty and white-livered respectability!" and so forth; but he does so as a defier of God, a public enemy, a Satanic hero. The gentleman really believes that he is a creator of national prestige, a defender of the faith, a pillar of society; and with this conviction to strengthen him he is utterly unscrupulous in his misplaced pride and honor, and plays the wholesaler in evil to the criminal's petty retail enterprises. (CC-228)

The Model Employer. "So long as you come here honestly as a self-respecting, thorough, convinced scoundrel, justifying your scoundrelism and proud of it, you are welcome. But I wont have you here snivelling about being a model employer and a converted man when youre only an apostate with your coat turned for the sake of a County Council contract." (*Morell,* C-18)

Man Must Justify His Existence. In a civilized community
life is not a matter of course: it can be maintained only on complicated artificial conditions; and whoever enlarges his life by violating these conditions enlarges it at the expense of others. The
extent to which we tolerate such vital embezzlement at present
is quite outrageous: we have whole classes of persons who waste,
squander, and luxuriate in the hard-earned income of the nation
without even a pretence of social service or contribution of any
kind; and instead of sternly calling on them to justify their existence or go to the scrap heap, we encourage and honor them, and
indeed conduct the whole business of the country as if its object
were to produce and pamper them. How can a prison chaplain
appeal with any effect to the conscience of a professional criminal
who knows quite well that his illegal and impecunious modes of
preying on society are no worse morally, and enormously less mischievous materially, than the self-legalized plutocratic modes practised by the chaplain's most honored friends with the chaplain's
full approval? The moment we cease asking whether men are good
or bad, and ascertain simply whether they are pulling their weight
in the social boat, our persistent evildoers may have a very unpleasant surprise. Far from having an easy time under a Government of soft-hearted and soft-headed sentimentalists, cooing that
"to understand everything is to pardon everything," they may find
themselves disciplined to an extent at present undreamed of by
the average man-about-town. (CC-218-219)

Torture as Justice. It is true that between self-controlled
people and ungovernable people there is a narrow margin of moral
malingerers who can be made to behave themselves by the fear
of consequences; but it is not worth while maintaining an abominable system of malicious, deliberate, costly and degrading ill-
treatment of criminals for the sake of these marginal cases. For
practical dealing with crime, Determinism or Predestination is
quite a good working rule. People without self-control enough for
social purposes may be killed, or may be kept in asylums with a
view to studying their condition and ascertaining whether it is

curable. To torture them and give ourselves virtuous airs at their expense is ridiculous and barbarous; and the desire to do it is vindictive and cruel. And though vindictiveness and cruelty are at least human qualities when they are frankly proclaimed and indulged, they are loathesome when they assume the robes of justice. . . .

I need not elaborate the argument further . . . I have only to point out that we have been judging and punishing ever since Jesus told us not to; and I defy anyone to make out a convincing case for believing that the world has been any better than it would have been if there had never been a judge, a prison, or a gallows in it all that time. We have simply added the misery of punishment to the misery of crime, and the cruelty of the judge to the cruelty of the criminal. We have taken the bad man, and made him worse by torture and degradation, incidentally making ourselves worse in the process. It does not seem very sensible, does it? It would have been far easier to kill him as kindly as possible, or to label him and leave him to his conscience, or to treat him as an invalid or a lunatic is now treated. . . . (P-AL-65-66)

Contracting-Out of the Moral Code. We shall never have real moral responsibilty until everyone knows that his deeds are irrevocable, and that his life depends on his usefulness. Hitherto, alas! humanity has never dared face these hard facts. We frantically scatter conscience money and invent systems of conscience banking, with expiatory penalties, atonements, redemptions, salvations, hospital subscription lists and what not, to enable us to contract out of the moral code. Not content with the old scapegoat and sacrificial lamb, we deify human saviors, and pray to miraculous virgin intercessors. We attribute mercy to the inexorable; soothe our consciences after committing murder by throwing ourselves on the bosom of divine love; and shrink even from our own gallows because we are forced to admit that it, at least, is irrevocable —as if one hour of imprisonment were not as irrevocable as any execution! (P-MB-239-240)

Democracy

Democracy in the most democratic modern republics: France and the United States for example, is an imposture and a delusion.

(P-AL-60)

"Democracy reads well; but it doesnt act well, like some people's plays." (*Lord Summerhays*, M-129)

Democracy: The Vision & The Reality. "Democracy was a great thing when I was young and we had no votes. We talked about public opinion and what the British people would stand and what they wouldnt stand. And it had weight, I tell you, sir: it held Governments in check: it frightened the stoutest of the tyrants and the bosses and the police: it brought a real reverence into the voices of great orators like Bright and Gladstone. But that was when it was a dream and a vision, a hope and faith and a promise. It lasted until they dragged it down to earth, as you might say, and made it a reality by giving everybody votes. The moment they gave the working men votes they found theyd stand anything. They gave votes to the women and found they were worse than the men; for men would vote for men—the wrong men, but men all the same—but the women wouldnt even vote for women. Since then politics have been a laughing stock. Parliamentary leaders say one thing on Monday and just the opposite on Wesdnesday; and nobody notices any difference. They put down the people in Egypt, in Ireland,

and in India with fire and sword, with floggings and hangings, burning the houses over their heads and bombing their little stores for
the winter out of existence; and at the next election theyd be sent
back to Parliament by working class constituencies as if they were
plaster saints, while men and women like me, that had spent their
lives in the service of the people, were booted out at the polls like
convicted criminals. It wasnt that the poor silly sheep did it on
purpose. They didnt notice: they didnt remember: they couldnt
understand: they were taken in by any nonsense they heard at the
meetings or read in the morning paper. You could stampede them
by crying out that the Russians were coming, or rally them by
promising them to hang the Kaiser, or Lord knows what silliness
that shouldnt have imposed on a child of four. That was the
end of democracy for me; though there was no man alive that had
hoped as much from it, nor spoke deeper from his heart about all
the good things that would happen when the people came to their
own and had votes like the gentry." (*Hipney*, OR-325-326)

Anarchism's Supreme Achievement.   The ordinary man— we
have to face it: it is every bit as true of the ordinary Englishman
as of the ordinary American—is an anarchist. He wants to do as he
likes. He may want his neighbor to be governed, but he himself
doesnt want to be governed. He is mortally afraid of government
officials and policemen. He loathes tax collectors. He shrinks from
giving anybody any official power whatever. This anarchism has
been at work in the world since the beginnings of civilization; and
its supreme achievement up to date is the American Constitution.
(FPSA-6)

Slaves Will Be Slaves.   The Anarchists are right when they
say that Governments, like schoolmasters, try to simplify their
task by destroying liberty and glorifying authority, especially their
own. But the difficulty of combining law and order with free institutions is not a natural one. It is a matter of inculcation. If people
are brought up to be slaves, it is useless and dangerous to let them
loose at the age of twenty-one and say "Now you are free." No one

with the tamed soul and broken spirit of a slave can be free. It is like saying to a laborer brought up on a family income of thirteen shillings a week, "Here is one hundred thousand pounds: now you are wealthy." Nothing can make such a man really wealthy. Freedom and wealth are difficult and responsible conditions to which men must be accustomed and socially trained from birth. A nation that is free at twenty-one is not free at all; just as a man first enriched at fifty remains poor all his life, even if he does not curtail it by drinking himself to death in the first wild ecstasy of being able to swallow as much as he likes for the first time. You cannot govern men brought up as slaves otherwise than as slaves are governed. You may pile Bills of Right and Habeas Corpus Acts on Great Charters; promulgate American Constitutions; burn the châteaux and guillotine the seigneurs; chop off the heads of kings and queens and set up Democracy on the ruins of feudalism: the end of it all for us is that already in the twentieth century there has been as much brute coercion and savage intolerance, as much flogging and hanging, as much impudent injustice on the bench and lustful rancor in the pulpit, as much naive resort to torture, persecution, and suppression of free speech and freedom of the press, as much war, as much as the vilest excess of mutilation, rapine, and delirious indiscriminate slaughter of helpless non-combatants, old and young, as much prostitution of professional talent, literary and political, in defence of manifest wrong, as much cowardly sycophancy giving fine names to all this villainy or pretending that it is "greatly exaggerated," as we can find any record of from the days when the advocacy of liberty was a capital offence and Democracy was hardly thinkable." (P-M-101-102)

The Constitution: A Great Protest. In England we have the British constitution; but nobody knows what it is: it is not written down anywhere; and you can no more amend it than you can amend the east wind. But in the United States you have a real tangible readable document. I can nail you down to every one of its sentences.

And what does it amount to? A great protest against the tyranny of law and order. A final manifesto from the centuries of revolutionary anarchism in which the struggle went on against government as such, against government by feudal barons, by autocratic kings, by the Pope and his cardinals, by the parliaments which have gradually ousted all these authorities, each of them in turn being used to disable the others in the glorified cause of what people called Liberty, until, when the power of the king was destroyed, the power of the barons destroyed, the power of the Church destroyed, and finally all effective parliamentary governing power destroyed, you found yourselves hopelessly in the power of your private racketeers, from the humble gunman to the great financial magnate, each playing for his own hand without status, without national authority or responsibility, without legal restraint, and without any sense of public government. You had perfected a Constitution of negatives to defend liberty, liberty, liberty—life, liberty and the pursuit of happiness—against the only checks on anarchy that could secure them, and fortified it by a Supreme Court which dealt out nothing but prohibitions, and a political party machinery of legislatures and senates which was so wonderfully devised that when you sent in one body of men to govern the country you sent in another body of men along with them to prevent their doing it. In your dread of dictators you established a state of society in which every ward boss is a dictator, every financier a dictator, every private employer a dictator, all with the livelihood of the workers at their mercy, and no public responsibility. (FPSA-6-7)

The Government: A Gabble Shop. "The government of your country! *I* am the government of your country. I, and Lazarus. Do you suppose that you and half a dozen amateurs like you, sitting in a row in that foolish gabble shop, can govern Undershaft and Lazarus? No, my friend: you will do what pays us. You will make war when it suits us, and keep peace when it doesnt. You will find out that trade requires certain measures when we have decided on those measures. When I want anything to keep my dividends up, you will discover that my want is a national need. When other people want something to keep my dividends down, you will call out the police and military. And in return you shall have the support and applause of my newspapers, and the delight of imagining that you are a great statesman. Government of your country! Be off with you, my boy, and play with your caucuses and leading articles and historic parties and great leaders and burning questions and the rest of your toys. *I* am going back to my counting-house to pay the piper and call the tune." (*Undershaft*, MB-312)

Democracy's Pretences. Democracy as it exists today has little more to say for itself than that its hopes and possibilities are infinite, whereas the possibilities of oligarchy and autocracy are limited to such an extent by their fundamental economic and psychic unsoundness that they can hardly be said to hold out any hopes at all. But they are not fraudulent except when they pretend to be democratic; and of this particular fraud the republics are ten times more guilty than the monarchies. Lincoln's famous formula of government of the people by the people for the people was always impossible as to its second count; for the people can no more govern than they can write plays or use the infinitesimal calculus. Even government by consent of the governed is impossible as long as people are so uneducated politically that they will not consent to be governed at all, and must therefore be governed, under one pretence or another, by main force. But government of the people for the people is possible, and is the goal of democracy. Now no political system at present existing on earth attains that goal, or is even visibly tending towards it. It has proved safer to be a frank traitor under the Hohenzollerns, like Liebknecht, even in war time, than to be a Conservative Non-Interventionist in the United States of America; and Mr. Wilson goes into the Peace Conference with the knowledge that if recriminations begin as to the condition of the people, the reasonableness of the distribution of the national income, the exploitation of child labor, the prevalence of Lynch law, the toleration of heterodox or anti-governmental opinion (even under Mr. Wilson's own rule), the general level of culture, the cruelty of the criminal codes and the guarantees for justice in their administration, the honesty of the police, and the freedom of municipal and national politics from corruption, American republicanism will come out of the comparison with constitutional monarchy so badly that it will be very difficult for him with any countenance to take the position of a moral dictator imposing superior American political institutions on the rest of the world. Feudal barons are not so much worse than beef barons, or Hohenzollern and Hapsburg kings than railway and kerosene kings, that he can offer a substitution of one for the other as a contribution to the emancipation of the human race. (PCH-46-48)

Democracy: Unashamed Plutocracy. Modern Liberal Democracy claims unlimited opportunities for tyranny: qualification for rule by heredity and class narrows it and puts it in harness and blinkers. Especially does such democracy favor money rule. It is in fact not democracy at all, but unashamed plutocracy. And as the meanest creature can become rich if he devotes his life to it, and the people with wider and more generous interests become or remain poor with equal certainty, plutocracy is the very devil socially, because it creates a sort of Gresham law by which the baser human currency drives out the nobler coinage. This is quite different from the survival of the fittest in the contests of character and talent which are independent of money. If Moses is the only tribesman capable of making a code of law, he inevitably becomes Lawgiver to all the tribes, and, equally inevitably, is forced to add to what he can understand of divine law a series of secular regulations designed to maintain his personal authority. If he finds that it is useless to expect the tribesmen to obey his laws as a matter of common sense, he must persuade them that his inspiration is the result of direct and miraculous communication with their deity. Moses and Mahomet and Joseph Smith the Mormon had to plead divine revelations to get them out of temporary and personal difficulties as well as out of eternal and impersonal ones. As long as an individual of their calibre remains the indispensable man (or woman) doing things that the common man can neither do without nor do for himself, he will be, up to a point, the master of the common man in spite of all the democratic fudge that may be advanced to the contrary. (P-TM-108)

Limits of the Indispensable Man. Of course, there are limits. He cannot go to the lengths at which the common man will believe him to be insane or impious: when measures of that complexion are necessary, as they very often are, he must either conceal them or mask them as follies of the sort the common man thinks splendid. If the ruler thinks it well to begin a world war he must persuade his people that it is a war to end war, and that the people he wants them to kill are diabolical scoundrels; and if he is forced to suspend hostilities for a while, and does so by a treaty which contains the seeds of half a dozen new wars and is impossible enough in its conditions to make its violation certain, he must create a general belief that it is a charter of eternal peace and a monument of retributive justice.

In this way the most honest ruler becomes a tyrant and a fabricator of legends and falsehoods, not out of any devilment in himself, but because those whom he rules do not understand his business, and, if they did, would not sacrifice their own immediate interests to the permanent interests of the nation or the world. In short, a ruler must not only make laws, and rule from day to day: he must, by school instruction and printed propaganda, create and maintain an artificial mentality which will endorse his proceedings and obey his authority. This mentality becomes what we call Conservatism; and the revolt against it when it is abused oppressively or becomes obsolete as social conditions change, is classed as sedition, and reviled as Radicalism, Anarchism, Bolshevism, or what you please. (P-TM-108-109)

"Air, Promise Crammed." It was part of the democratic dream that Parliament was an instrument for carrying out the wishes of the voters, absurdly called its constituents. And as, in the nineteenth century, it was still believed that British individual liberty forbad Parliament to do anything that it could pos-

sibly leave to private enterprise, Parliament was able to keep up its reputation by simply maintaining an effective police force and enforcing private contracts. Even Factory Acts and laws against adulteration and sweating were jealously resisted as interference with the liberty of free Britons. If there was anything wrong, the remedy was an extension of the franchise. Like Hamlet, we live on the chameleon's dish "air, promise crammed."

But you cannot create a mentality out of promises without having to face occasional demands for their materialization. The Treasury Bench was up for auction at every election, the bidding being in promises. The political parties, finding it much less troublesome to give the people votes than to carry out reforms, at last established adult suffrage.

The result was a colossal disappointment and disillusion. The phantom of Democracy, *alias* Public Opinion, which, acting as an artificial political conscience, had restrained Gladstone and Disraeli, vanished. The later parliamentary leaders soon learnt from experience that they might with perfect impunity tell the nation one thing on Tuesday and the opposite on Friday without anyone noticing the discrepancy. The donkey had overtaken the carrots at last; and instead of eating them he allowed them to be snatched away from him by any confidence trickster who told him to look up into the sky. (P-TM-113-114)

The Mountebank Catches the Votes. The politician who once had to learn how to flatter Kings has now to learn how to fascinate, amuse, coax, humbug, frighten or otherwise strike the fancy of the electorate; and though in advanced modern States, where the artizan is better educated than the King, it takes a much bigger man to be a successful demagogue than to be a successful courtier, yet he who holds popular convictions with prodigious energy is the man for the mob, whilst the frailer sceptic who is cautiously feeling his way towards the next century has no chance unless he happens by accident to have the specific artistic talent of the mountebank as well, in which case it is as a mountebank that he catches votes, and not as a meliorist. Consequently the

demagogue, though he professes (and fails) to readjust matters in
the interests of the majority of the electors, yet stereotypes mediocrity, organizes intolerance, disparages exhibitions of uncommon
qualities, and glorifies conspicuous exhibitions of common ones. He
manages a small job well: he muddles rhetorically through a large
one. When a great political movement takes place, it is not consciously led nor organized: the unconscious self in mankind breaks
its way through the problem as an elephant breaks through a
jungle; and the politicians make speeches about whatever happens
in the process, which, with the best intentions, they do all in their
power to prevent. (RHPC-197)

Democracy: Anarchy. What the extension of political power
to the whole community (Democracy, as they call it) has produced is a reinforcement of the popular resistance to government
and taxation at a moment when nothing but a great extension of
government and taxation can hope to control the Gadarene rush
of Capitalism towards the abyss. And this has produced a tendency
which is the very last that the old Suffragists and Suffragettes
dreamt of, or would have advocated if they had dreamt of it:
namely, a demand for the abandonment of parliamentary government and the substitution of a dictatorship. In desperation at the
failure of Parliament to rescue industry from the profiteers, and
currency from the financiers (which means rescuing the livelihood of the people from the purely predatory side of Capitalism),
Europe has begun to clamor for political disciplinarians to save
her. Victorious France, with her currency in the gutter, may be said
to be advertising for a Napoleon or a political Messiah. Italy has
knocked its parliament down and handed the whip to Signor
Mussolini to thrash Italian democracy and bureauocracy into some
sort of order and efficiency. In Spain the king and the military
commander-in-chief have refused to stand any more democratic
nonsense, and taken the law into their own hands. In Russia
a minority of devoted Marxists maintain by sheer force such government as is possible in the teeth of an intensely recalcitrant
peasantry. In England we should welcome another Cromwell but

for two considerations. First, there is no Cromwell. Second, history teaches us that if there were one, and he again ruled us by military force after trying every sort of parliament and finding each worse than the other, he would be worn out or dead after a few years; and then we should return like the sow to her wallowing in the mire and leave the restored profiteers to wreak on the corpse of the worn-out ruler the spite they dared not express whilst he was alive. Thus our inability to govern ourselves lands us in such a mess that we hand the job over to any person strong enough to undertake it; and then our unwillingness to be governed at all makes us turn against the strong person, the Cromwell or Mussolini, as an intolerable tyrant, and relapse into the condition of Bunyan's Simple, Sloth, and Presumption the moment his back is turned or his body buried. We clamor for a despotic discipline out of the miseries of our anarchy, and, when we get it, clamor out of the severe regulation of our law and order for what we call liberty. At each blind rush from one extreme to the other we empty the baby out with the bath, learning nothing from our experience, and furnishing examples of the abuses of power and the horrors of liberty without ascertaining the limits of either. (IWGSC-317-318)

Democracy versus Time. The worst features of our sham-democratic misgovernment are caused, not by incurable mental incapacity, but by an ignorance that is essentially mathematical. None of our politicians seems to know that political action, like all earthly action, must take place in a world of four dimensions, not three. The fourth dimension is that of Time. To ignore it is to be pre-Einstein, which is as out-of-date as to be pre-Marx. Fortunately it can be taught, just as the theories of rent and value can be taught; and those who learn it see that our British parliamentary system is far too slow for twentieth century social organization. (P-FF-82)

Democracy's Extravagant Hopes. The naked truth is that democracy, or government by the people through votes for everybody, has never been a complete reality; and to the very limited extent to which it has been a reality it has not been a success. The extravagant hopes which have been attached to every extension of it have been disappointed. A hundred years ago the great Liberal Reform Bill was advocated as if its passage into law would produce the millenium. Only the other day the admission of women to the electorate, for which women fought and died, was expected to raise politics to a nobler plane and purify public life. But at the election which followed the women voted for hanging the Kaiser; rallied hysterically round the worst male candidates; threw out all the women candidates of tried ability, integrity, and devotion; and elected just one titled lady of great wealth and singular damagogic fascination, who, though she justified their choice subsequently, was then a beginner. In short, the notion that the female voter is more politically intelligent or gentler than the male voter proved as great a delusion as the earlier delusions that the business man was any wiser politically than the country gentleman or the manual worker than the middle class man. If there were any disfranchised class left for our democrats to pin their repeatedly disappointed hopes on, no doubt they would still clamor for a fresh set of votes to jump the last ditch into their Utopia; and the vogue of democracy might last a while yet. Possibly there may be here and there lunatics looking forward to votes for children, or for animals, to complete the democratic structure. But the majority shows signs of having had enough of it. Discipline for Everybody and Votes for Nobody is the fashion in Spain and Italy; and for some years past in Russia the proletarian Government has taken no more notice of an adverse vote than the British Raj of an Indian jury's verdict, except when it turns the majority out of doors in the manner of Bismarck or Cromwell. (IWGSC-452-453)

Democracy & the Madness of God. There is a story told of a pious man who was sustained through a lifetime of crushing misfortune by his steady belief that if he fought the good fight to the end he would at last stand in the presence of God. In due course he died, and presented himself at the gates of heaven for his reward. St Peter, who was for some reason much worried, hastily admitted him and bade him go and enjoy himself. But the good man said that he did not want to enjoy himself: he wanted to stand in the presence of God. St Peter tried to evade the claim, dwelling on the other delights of heaven, coaxing, bullying, arguing. All in vain: he could not shake the claimant and could not deny his right. He sent for St Paul, who was as worried and as evasive as his colleague; but he also failed to induce the newcomer to forego his promised privilege. At last they took him by the arms and led him to a mighty cathedral, where, entering by the west door, he saw the Ancient of Days seated in silent majesty on a throne in the choir. He sprang forward to prostrate himself at the divine feet, but was held back firmly by the apostles. "Be quiet" said St Paul. "He has gone mad; and we dont know what to do." "Dont tell anybody" added St Peter. And there the story ends.

But that is not how the story ends on earth. Make any common fellow an autocrat and at once you have the Beggar on Horseback riding to the devil. Even when, as the son of his father, he has been trained from infancy to behave well in harness and blinkers, he may go as mad sadistically as a Roman emperor or a Russian Tsar. But that is only the extreme case. Uncommon people, promoted on their merits, are by no means wholly exempt from megalomania. Morris's simple and profound saying that "no man is good enough to be another man's master" holds good unless both master and man regard themselves as equally the servants of God in States where God still reigns, or, in States where God is dead, as the subjects and agents of a political constitution applying humane principles which neither of them may violate. In that case autocrats are no longer autocrats. Failing any such religious or political creed all autocrats go more or less mad. That is a plain fact of political pathology.

Judged in this light our present predicament is lamentable. We no longer believe in the old "sanctions" (as they are called nowadays) of heaven and hell; and except in Russia there is not in force a single political constitution that enables and enjoins the citizen to earn his own living as a matter of elementary honesty, or that does not exalt vast personal riches and the organization of slaughter and conquest above all other conditions and activities. The financier and the soldier are the cocks of the walk; and democracy means that their parasites and worshippers carry all before them. (P-TM-121-123)

Political Proselytizing. Unfortunately it is easier to produce a nation of artistic than of political connoisseurs. Our schools and universities do not concern themselves with fine art, which they despise as an unmanly pursuit. It is possible for a young gentleman to go through the whole educational mill of preparatory school, public school, and university with the highest academic honors without knowing the difference between a chanty and a symphony, a tavern sign and a portrait by Titian, a ballad by Macaulay and a stanza by Keats. But at least he is free to find out all this for himself if he has a fancy that way.

Not so in political science. Not so in religion. In these subjects he is proselytized from the beginning in the interests of established institutions so effectually that he remains all his life firmly convinced that his greatest contemporaries are rascally and venal agitators, villainous blasphemers, or at best seditious cads. He will listen to noodles' orations, read pompous leading articles, and worship the bloodthirsty tribal idols of Noah and Samuel with a gravity and sincerity that would make him infinitely pitiable if they did not also make him infinitely dangerous. He will feed his mind on empty phrases as Nebuchadnezzar fed his body on grass; and any boss who has mastered these phrases can become his dictator, his despot, his evangelist, and in effect his god-emperor. (P-TM-128)

The Two Inseparable Problems. We have to solve two inseparable main problems: the economic problem of how to produce and distribute our subsistence, and the political problem of how to select our rulers and prevent them from abusing their authority in their own interests or those of their class or religion. Our solution of the economic problem is the Capitalist system, which achieves miracles in production, but fails so ludicrously and disastrously to distribute its products rationally, or to produce in the order of social need, that it is always complaining of being paralysed by its "overproduction" of things of which millions of us stand in desperate want. Our solution of the political problem is Votes for Everybody and Every Authority Elected by Vote, an expedient originally devised to prevent rulers from tyrannizing by the very effectual method of preventing them from doing anything, and thus leaving everything to irresponsible private enterprise. But as private enterprise will do nothing that is not profitable to its little self, and the very existence of civilization now depends on the swift and unhampered public execution of enterprises that supersede private enterprise and are not merely profitable but vitally necessary to the whole community, this purely inhibitive check on tyranny has become a stranglehold on genuine democracy. Its painfully evolved machinery of Parliament and Party System and Cabinet is so effective in obstruction that we take thirty years by constitutional methods to do thirty minutes work, and shall presently be forced to clear up thirty years arrears in thirty minutes by unconstitutional ones unless we pass a Reform Bill that will make a complete revolution in our political machinery and procedure. When we see parliaments like ours kicked into the gutter by dictators, both in kingdoms and republics, it is foolish to wait until the dictator dies or collapses, and then do nothing but pick the poor old things up and try to scrape the mud off them: the only sane course is to take the step by which the dictatorship could have been anticipated and averted, and construct a political system for rapid positive work instead of slow nugatory work, made to fit into the twentieth century instead of into the sixteenth. (P-AC-11-13)

Democracy a Nuisance. All reformers who use democracy as a stepping stone to power find it a nuisance when they get there. The more power the people are given the more urgent becomes the need for some rational and well-informed superpower to dominate them and disable their inveterate admiration of international murder and national suicide. Voltaire said that there is one person wiser than Mrs Anybody, and that is Mrs Everybody; but Voltaire had not seen modern democracy at work: the democracy he admired in England was a very exclusive oligarchy; and the mixture of theocracy and hereditary autocracy that disgusted him in France was not a fair test of aristocracy, or government by the best qualified. We now know that though Mrs Everybody knows where the shoe pinches and must therefore have a say in the matter, she cannot make the shoe, and cannot tell a good shoemaker from a bad one by his output of hot air on a platform. Government demands ability to govern: it is neither Mrs Everybody's business nor Mrs Anybody's, but Mrs Somebody's. Mrs Somebody will never be elected until she is protected from the competition of Mrs Noodle and Mrs Bounder and Mrs Noisy Nobody and Mrs Kin-and-Country and Mrs Class War and Mrs Hearth-and-Home and Mrs Bountiful and Mrs Hands-off-the-Church and Mrs Please-I-want-everybody-to-love-me. If democracy is not to ruin us we must at all costs find some trustworthy method of testing the qualifications of candidates before we allow them to seek election. When we have done that we may have great trouble in persuading the right people to come forward. We may even be driven to compel them; for those who fully understand how heavy are the responsibilities of government and how exhausting its labor are the least likely to shoulder them voluntarily. As Plato said, the ideal candidate is the reluctant one. When we discover such a test you will still have your electoral choice between several Mrs Somebodys, which will make them all respect you; but you will not be taken in by Mrs Noodle & Co. because they will not be eligible for election. Meanwhile, Heaven help us! we must do the best we can. (IWGSC-454-455)

The State: Robber & Slavedriver. I fully admit and vehemently urge that the State at present is simply a huge machine for robbing and slavedriving the poor by brute force. You may, if you

are a stupid or comfortably-off person, think that the policeman
at the corner is the guardian of law and order—that the gaol,
with those instruments of torture, the treadmill, plank bed, solitary
cell, cat-o'-nine tails, and gallows, is a place to make people cease
to do evil and learn to do well. But the primary function of the
policeman, and that for which his other functions are only blinds,
is to see that you do not lie down to sleep in this country without paying an idler for the privilege; that you do not taste bread
until you have payed the idler's toll in the price of it; that you
do not resist the starving blackleg who is dragging you down to
his level for the idler's profit by offering to do your work for a
starvation wage. Attempt any of these things, and you will be haled
off and tortured in the name of law and order, honesty, social
equilibrium, safety of property and person, public duty, Christianity, morality, and what not, as a vagrant, a thief, and a rioter.
Your soldier, ostensibly a heroic and patriotic defender of his
country, is really an unfortunate man driven by destitution to offer
himself as food for powder for the sake of regular rations, shelter,
and clothing; and he must, on pain of being arbitrarily imprisoned,
punished with petty penances like a naughty child, pack-drilled,
flogged, or shot, all in the blessed name of "discipline," do anything
he is ordered to, from standing in his red coat in the hall of an
opera house as a mere ornament, to flogging his comrade, or committing murder. And his primary function is to come to the aid
of the policeman when the latter is overpowered. Members of
parliament whose sole qualifications for election were £1000 loose
cash, an "independent" income, and a vulgar strain of ambition;
parsons quoting scripture for the purposes of the squire; lawyers
selling their services to the highest bidder at the bar, and maintaining the supremacy of the moneyed class on the bench; juries
of employers masquerading as the peers of proletarians in the
dock; University professors elaborating the process known as the
education of a gentleman; artists striving to tickle the fancy or
flatter the vanity of the aristocrat or plutocrat; workmen doing
their work as badly and slowly as they dare so as to make the
most of their job; employers starving and overworking their hands

and adulterating their goods as much as *they* dare: these are the actual living material of those imposing abstractions known as the State, the Church, the Law, the Constitution, Education, the Fine Arts, and Industry. (IOA-96-97)

The People against the Classes. It is easy to say, Abolish the State; but the State will sell you up, lock you up, blow you up, knock you down, bludgeon, shoot, stab, hang—in short, abolish you, if you lift a hand against it. Fortunately, there is, as we have seen, a fine impartiality about the policeman and the soldier, who are the cutting edge of the State power. They take their wages and obey their orders without asking questions. If those orders are to demolish the homestead of every peasant who refuses to take the bread out of his children's mouths in order that his landlord may have money to spend as an idle gentleman in London, the soldier obeys. But if his orders were to help the police to pitch his lordship into Holloway Gaol until he had paid an Income Tax of twenty shillings on every pound* of his unearned income, the soldier would do that with equal devotion to duty, and perhaps with a certain private zest that might be lacking in the other case. Now these orders come ultimately from the State—meaning, in this country, the House of Commons. A House of Commons consisting of 660 gentlemen and 10 workmen will order the soldier to take money from the people for the landlords. A House of Commons consisting of 660 workmen and 10 gentlemen will probably, unless the 660 are fools, order the soldier to take money from the landlords for the people. With this hint I leave the matter, in the full conviction that the State, in spite of the Anarchists, will continue to be used against the people by the classes until it is used by the people against the classes with equal ability and equal resolution. (IOA-99)

* Amounting to 100-per-cent taxation.

Capitalism

The Single Taxers are not wrong in principle; but they are
behind the times. Out of landowning there has grown a lazier
way of living on other people's labor without doing anything for
them in return. Land is not the only property that returns a rent
to the owner. Spare money will do the same if it is properly used.
Spare money is called Capital; its owner is called a capitalist; and
our system of leaving all the spare money in the country in private hands like the land is called Capitalism. Until you understand Capitalism you do not understand human society as it
exists at present. You do not know the world, as the saying is.
You are living in a fool's paradise; and Capitalism is doing its
best to keep you there. You may be happier in a fool's paradise;
and as I must now proceed to explain Capitalism, you will read
the rest of this book at the risk of being made unhappy and rebellious, and even of rushing into the streets with a red flag and
making a greater fool of yourself than Capitalism has ever made
of you. On the other hand, if you do not understand Capitalism
you may easily be cheated out of all your money, if you have any,
or, if you have none, duped into sacrificing yourself in all sorts
of ways for the profit of mercenary adventurers and philanthropic
humbugs under the impression that you are exercising the noblest virtues. Therefore I will risk letting you know where you
are and what is happening to you. (IWGSC-127)

ABILITY UNDER CAPITALISM

The Eternal War. "There is the eternal war between those who are in the world for what they can get out of it and those who are in the world to make it a better place for everybody to live in." (*Sir Arthur Chavender,* OR-319)

To Whom Should Go the Product of Ability? What on earth use would Ability be to us if it did not lighten our toil and increase our gain? We support and encourage Ability in order that we may get as much as possible out of it, not in order that it may get as much as possible out of us. Mr. Mallock seems to regard this as dishonest. Possibly it is; but it is the sole safeguard for the existence of men of Ability. Give them and their heirs the entire product of their ability, so that they shall be enormously rich whilst the rest of us remain just as poor as if they had never existed; and it will become a public duty to kill them, since nobody but themselves will be any the worse, and we shall be much the better for having no further provocation to the sin of envy. (SSB-261-262)

Capitalism's Waste of Ability. Let us consider now how far
exceptional payments depend really on the ability of the earner,
and how far on the social conditions under which they occur.
To begin with a striking instance. A famous painter charges, and
gets, 2,000 guineas* for painting a portrait. Such a price is rendered
possible solely by the existence of a class of patrons so rich that
the payment of 2,000 guineas inflicts less privation on them than
the payment of sixpence to an itinerant photographer on Hamp-
stead Heath inflicts on a courting costermonger. These portraits
are as often as not portraits of persons of average or inferior
ability. If such persons had to earn the price of their portraits
by their own labor, they would not pay two guineas, much less
2,000, for a portrait. On the other hand, the painter demands
2,000 guineas solely because he finds that he can get it, not in
the least because his genius refuses to operate under a weaker
stimulus. He will paint as good a portrait for £50 as for £2,000
if £50 is the top of his market: greater painting than any yet
produced in Melbury Road or Fitzjohn's Avenue has been worse
paid than that. The fashionable physician, the surgeon pre-
eminently skilled in some dangerous operation, the Parliamentary
barrister, all owe the excess of their incomes over that of, say,
a cabinet minister, to the competition among enormously rich
people or huge companies for their services. In order to state the
case in the most foolish possible way, let me put it that modern
Capitalism has created thousands of guineas' worth of professional
ability where only tens and hundreds existed before. All that this
means is that it has raised the price of certain sorts of ability
twenty-fold without at all improving their quality. And in enabling
idle rich people to buy up the best of this ability, it has greatly
wasted and nullified it. The eminent painter paints unmemorable
people; the fashionable physician preserves the lives of useless
people; the Parliamentary barrister would be more useful to society
as an upper division clerk in the legal branch of some public
service. Generally speaking, it may be said that our capitalists pay
men of ability very highly to devote their ability to the service

* A guinea contains 21 shillings (one more than a pound).

of Capitalism; and the moment society begins to outgrow the capitalistic system, it is no longer permissible to assume that ability devoted to the service of Capitalism is serviceable to society, or, indeed, that ability which can only flourish in that way is, from the social point of view, ability at all. (SSB-268-269)

Artificial Ability. As "the defenders of the system of Conservatism" well know, we have for centuries made able men out of ordinary ones by allowing them to inherit exceptional power and status; and the success of the plan is the phase of social development to which it was proper was due to the fact that, provided only the favored man were really an ordinary man, and not a duffer, the extraordinary power conferred on him did effectually create extraordinary ability as compared with that of an agricultural laborer, for example, of equal natural endowments. The gentleman, the lord, the king, all discharging social functions of which the laborer is incapable, are products as artificial as queen bees. Their superiority is produced by giving them a superior status, just as the inferiority of the laborer is produced by giving him an inferior status. But the superior income which is the appanage of superior status is not rent of ability. It is a payment made to a man to exercise normal ability in an abnormal situation. Rent of ability is what a man gets by exercising abnormal ability in a normal situation. (SSB-271)

Imaginary Ability. . . . The public is often a very bad judge of ability. For example, there died a short time ago a barrister who once acquired extraordinary celebrity as an Old Bailey advocate, especially in murder cases. When he was at his zenith I read all his most famous defenses, and can certify that he always missed the strong point in his client's case and the weak one in the case for the prosecution, and was, in short, the most homicidally incompetent impostor that ever bullied a witness or made a "moving" but useless appeal to a jury. Fortunately for him the murderers were too stupid to see this: besides, their imaginations were powerfully impressed by the number of clients of his who

were hanged. So they always engaged him, and added to his fame
by getting hanged themselves in due course. In the same way
a surgeon will get a reputation as the only possible man to consult
in cancer cases simply because he has cut off more breasts than
anyone else. The fact that in all the professions there is one first
favorite means no more than the fact that there is only one
editor of The Times. It is not the man who is singular, but the
position. The public imagination demands a best man everywhere;
and if Nature does not supply him the public invents him. The art
of humbug is the art of getting invented in this way. Every generation invents great men at whom posterity laughs when some
accident makes it aware of them. Even in business, the greatest
reputations are sometimes the result of the glamor of city superstition. I could point to railway chairmen reputed indispensable,
whom the shareholders and the travelling public might with great
profit and comfort to themselves send to St. Helena with a pension
of £10,000 a year. (SSB-266-267)

Merit & Difference in Income.   Nothing hides the difference
in merit between one person and another so much as difference in
income. Take for example a grateful nation making a parliamentary grant of twenty thousand pounds to a great explorer, or
a great discoverer, or a great military commander (I have to make
my example a man: women get only statues after their death).
Before he has walked half way down the street on his way home
to tell his wife about it he may meet some notorious fool or scan-
dalous libertine, or some quite ordinary character, who has not
merely twenty thousand pounds but twenty thousand a year or
more. The great man's twenty thousand pounds will bring him in
only a thousand a year; and with this he finds himself in our
society regarded as "a poor devil" by tradesmen and financiers
and quacks who are ten times as rich because they have never
in their lives done anything but make money for themselves with
entire selfishness, possibly by trading in the vices or on the credulity
of their fellow-countrymen. It is a monstrous thing that a man
who, by exercising a low sort of cunning, has managed to grab

three or four millions of money selling bad whiskey, or fore-stalling the wheat harvest and selling it at three times its cost, or providing silly newspapers and magazines for the circulation of lying advertisements, should be honored and deferred to and waited on and returned to Parliament and finally made a peer of the realm, whilst men who have exercised their noblest faculties or risked their lives in the furtherance of human knowledge and welfare should be belittled by the contrast between their pence and the grabber's pounds. (IWGSC-70-71)

Why Idiots Favor Inequality. Between persons of equal income there is no social distinction except the distinction of merit. Money is nothing: character, conduct, and capacity are everything. Instead of all the workers being levelled down to low wage standards and all the rich levelled up to fashionable income standards, everybody under a system of equal incomes would find her and his own natural level. There would be great people and ordinary people and little people; but the great would always be those who had done great things, and never the idiots whose mothers had spoiled them and whose fathers had left them a hundred thousand a year; and the little would be persons of small minds and mean characters, and not poor persons who had never had a chance. That is why idiots are always in favor of inequality of income (their only chance of eminence), and the really great in favor of equality. (IWGSC-71)

The Real Great. Capitalism can be made to look very well on paper. But beware of allowing your dillusion to disable you by plunging you into disgust and general cynical incredulity. Our thrilling columns of national self-praise and mutual admiration must not be dismissed as mere humbug. Without great discoverers and inventors and explorers, great organizers and engineers and soldiers, hardy and reckless sailors, great chemists and mathematicians, devoted missionaries and desperate adventurers, our capitalists would be no better off today than they would have remained in Greenland or Thibet. But the extraordinary men whose exploits have made the capitalists rich were not themselves capitalists. The best of them received little or no encouragement from capitalists, because there was seldom any prospect of immediate profit from their labors and adventures. Many of them were and are not only poor but persecuted. And when the time comes, mostly after their deaths, to bring their discoveries and conquests into everyday use, the work is done by the hungry ones: the capitalists providing only the spare food they have neither sown nor reaped, baked nor brewed, but only collected from the hungry as rent or interest, and appropriated under laws made by capitalist legislators for that purpose. British brains, British genius, British courage and resolution have made the great reputation of Britain, as the same qualities in other nations have made the other great national reputations; but the capitalists as such have provided neither brains, genius, courage, nor resolution. Their contribution has been the spare food on which the geniuses have lived; and this the capitalists did not produce: they only intercepted it during its transfer from the hungry ones who made it to the hungry ones who consumed it. (IWGSC-310-311)

Capitalists as Such. It is not likely that a born capitalist (that is, the inheritor of a fortune) will be a genius, because it is not likely that anybody will be born a genius, the phenomenon being naturally rare; but it may happen to capitalists occasionally, just as it has happened to princes. Queen Elizabeth was able to tell her ministers that if they put her into the street without anything but her petticoat she could make her living with the best of them. At the same time Queen Mary of Scotland was proving that if she had been put into the street with a hundred millions of money and an army of fifty thousand men she would have made a mess of it all somehow and come to a bad end. But their being queens had nothing to do with that: it was their personal quality as women that made the difference. In the same way, when one born capitalist happens to be a genius and another a waster, the capital produces neither the ability nor the worthlessness. Take away their capital, and they remain just the same:

double it, and you double neither their ability nor their imbecility. The stupidest person in the country may be the richest: the cleverest and geatest may not know where tomorrow's dinner is to come from. I repeat, capitalists as such need no special ability, and lose nothing by the lack of it. (IWGSC-311-312)

Exceptional Ability Needs no Special Inducement. Let us therefore dismiss the fear that persons of exceptional ability need special inducements to exercise that ability to the utmost. Experience proves that even the most severe discouragements and punishments cannot restrain them from trying to do so. Let us return to the real social problem: that of preventing them from taking advantage of the vital necessity and relative scarcity of certain kinds of ability to extort excessive incomes.

In socialized services no difficulty arises. The civil servant, the judge, the navy captain, the field marshal, the archbishop, however extraordinarily able, gets no more than any routincer of his rank and seniority. A real gentleman is not supposed to sell himself to the highest bidder: he asks his country for a sufficient provision and a dignified position in return for the best work he can do for it. A real lady can say no less. But in capitalist commerce they are both forced to be cads: that is, to hold up to ransom those to whom their services are indispensable, and become rich at their expense. The mere disciplinarian cannot extort very much because disciplinarians of one sort or another are not very scarce. But the organizer and financier is in a strong position. The owner of a big business, if his employees ask for anything more than a subsistence wage as their share of its product, can always say "Well, if you are not satisfied, take the business and work it yourself without me." This they are unable to do. The Trade Union to which his employees belong may be tempted to take him at his word; but it soon finds itself unable to carry on, that sort of management not being its job. He says in effect, and often in so many words, "You cannot do without me; so you must work on my terms." They reply with perfect truth "Neither can you do without us; let us see you organize without any workers to organize." But he beats them; and the reason is not that he can do without them any more than they can do without him (or her), but that his bargain for the use of his ability is not really made with them but with the landlords whose land he is using and the capitalists who have lent him the capital for his enterprise. It is to them that he can say unanswerably "You cannot do without me." They may say "Yes we can. We can tell the workers that unless they give up everything they can make out of our land and capital to us except what is enough to keep them alive and renew themselves from generation to generation they shall starve; because they cannot produce without land and capital, and we own all there is available of both." "That is true" retorts the able organizer and financier; "but please to remember that without an elaborate scientific organization of their labor they can produce no more than a mob of allotment holders, or of serfs on a tenth century manor, whereas if I organize them for you industrially and financially I can multiply their product a thousandfold. Even if you have to pay me a large share of the increase due to my ability you are still far richer than if you did without me." And to this there is no reply. In this way there rises under Capitalism not only a rent of land and a rent of capital (called interest), but a rent of ability (called profit); and just as in order to secure equality of income it becomes necessary to nationalize land and capital, so it becomes necessary to nationalize ability. We already do this in part by taxing profits. But we do it completely only when, as in the public services, we give it direct national or municipal employment. (IWGSC-339-341)

Capitalist Parasites. Great astronomers, chemists, mathematicians, physicists, philosophers, explorers, discoverers, teachers, preachers, sociologists, and saints may be so poor that their wives are worn-out in a constant struggle to keep up appearances and make both ends meet; but the business organizers pile millions on millions whilst their unfortunate daughters carry about diamonds and sables to advertize their parent's riches, and drink cocktails until they feel so bad inside that they pay large sums to surgeons to cut them open and find out what is the matter with them. If you reproach these organizers for their inordinate gains, they tell you—or they would tell you if they understood their own position and could express it intelligibly—that every penny they make is made by making money for other people as well; that before they can spend a farthing on themselves they must provide rent for the landlord, interest for the capitalists, and wages for the proletarian on a scale that would be impossible without them; and that England can support five times the number of people she could a hundred years ago because her industries are better organized and more amply financed by them and their like. This is true; but you need not be abashed by it; for which of us has not to provide rent for the landlord, interest for the capitalist, and wages for the laborer before we can spend a penny on ourselves? And why should the organizer and financier be paid more for the exercise of his particular faculty than we who have to co-operate with him by the exercise of our particular faculties before he can produce a loaf of bread or a glass of milk? It is not natural necessity but the capitalist system that enables him to snatch more than his fellow workers from the welter of competitive commerce; and while this lasts we shall have the financier's daughter saying to the scavenger's daughter "What would your dirty common father do without my father, who is going to be made a lord?" and the scavenger's daughter retorting "What would your greedy robber of a father do if my father did not keep the streets clean for him?" Of course you have never heard a lady or a young person talk like that. And probably you never will. They are too polite and too thoughtless to discuss their father's positions. Besides, they never speak to one another. But if they did, and anything upset their tempers, their last words before they came to blows would be just those which I have imagined. If you doubt it, read what the capitalist papers say about Trade Unionists and Socialists, and what the proletarian papers say about landlords and capitalists and bosses. Do you suppose that the charwoman, who has worked in her own necessary way all her life as hard as or harder than any financier, and in the end has nothing to leave to her daughter but her pail and scrubbing brush, really believes, or ever will believe, that Lady Billionham, inheriting a colossal income from her father the financier, has any moral right to her money? (IWGSC-341-343)

The Ignoramus, the Visionary, & the Fool. It is fortunate for us that few of our tradesmen are so vile or so silly as the commercial theory by which theorists attempt to justify them. The man who has "made" £20,000 a year for himself knows very well that his success does not afford the smallest presumption that his services have been more important than those of a police constable with 24s. a week. He does not dream of posing as the superior of the captain of a battleship with a modest income of three figures. Mr. Carnegie "divides up" his surplus millions, and makes wildly Socialistic proposals, never for a moment suggesting that he is 50 times as clever as Mr. Mallock because he is 50 times as rich. I am not supposed to be an exceptionally modest man; but I did not advance the fact that I have made more money by a single play than Shakespear did by all his plays put together as a simple proof that I am enormously superior to Shakespear as a playwright. Our millionaires unload—awkwardly and unwisely sometimes, it is true, but still they unload—and do not talk nonsense about being 650 times as clever or as sober or as industrious as a dock-laborer because they have 650 times his income. The man who pretends that the distribution of income in this country reflects the distribution of ability or character is an ignoramus. The man who says that it could by any possible political device be made to do so is an unpractical visionary. But the man who says that it ought to do so is something worse than an ignoramus and more disastrous than a visionary: he is, in the profoundest Scriptural sense of the word, a fool. (SSB-253-254)

CAPITALIST MORALS & CONSCIENCE

The Source of Income: Don't Look Too Close. "Why the devil shouldn't I invest my money that way? I take the interest on my capital like other people: I hope you don't think I dirty my own hands with the work. Come: you wouldn't refuse the acquaintance of my mother's cousin, the Duke of Belgravia, because some of the rents he gets are earned in queer ways. You wouldn't cut the Archbishop of Canterbury, I suppose, because the Ecclesiastical Commissioners have a few publicans and sinners among their tenants? Do you remember your Crofts scholarship at Newnham? Well, that was founded by my brother the M.P. He gets his 22 per cent out of a factory with 600 girls in it, and not one of them getting wages enough to live on. How d'ye suppose most of them manage? Ask your mother. And do you expect me to turn my back on 35 per cent when all the rest are pocketing what they can, like sensible men? No such fool! If you're going to pick and choose your acquaintances on moral principles, you'd better clear out of this country, unless you want to cut yourself out of all decent society." (*Sir George Crofts*, MWP-220-221)

Approve or Be Ruined. Capitalism, in its ceaseless search for investment, its absolute necessity for finding hungry men to eat its spare bread before it goes stale, breaks through every barrier, rushes every frontier, swallows every religion, levels every institution that obstructs it, and sets up any code of morals that facilitates it, as soullessly as it sets up banks and lays cables. And you must approve and conform, or be ruined, and perhaps imprisoned or executed. (IWGSC-314)

Imported Profits of Cheap Labor. "No: we have not abolished poverty and hardship. Our big business men have abolished them. But how? By sending their capital abroad to places where poverty and hardship still exist: in other words, where labor is cheap. We live in comfort on the imported profits of that capital. We are all ladies and gentlemen now." (*Magnus*, AC-60)

Why Lust for Money & Power Prevail. The reason that lust for money and power prevail as they do against the nobler sentiments is simply that the people who want more money and more power have organized armaments to coerce those who desire to establish the kingdom of heaven on earth, and have also organized the Press and the public schools to persuade the masses that the pursuit of more money and more power is virtuous, heroic, and patriotic. This they do with the enormous advantage of being single-minded in the knowledge of what they want and the determination to get it at all costs (though, having got it, they become at once the most charming people imaginable) . . . The single-minded "divide and govern," because they have a common religion and a common philosophy of life. The religion may be the worship of Mammon, and the philosophy that of a pirate; but they are all effectively agreed on it, and will cut throats for its sake; and so they will triumph until their opponents learn the lesson and find unity in a common religion and philosophy of their own. (PCH-38-39)

The Weapons of the Have-and-Holders. People who are shown by their inner light the possibility of a better world based on the demand of the spirit for a nobler and more abundant life, not for themselves at the expense of others, but for everybody, are naturally dreaded and therefore hated by the Have-and-Holders, who keep always in reserve two sure weapons against them. The first is a persecution effected by the provocation, organization, and arming of that herd instinct which makes men abhor all departures from custom, and, by the most cruel punishments and the wildest calumnies, force eccentric people to behave and profess exactly as other people do. The second is by leading the herd to war, which immediately and infallibly makes them forget every-thing, even their most cherished and hardwon public liberties and private interests, in the irresistible surge of their pugnacity and the tense preoccupation of their terror. (E-AL-145)

The Height of Honor & Success. Now outside Russia the height of honor and success is to be a gentleman or lady, which means that your living is earned for you by other people (mostly untouchables), and that, far from being under an obligation to work, you are so disgraced by the mere suggestion of it that you dare not be seen carrying a parcel along a fashionable thorough-fare. Nobody has ever seen a lady or gentleman carrying a jug of milk down Bond Street or the *rue de la Paix.* A white person doing such a thing in Capetown would be socially ruined. The physical activities called Sport, which are needed to keep the gentry in health, must be unpaid and unproductive: if payment is accepted for such activities the payee loses caste and is no longer called Mister. Labor is held to be a cross and a disgrace; and the lowest rank known is that of laborer. The object of everyone's ambition is an unearned income; and hundreds of millions of the country's income are lavished annually on ladies and gentlemen whilst laborers are underfed, ill clothed, and sleep-ing two or three in a bed and ten in a room. (P-SUI-8)

Limited Liability in Morals. Our "free" British citizens can ascertain exactly what they may do and what they may not do if they are to keep out of the hands of the police. Our financiers know that they must not forge share certificates nor overstate their assets in the balance sheets they send to their shareholders. But provided they observe a few conditions of this kind they are free to enter upon a series of quite legitimate but not the less nefarious operations. For example, making a corner in wheat or copper or any other cornerable commodity and forcing up prices so as to make enormous private fortunes for themselves, or making mischief between the nations through the Press to stimulate the private trade in armaments. Such limited liability no longer exists in Russia, and is not likely to exist in the future in any highly civilized state. It may be quite impossible to convict a forestaller or regrator under a criminal code of having taken a single illegal step, but quite easy to convince any reasonable body of judges that he is what the people call "a wrong one." In Russia such a conviction would lead to his disappearance and the receipt by his family of a letter to say that they need not wait up for him, as he would not return home any more.[1] In our country he would enjoy his gains in high honor and personal security, and thank his stars that he lived in a free country and not in Communist Russia. (P-OR-196-197)

Property, Property, Property. I, an old Irishman, am too used to Coercion Acts, suspensions of the Habeas Corpus Act, and the like, to have any virtuous indignation left to spare for the blunders and excesses into which the original Tcheka, as a body of well intentioned amateurs, no doubt fell before it had learnt the limits of its business by experience. My object in citing it is to draw attention to the legal novelty and importance of its criterion of human worth. I am careful to say legal novelty because of course the criterion must have been used in the world long before St. Paul commanded that "if any would not work, neither should he eat." But our courts have never taken that Communist view: they have always held unconditional property, private property, real property, do-what-you-like-with-your-own-property, which, when

---

[1] Note, however, that a sentence of extermination should never be so certain as to make it worth the delinquent's while to avoid arrest by murdering his or her pursuers.

it is insanely extended to the common earth of the country, means the power to make landless people earn the proprietors' livings for them. Such property places the social value of the proprietor beyond question. The propertyless man may be challenged as a rogue and a vagabond to justify himself by doing some honest work; but if he earns a gentleman's living for him he is at once vindicated and patted on the back. Under such conditions we have lost the power of conceiving ourselves as responsible to society for producing a full equivalent of what we consume, and indeed more. On the contrary, every inducement to shirk that primary duty is continually before us. (P-SUI-11)

"Get Off the Earth." "Do you forget how your family drove a whole countryside of honest hardworking Scotch crofters into the sea, and turned their little farms into deer forests because you could get more shooting rents out of them in that way? Do you forget that women in childbirth were carried out by your bailiffs to die by the roadside because they clung to their ancient homesteads and ignored your infamous notices to quit? Would it surprise you to learn that I am only one of thousands of young women who have read the hideous story of this monstrous orgy of house-breaking and murder, and sworn to ourselves that never, if we can help it, will it again be possible for one wicked rich man to say to a whole population 'Get off the earth.'" (*Aloysia*, OR-302-303)

The Business Principle. Among ourselves, though robbery and violence are forbidden, we still allow business to be conducted on the principle of letting everyone make what he can out of it without respecting anyone but himself. A shopkeeper or a coal merchant may not pick your pocket; but he may overcharge you as much as he likes. Everyone is free in business to get as much and give as little for his money as he can induce his customers to put up with. (IWGSC-129)

The Slum Rent Collector. "Mark my words, gentlemen: he'll find what a man he's lost the very first week's rents the man'll

bring him. You'll find the difference yourself, Dr. Trench, if you
or your children come into the property. I have got money when
no other collector alive would have wrung it out. And this is
the thanks I get for it! Why, see here, gentlemen! Look at that
bag of money on the table. Hardly a penny of that but there was
a hungry child crying for the bread it would have bought. But I got
it for him—screwed and worried and bullied it out of them. I—
look here, gentlemen: I'm pretty well seasoned to the work; but
there's money there that I couldn't have taken if it hadn't been
for the thought of my own children depending on me for giving
him satisfaction. And because I charged him four-and-twenty
shillin' to mend a staircase that three women have been hurt on,
and that would have got him prosecuted for manslaughter if it
had been let go much longer, he gives me the sack." (*Lickcheese*,
WH-34)

The Conspiracies for Limiting Supply. We . . . see how
man's control over the value of commodities consists solely in his
power of regulating their supply. Individuals are constantly
trying to decrease supply for their own advantage. Gigantic conspiracies have been entered into to forestall the world's wheat and
cotton harvests, so as to force their value to the highest possible
point. Cargoes of East Indian spices have been destroyed by the
Dutch, as cargoes of fish are now destroyed in the Thames, to
maintain prices by limiting supply. All rings, trusts, corners, combinations, monopolies, and trade secrets have the same object.
Production and the development of the social instincts are alike
hindered by each man's consciousness that the more he stints the
community the more he benefits himself, the justification, of
course, being that when every man has benefited himself at the
expense of the community, the community will benefit by every
man in it being benefited. (EBS-17-18)

Breakages, Limited: A Finger in Every Pie. "Here am I,
the Powermistress Royal. I have to organize and administer all
the motor power in the country for the good of the country. I have

to harness the winds and the tides, the oils and the coal seams. I have to see that every little sewing machine in the Hebrides, every dentist's drill in Shetland, every carpet sweeper in Margate, has its stream of driving power on tap from a switch in the wall as punctually as the great thundering dynamos of our big industrial plants. I do it; but it costs twice as much as it should. Why? Because every new invention is bought up and suppressed by Breakages, Limited. Every breakdown, every accident, every smash and crash, is a job for them. But for them we should have unbreakable glass, unbreakable steel, imperishable materials of all sorts. But for them our goods trains could be started and stopped without battering and tearing the vitals out of every wagon and sending it to their repair shops once a week instead of once a year. Our national repair bill runs up to hundreds of millions. I could name you a dozen inventions within my own term of office which would have effected enormous economies in breakages and breakdowns; but these people can afford to pay an inventor more for his machine or his process or whatever it may be than he could hope to make by a legitimate use of it; and when they have bought it they smother it. When the inventor is poor and not good at defending himself they make bogus trials of his machine and report that it is no use. I have been shot at twice by inventors driven crazy by this sort of thing: they blamed me for it—as if I could stand up against this monster with its millions and its newspapers and its fingers in every pie. It is heartbreaking. I love my department: I dream of nothing but its efficiency: with me it comes before every personal tie, every happiness that common women run after. I would give my right hand to see these people in the bankruptcy court with half their business abolished and the other half done in public workshops where public losses are not private gains. You stand for that, sir; and I would be with you to the last drop of my blood if I dared. But what can I do? If I said one word of this in public, not a week would pass in the next two years without an article on the inefficiency and corruption of all Government departments, especially departments managed, like mine, by females. They would dig up the very machines they have buried, and make out that it is my fault that they have never been brought into use. They would set their private police to watch me day and night to get something against my private character. One of their directors told me to my face that by lifting up his finger he could get my windows broken by the mob; and that Breakages, Limited, would get the job of putting in new glass." (*Lysistrata*, AC-79-81)

A *Self-Acting Millenium*. The rough and ready conclusion as to market prices is that sellers will compete for custom by underbidding one another, and that thus free competition will secure the utmost possible cheapness to the consumer. The simple reply to this optimistic receipt for a self-acting millenium is that as soon as sellers find this out they stop competing; and competition is replaced by conspiracy. The far-seeing and capable heads of the trade combine, and finally get the whole trade into their own hands, even if they have to sell at less than cost for long enough to ruin all the small manufacturers who are too poor or too stupid to join the combination. A monopoly being thus established, a market price is fixed, and retailers are supplied only on condition of their selling at that price. (CSMT-199)

Anti-Socialism of Private Enterprise. The tendency of private enterprise, with its preference for "a high class connection," and its natural desire to make the rate of profit as high as possible, is to keep up prices to the point beyond which the contraction of the market would make the trade unstable. The sudden reintroduction of competition by a new departure—for example, the tube railway suddenly upsetting the monopoly of the old underground in London—always brings down prices, a fact which proves that private enterprise maintains the highest price that will pay instead of the lowest. This tendency is clearly an anti-social one. Through its operation the various inventions which are the sole real assets of modern civilization, instead of raising the standard of life of the whole population, may remain for a long time the toys of the rich, who themselves cannot escape from an overwhelming environment of primitive poverty, to which more civilization means only less air, less house room, less decency, less health, and less freedom. (CSMT-204-205)

Trade Morals. Herbert Spencer's essay on the laxity of the morals of trade have called no trader successfully to repentence. It is not too much to say that any contractor in Europe or America who does not secure business by tenders and estimates and specifications for work and materials which he has not the smallest intention of doing or putting in, and who does not resort to bribery to have the work and materials he actually does do and put in passed by anybody whose duty it is to check them, is an exceptional man. The usage is so much a matter of course, and competition has made it so compulsory, that conscience is awakened only when the fraud is carried to some unusual length. I can remember two cases which illustrate what I mean very well. A builder of high commercial standing contracted to put up a public building. When the work began he found that the clerk of the works, whose business it was to check the work on behalf of the purchaser, lived opposite the building site. The contractor immediately protested that this was not part of the bargain, and that his estimate had been obtained on false pretences. The other is the case of the omnibus conductors of London when the alarum punch was invented and introduced. They immediately struck for higher wages, and got them, frankly on the ground that the punch had cut off the percentage they had been accustomed to add to their wages by peculation, and that it should be made up to them.

Both these cases prove that dishonesty does not pay when it becomes general. The contractor might just as well estimate for the work he really does and the material he actually uses; for, after all, since his object is to tempt the purchaser by keeping prices down, he has to give him the benefit of the fraud. If the purchaser finds him out and says, for example, "You estimated for galvanized pipes; and you have put in plain ones," the contractor can reply, "If I had put in galvanized pipes I should have had to charge you more." In the same way, the bus conductors might just as well have struck for an increase of wages as stolen it: they even proved they could have got it. But they thought they could secure employment more easily by asking for a low wage and making it up to their needs surreptitiously. It is one of the grievances of clerks in many businesses that they have to connive at dishonest practices as part of the regular routine of office; but neither they nor their employers are any the richer, because business always finally settles down to the facts, and is conducted in terms not of the pretence but of the reality. (CC-201-202)

The Right To Strike Defined. "My dear Mr. Mayor, what is the right to strike? The right to starve on your enemy's doorstep and set the whole public against you. Which of you starves first when it comes to the point?" (*Sir Arthur Chavender, OR-299*)

Quieting the Unemployed. "The police brought the Chancellor of the Exchequer to make a speech to the unemployed to quiet them. The first thing we heard him say was 'Gentlemen: be patient. I promise you you will soon see the one thing that can revive our industries and save our beloved country: a rise in prices.' The mob just gave one howl and went for him. Then the police drew their batons and charged." (*David, OR-269*)

Proletarian Capitalism. Trade Unionism is not Socialism: it is the Capitalism of the Proletariat. (IWGSC-186)

The Three-Brick Joke. You must be tired by this time of the silly joking of the Capitalist newspapers about bricklayers who are not allowed by their unions to lay more than three bricks a day. A bricklayer has clearly as much right to charge a day's wages for laying three bricks as the employer has to sell the house when it is built for the biggest price he can get for it. Those who condemn either of them are condemning the capitalist system, like good Bolshevists. The three-brick joke is only a comic exaggeration of what actually occurs. The employers, to find out how much work can be got out of a man, pick out an exceptionally quick and indefatigable man called a slogger, and try to impose what he can do in a day on all the rest. The unions naturally retort by forbidding any of their members to lay a brick more than he must do if he is to be worth employing at all. This practice of deliberately doing the least they dare instead of the most they can is the ca'canny of which the employers complain so much, though they all do the same thing themselves under the more respectable name of "restricting output" and selling in the dearest market. It is the principle on which the Capitalist system is avowedly founded. (IWGSC-208)

Sweatshop. "It's a cheap labor business. As long as I get women to work for their natural wage, I can get along; but no luxuries, mind you. No trade union wages. No sanitary arrangements as you call them. No limewashings every six months. No separate rooms to eat in. No fencing in of dangerous machinery or the like of that: not that I care; for I have nothing but the old gas engine that wouldnt hurt a fly, though it brings me under the blasted Workshop Act as you spotted all right. I have no big machinery; but I have to undersell those that have it. If I put up my prices by a farthing theyd set their machinery going and drop me. You might as well ask me to pay trade union wages as do all that the inspector wants: I should be out of business in a week." (*The Man,* TM-173-174)

The Deadlock. Thus Capitalism drives the employers to do their worst to the employed, and the employed to do the least for them. And it boasts all the time of the incentive it provides to both to do their best! You may ask why this does not end in a deadlock. The answer is it is producing deadlocks twice a day or thereabouts. The King's speeches in opening Parliament now contain regularly an appeal to the workers and employers to be good boys and not paralyse the industry of the nation by the clash of their quite irreconcilable interests. The reason the Capitalist system has worked so far without jamming for more than a few months at a time, and then only in places, is that it has not yet succeeded in making a conquest of human nature so complete that everybody acts on strictly business principles. The mass of the nation has been humbly and ignorantly taking what the employers offer and working as well as it can, either believing that it is doing its duty in that station of life to which it has pleased God to call it, or not thinking about the matter at all, but suffering its lot as something that cannot be helped, like the weather. (IWGSC-208)

The Spread of Socialism? If the matter were not so serious for all of us one could laugh at the silly way in which people talk of the spread of Socialism when what is really threatening them is the spread of Capitalism. The moment that propertyless workers refuse to see the finger of God in their property, and begin organizing themselves in unions to make the most money they can out of their labor exactly as they find the landlord doing with his land, the capitalist with his capital, the employer with his knowledge of business, and the financier with his art of promotion, the industry of the country, on which we all depend for our existence, begins rolling faster and faster down two opposite slopes, at the bottom of which there will be a disastrous collision which will bring it to a standstill until either Property drives Labor by main force into undisguised and unwilling slavery, or Labor gains the upper hand, and the long series of changes by which the mastery of the situation has already passed from the landlord-capitalist to the individual employer, from the individual employer to the joint stock company, and from the joint stock company to the Trust, and finally from the industrialists in general to the financiers, will culminate in its passing to capitalized Labor. The battle for this supremacy is joined; and here we are in the thick of it, our country ravaged by strikes and lockouts, a huge army of unemployed billeted upon us, the ladies and gentlemen declaring that it is all the fault of the workers, and the workers either declaring that it is all the fault of the ladies and gentlemen, or else, more sensibly, concluding that it is the fault of the Capitalist system, and taking to Socialism not so much because they understand it as because it offers a way out. (IWGSC-209)

Deliver Us from Capitalist Trade Unionism! Just as the owners of property, when they controlled Parliament, used their power to extort the utmost farthing from Labor, Labor can and probably will use its power to extort the utmost farthing from Property unless equal distribution for all is made a fundamental constitutional dogma. At present the propertied classes are looking to capitalist Trade Unions to save them from Socialism. The time is coming when they will clamor for Socialism to save them from capitalist Trade Unionism: that is, from Capitalized Labor. Already in America Trade Unionism is combining with Big Business to squeeze the sleeping partner. (IWGSC-225)

The Free Press? As people get their opinions so largely from the newspapers they read, the corruption of the schools would not matter so much if the Press were free. But the press is not free. As it costs at least quarter of a million of money to establish a daily newspaper in London, the newspapers are owned by rich men. And they depend on the advertisements of other rich men. Editors and journalists who express opinions in print that are opposed to the interests of the rich are dismissed and replaced by subservient ones. The newspapers therefore must continue the work begun by the schools and colleges; so that only the strongest and most independent and original minds can escape from the mass of false doctrine that is impressed on them by the combined and incessant suggestion and persuasion of Parliament, the law-courts, the Church, the schools, and the Press. We are all brought up wrongheaded to keep us willing slaves instead of rebellious ones.

What makes this so hard to discover and to believe is that the false teaching is mixed up with a great deal of truth, because up to a certain point the interests of the rich are the same as the interests of everybody else. It is only where their interests differ from those of their neighbors that the deception begins. For example, the rich dread railway accidents as much as the poor; consequently the law on railway accidents, the sermons about railway accidents, the school teaching about railway accidents, and the newspaper articles about them are all quite honestly directed to the purpose of preventing railway accidents. But when anyone suggests that there would be fewer railway accidents if the railwaymen worked fewer hours or had better wages, or that in the division of the railway fares between the shareholders and the workers the shareholders should get less and the workers more, or that railway travelling would be safer if the railways were in the hands of the nation like the posts and the telegraph, there is an immediate outcry in the Press and in Parliament against such suggestions, coupled with denunciations of those who make them as Bolsheviks or whatever other epithet may be in fashion for the moment as a term of the most infamous discredit. (IWGSC-64-65)

Should I Be Shot in Russia?   I am told that I should be shot in Russia if I dared to pontificate against the Government there as I often do here, and that Freedom of the Press, the glory of England, does not and cannot exist under Communist tyranny.

As a matter of fact the Russian newspapers are full of complaints and grievances. There is a Government Department whose function it is to receive and deal with such complaints. Here in England I, an old journalist and agitator, know only too well that both platform and press are gagged by such an irresponsible tyranny of partisan newspaper proprietors and shamelessly mendacious advertizers, and by the law against seditious and blasphemous libel, that my speeches were never reported, and my letters and articles inserted only when I could combine what I believed and wanted to say with something that the paper wanted to have said, or when I could disguise it as an attractively readable art criticism, the queer result being that my reputation was made in Conservative papers whilst the Liberal, Radical, and Socialist editors dared not mention my name except in disparagement and repudiation. I owe more of my publicity to The Times than to any other daily newspaper. The same is true of my Fabian colleagues. The Webbs, now in Westminster Abbey, never could get into the British daily newspapers. In Russia, when Fabians were despised there as bourgeois Deviators, the Webbs were translated by Lenin.

As a playwright I was held up as an irreligious pornographer, and as such a public enemy, not to say a thorough-paced cad, for many years by an irresponsible censorship which could not be challenged in parliament or elsewhere. No such misfortune has happened to me in Russia. (FF-76-77)

How Your Taxes May Enrich the Profiteers. At the beginning of the war, the influence of the profiteers was so strong that they persuaded the government to allow them to make all the shells instead of having them made in national factories. The result was that you were paying taxes to keep workmen standing idle in Woolwich Arsenal at full wages in order that the profiteering firms should have all the work at a profit. You had to pay their workmen too, and the profit into the bargain. It soon turned out that they could not make nearly enough shells. Those they did make were unnecessarily expensive and not always explosive. The result was an appalling slaughter of our young men in Flanders, who were left almost defenceless in the trenches through the shortage of munitions; and we were on the verge of being defeated by simple extermination when the Government, taking the matter in hand itself, opened national factories (you may have worked in some of them) in which munitions were produced on such a scale that we have hardly yet got rid of what was left of them when the war ended, besides controlling the profiteers, teaching them their business (they did not know even how to keep proper accounts, and were wasting money like water), and limiting their profits drastically. And yet, in the face of this experience (which was of course a tremendous triumph for the advocates of nationalized industries), the war was no sooner at an end than the capitalist papers began again with their foolish and corrupt declarations that Governments are such incompetent and dishonest and extravagant jobbers, and private firms so splendidly capable and straightforward, that Governments must never do anything that private firms can make profits by doing; and very soon all the nationalized factories were sold for an old song to the profiteers, and the national workers were in the streets with the demobilized soldiers, living on the dole, two millions strong.

This is only a sensational instance of something that is always going on: namely, the wasting of your money by employing profiteering contractors to do the work that could be done better by the authorities themselves without charging you any profit. (IWGSC-116-117)

Capitalism & Prostitution. . . . Let not anyone imagine that men escape prostitution under Capitalism. If they do not sell their bodies they sell their souls. The barrister who in court strives "to make the worse appear the better cause" has been held up as a stock example of the dishonesty of misrepresenting for money. Nothing could be more unjust. It is agreed, and necessarily agreed, that the best way of learning the truth about anything is not to listen to a vain attempt at an impartial and disinterested statement, but to hear everything that can possibly be said for it, and then everything that can possibly be said against it, by skilled pleaders on behalf of the interested parties on both sides. A barrister is bound to do his utmost to obtain a verdict for a client whom he privately believes to be in the wrong, just as a doctor is bound to do his utmost to save the life of a patient whose death would, in his private opinion, be a good riddance. The barrister is an innocent figure who is used to distract our attention from the writer and publisher of lying advertisements which pretend to prove the worse the better article, the shopman who sells it by assuring the customer that it is the best, the agents of drugging and drink, the clerk making out dishonest accounts, the adulterator and giver of short weight, the journalist writing for Socialist papers when he is a convinced Liberal, or for Tory papers when he is an Anarchist, the professional politician working for his party right or wrong, the doctor paying useless visits and prescribing bogus medicines to hypochondriacs who need only Abernathy's advice, "Live on sixpence a day, and earn it," the solicitor using the law as an instrument for the oppression of the poor by the rich, the mercenary soldier fighting for a country which he regards as the worst enemy of his own, and the citizens of all classes who have to be obsequious to the rich and insolent to the poor. These are only a few examples of the male prostitutions, so repeatedly and vehemently denounced by the prophets in the Bible as whoredoms and idolatries, which are daily imposed on me by Capitalism. (IWGSC-202-203)

Belief Mostly Bias. What have Socialism and Capitalism to do with the fact that belief is mostly bias. It is very simple. If by inequality of income you give your doctors, your lawyers, your clergymen, your landlords, or your rulers an overwhelming economic interest in any sort of belief or practice, they will immediately begin to see all the evidence in favor of that sort of belief and practice, and become blind to all the evidence against it. Every doctrine that will enrich doctors, lawyers, landlords, clergymen, and rulers will be embraced by them eagerly and hopefully; and every doctrine that threatens to impoverish them will be mercilessly criticized and rejected. There will inevitably spring up a body of biassed teaching and practice in medicine, law, religion, and government that will become established and standardized as scientifically, legally, religiously, constitutionally, and morally sound, taught as such to all young persons entering these professions, stamping those who dare dissent as outcast quacks, heretics, sedition mongers, and traitors. Your doctor may be the honestest, kindliest doctor on earth; your solicitor may be a second father or mother to you; your clergyman may be a saint; your member of Parliament another Moses or Solon. They may be heroically willing to put your health, your prosperity, your salvation, and your protection from injustice before their interest in getting a few extra pounds out of you; but how far will that help you if the theory and practice of their profession, imposed on them as a condition of being allowed to pursue it, has been corrupted at the root by pecuniary interest? They can proceed only as the hospitals and medical schools teach them and order them to proceed, as the courts proceed, as the Church proceeds, as Parliament proceeds: that is their orthodoxy; and if the desire to make money and obtain privileges has been operating all the time in building up that orthodoxy, their best intentions and endeavors may result in leaving you with your health ruined, your pocket empty, your soul damned, and your liberties abrogated by your best friends in the name of science, law, religion, and the British Constitution. Ostensibly you are served and protected by learned professions and political authorities whose duty it is to save life, minimize suffering, keep the public health as tested by vital statistics at the highest attainable pitch, instruct you as to your legal obligations and see that your legal rights are not infringed, give you spiritual help and disinterested guidance when your conscience is troubled, and make and administer, without regard to persons or classes, the laws that protect you and regulate your life. But the moment you have direct personal occasion for these services you discover that they are all controlled by Trade Unions in disguise, and that the high personal honor and kindliness of their individual members is subject to the morality of Trade Unionism, so that their loyalty to their union, which is essentially a defensive conspiracy against the public, comes first, and their loyalty to you as patient, client, employer, parishioner, customer or citizen, next. (IWGSC-461-462)

Capitalist Crust.   The Capitalists, though they are very angry when the hungry ask for Government help of any kind, have no scruples about asking it for themselves. The railways ask the Government to guarantee their dividends; the air services ask for large sums from the Government to help them to maintain their aeroplanes and make money out of them; the coalowners and the miners between them extort subsidies from the Government by threatening a strike if they do not get it; and the Government, under the Trades Facilities Acts, guarantees loans to private capitalists without securing any share in their enterprises for the nation, which provides them with capital cheaply, but has to pay profiteering prices for goods and services all the same. In the end there is hardly any conceivable enterprise that can be made to pay dividends that Capitalism will not undertake as long as it can find spare money; and when it cannot it is quite ready to extract money from the Government—that is, to take it forcibly from the people by taxes—by assuring everyone that the Government can do nothing itself for the people, who must always come to the capitalists to get it done for them in return for substantial profits, dividends, and rents. Its operations are so enormous that it alters the size and meaning of what we call our country. Trading companies of capitalists have induced the Government to give them charters under which they have seized large and populous islands like Borneo, whole Empires like India, and great tracts of country like Rhodesia, governing them and maintaining armies in them for the purpose of making as much money out of them as possible. But they have taken care to hoist the British flag, and make use directly or indirectly of the British army and navy at the cost of the British taxpayers to defend these conquests of theirs; and in the end the British Commonwealth has had to take over their responsibilities and add the islands and countries they have seized to what is called the British Empire, with the curious result, quite unintended by the British people, that the centre of the British Empire is now in the East instead of in Great Britain, and out of every hundred of our fellow subjects only eleven are whites, or even Christians. Thus Capitalism leads us into enterprises of all sorts, at home and abroad, over which we have no control, and for which we have no desire. The enterprises are not necessarily bad: some of them have turned out well; but the point is that Capitalism does not care whether they turn out well or ill for us provided they promise to bring in money to the shareholders. We never know what Capitalism will be up to next; and we never can believe a word its newspapers tell us about its doings when the truth seems likely to be unpopular. (IWGSC-312-314)

The Capitalist Crusade. Do not be deceived by modern professions of toleration. Women are still what they were when the Tudor sisters sent Protestants to the stake and Jesuits to the rack and gallows; when the defenders of property and slavery in Rome set up crosses along the public roads with the crucified followers of the revolted gladiator slave Spartacus dying horribly upon them in thousands; and when the saintly Torquemada burnt alive every Jew he could lay hands on as piously as he told his beads. The difference between the Socialist versus Capitalist controversy and the Jew versus Christian controversy or the Roman Catholic versus Protestant controversy is not that the modern bigot is any more tolerant or less cruel than her ancestors, nor even that the proletarians are too numerous and the proprietors too powerful to be persecuted. If the controversy between them could be settled by either party exterminating the other, they would both do their worst to settle it in that way. History leaves us no goodnatured illusions on this point. From the wholesale butcheries which followed the suppression of the Paris Commune of 1871 to the monstrous and quite gratuitous persecution of Russians in the United States of America after the war of 1914-18, in which girls were sentenced to frightful terms of imprisonment for remarks that might have been made by any Sunday School teacher, there is abundant evidence that modern diehards are no better than medieval zealots, and that if they are to be restrained from deluging the world in blood and torture in the old fashion it will not be by any imaginary advance in toleration or in humanity. At this moment (1927) our proprietary classes appear to have no other conception of the Russian Soviet Government and its sympathizers than as vermin to be ruthlessly exterminated; and when the Russian Communist and his western imitators speak of the proprietors and their political supporters as "bourgeois," they make no secret of regarding them as enemies of the human race. The spirit of the famous manifesto of 1792, in which the Duke of Brunswick, in the name of the monarchs of Europe, announced that he meant to exterminate the French Republican Government and deliver up the cities which tolerated it to "military execution and total subversion," is reflected precisely in the speeches made by our own statesmen in support of the projected expedition against the Union of Soviet Republics which was countermanded a few years ago only because the disapproval of the British Proletarian voters became so obvious that the preparations for the Capitalist Crusade had to be hastily dropped. (IWGSC-368-369)

Shamefaced Leadership. When the Russian Bolsheviks went ruinously wrong by ignoring "the inevitability of gradualness" and attempting a catastrophic transfer of industry and agriculture from private to public ownership, it was the Englishman Sidney Webb and his Fabians who corrected them and devised the new economic policy Lenin had to announce, and Stalin to put in practice. Thus Englishmen can claim to have been pioneers in the revolutionary development of political organization since Cobdenism conquered us.

Unfortunately, whenever English parties effect an advance, they are so ashamed of it that they immediately throw away all credit for it by protesting that they are respectable citizens who would never dream of changing anything, and shouting their abhorrence of all the wicked foreigners who are in effect taking their advice. And then they are surprised when their disciples, especially in Russia, regard them as enemies, and the Marxist left wins more and more votes from them. (FF-95)

Capitalist Unconstitutionalism. Parliamentary constitutionalism holds good up to a certain point: the point at which the people who are outvoted in Parliament will accept their defeat. But on many questions people feel so strongly, or have such big interests at stake, that they leave the decision to Parliament only as long as they think they will win there. If Parliament decides against them, and they see any chance of a successful resistance, they throw Parliament over and fight it out. During the thirty years of the parliamentary campaign for Irish Home Rule there were always Direct Action men who said "It is useless to go to the English Parliament: the Unionists will never give up their grip of Ireland until they are forced to; and you may as well fight it out first as last." And these men, though denounced as wanton incendiaries, turned out to be right. The French had to cut off the heads of both king and queen because the king could not control the queen, and the queen would not accept a constitutional revolution, nor stop trying to induce the other kings of Europe to march their armies into France and slaughter the Liberals for her. In England we beheaded our king because he would not keep faith with the Liberal Parliament even after he had fought it and lost. In Spain at this moment the King and the army have suppressed Parliament, and are ruling by force of arms on the basis of divine right, which is exactly what Cromwell did in England after he had cut off King Charles's head for trying to do the same. Signor Mussolini, a Socialist, has overridden parliament in Italy, his followers having established what is called a reign of terror by frank violence.

These repudiations of constitutionalism in Spain and Italy have been made, not to effect any definite social change, but because the Spanish and Italian Governments had become so unbearably inefficient that the handiest way to restore public order was for some sufficiently energetic individuals to take the law into their own hands and just break people's heads if they would not behave themselves. And it may quite possibly happen that even if the most perfect set of Fabian Acts of Parliament for the constitutional completion of Socialism in this country be passed through Parliament by duly elected representatives of the people; swallowed with wry faces by the House of Lords; and finally assented to by the king and placed on the statute book, the capitalists may, like Signor Mussolini, denounce Parliament as unpatriotic, pernicious, and corrupt, and try to prevent by force the execution of the Fabian Acts. We should then have a state of civil war, with, no doubt, the Capitalist forces burning the cooperative stores, and the proletarians burning the country houses, as in Ireland, in addition to the usual war routine of devastation and slaughter. (IWGSC-371-372)

Capitalists at no Loss for Proletarian Troops.   In our examination of the effect of unequal distribution of income we found that it is not only the rich who live on the poor, but also the servants and tradesmen who live on the money the rich spend, and who have their own servants and tradesmen. In the rich suburbs and fashionable central quarters of the great cities, and all over the south of England where pleasant country houses are dotted over the pleasantest of the English counties, it is as hard to get a Labor candidate into Parliament as in Oxford University. If the unearned incomes of the rich disappeared, places like Bournemouth would either perish like the cities of Nineveh and Babylon, or else the inhabitants would have, as they would put it, to cater for a different class of people; and many of them would be ruined before they could adapt themselves to the new conditions. Add to these the young men who are out of employment, and will fight for anyone who will pay them well for an exciting adventure, with all the people who dread change of any sort, or who are duped by the newspapers into thinking Socialists scoundrels, or who would be too stupid to understand such a book as this if they could be persuaded to read anything but a cheap newspaper; and you will see at once that the line that separates those who live on rich customers from those who live on poor customers: in other words which separates those interested in the maintenance of Capitalism from those interested in its replacement by Socialism, is a line drawn not between rich and poor, capitalist and proletarian, but right down through the middle of the proletariat to the bottom of the very poorest section. In a civil war for the maintenance of Capitalism the capitalists would therefore find masses of supporters in all ranks of the community; and it is their knowledge of this that makes the leaders of the Labor Party so impatient with the extremists who talk of such a war as if it would be a Class War, and echo Shelley's very misleading couplet "Ye are many: they are few." And as the capitalists know it too, being reminded of it by the huge number of votes given for them by the poor at every election, I cannot encourage you to feel too sure that their present denunciations of Direct Action by their opponents mean that whenever their own sooner-or-later defeat by Labor in Parliament comes, they will take it lying down. (IWGSC-372-373)

THE RICH & RICHES

Moneymaking versus the World's Welfare. What is to be done with that section of the possessors of specific talents whose talent is for moneymaking? History and daily experience teach us that if the world does not devise some plan of ruling them, they will rule the world. Now it is not desirable that they should rule the world; for the secret of moneymaking is to care for nothing else and to work at nothing else; and as the world's welfare depends on operations by which no individual can make money, whilst its ruin by war and drink and disease and drugs and debauchery is enormously profitable to moneymakers, the supremacy of the moneymaker is the destruction of the State. A society which depends on the incentive of private profit is doomed. (P-TM-106)

"Evil: Be Thou My Good." By far the most unjust and mischievous privilege claimed by the rich is the privilege to be idle with complete impunity; and unfortunately they have established this privilege so firmly that we take it as a matter of course, and even venerate it as the mark of a real lady or gentleman, without ever considering that a person who consumes goods or

accepts services without producing equivalent goods or performing equivalent services in return inflicts on the country precisely the same injury as a thief does: in fact, that is what theft means. We do not dream of allowing people to murder, kidnap, break into houses, sink, burn, and destroy at sea or on land, or claim exemption from military service, merely because they have inherited a landed estate or a thousand a year from some industrious ancestor; yet we tolerate idling, which does more harm in one year than all the legally punishable crimes in the world in ten. The rich, through their majority in Parliament, punish with ruthless severity such forms of theft as burglary, forgery, embezzlement, pocket-picking, larceny, and highway robbery, whilst they exempt rich idling, and even hold it up as a highly honorable way of life, thereby teaching our children that working for a livelihood is inferior, derogatory, and disgraceful. To live like a drone on the labor and service of others is to be a lady or a gentleman: to enrich the country by labor and service is to be base, lowly, vulgar, contemptible, fed and clothed and lodged on the assumption that anything is good enough for hewers of wood and drawers of water. This is nothing else than an attempt to turn the order of nature upside down, and to take "Evil: be thou my good" as the national motto. If we persist in it, it must finally bring upon us another of those wrecks of civilization in which all the great empires in the past have crashed. Yet nothing can prevent this happening where income is unequally distributed, because the laws will inevitably be made by the rich; and the law that all must work, which should come before every other law, is a law that the rich never make. (IWGSC-58-59)

Genteel Economy's Illusion of Wealth. The moment a price is to be had for a luxury, it acquires exchange value, and labor is employed to produce it. A New York lady, for instance, having a nature of exquisite sensibility, orders an elegant rosewood and silver coffin, upholstered in pink satin, for her dead dog. It is made; and meanwhile a live child is prowling barefooted and hunger-stunted in the frozen gutter outside. The exchange value of the coffin is counted as part of the national wealth; but a nation which cannot afford food and clothing for its children cannot be allowed to pass as wealthy because it has provided a pretty coffin for a dead dog. Exchange value itself, in fact, has become bedevilled like everything else, and represents, no longer utility, but the cravings of lust, folly, vanity, gluttony, and madness, technically described by genteel economists as "effective demand." Luxuries are not social wealth: the machinery for producing them is not social wealth: labor skilled only to manufacture them is not socially useful labor: the men, women, and children who are making a living by producing them are no more self-supporting than the idle rich for whose amusement they are kept at work. It is the habit of counting as wealth the exchange values involved in these transactions that makes us fancy that the poor are starving in the midst of plenty. They are starving in the midst of plenty of jewels, velvets, laces, equipages, and racehorses; but not in the midst of plenty of food. In the things that are wanted for the welfare of the people we are abjectly poor. . . . (EBS-22-23)

The Rich Call the Tune. All the purchasing power that is left to buy men's souls with after their bodies are fed is in the hands of the rich; and everywhere, from the Parliament which wields the irresistible coercive forces of the bludgeon, bayonet, machine gun, dynamite shell, prison, and scaffold, down to the pettiest centre of shabby-genteel social pretension, the rich pay the piper and call the tune. Naturally, they use their power to steal more money to continue paying the piper; and thus all society becomes a huge conspiracy and hypocrisy. The ordinary man is insensible to the fraud just as he is insensible to the taste of water, which, being constantly in contact with his mucous membrane, seems to have no taste at all. The villainous moral conditions on which our social system is based are necessarily in constant contact with our moral mucous membrane, and so we lose our sense of their omnipresent meanness and dishonor. The insensibility, however, is not quite complete; for there is a period in life which is called the age of disillusion, which means the age at which a man discovers that his generous and honest impulses are incompatible with success in business; that the institutions he has reverenced are shams; and that he must join the conspiracy or go to the wall, even though he feels that the conspiracy is fundamentally ruinous to himself and his fellow-conspirators. (IOA-97-98)

Riches & Happiness. I . . . plead for a science of happiness to cure us of the miserable delusion that we can achieve it by becoming richer than our neighbors. Modern colossal fortunes have demonstrated its vanity. When country parsons were "passing rich with forty pounds a year" there was some excuse for believing that to be rich was to be happy, as the conception of riches did not venture beyond enough to pay for the necessities of a cultivated life. A hundred years ago Samuel Warren wrote a famous novel about a man who became enormously rich. The title of the novel was Ten Thousand a Year; and this, to any resident Irish family in my boyhood, represented an opulence beyond which only Lords Lieutenant and their like could aspire. The scale has changed since then. I have just seen in the papers a picture of the funeral of a shipping magnate whose income, if the capital value of the property left by him be correctly stated, must have been over four thousand pounds a day or a million and a half a year. If happiness is to be measured by riches he must have been fourteen thousand times as happy as the laborer lucky enough to be earning two pounds a week. Those who believe that riches are the reward of virtue are bound to conclude that he was also fourteen thousand times as sober, honest, and industrious, which would lead to the quaint conclusion that if he drank a bottle of wine a day the laborer must have drunk fourteen thousand. (P-TTTBG-6-7)

The Idle Rich. I maintain that nobody with a sane sense of values can feel that the sole prize which our villainous capitalist system has to offer, the prize of admission to the ranks of the idle rich, can possibly confer either happiness or health or freedom on its winner. No one can convict me of crying sour grapes; for

during the last thirty-five years I have been under no compulsion
to work, nor had any material privation or social ostracism to fear
as a consequence of not working. But, like all the intelligent rich
people of my acquaintance, I have worked as hard, ate and drunk
no more, and dressed no better than when I had to work or
starve. When my pockets were empty I did not buy any of the
luxuries in the London shops because I had no money to buy them
with. When later on, I had enough to buy anything that London
could tempt me with, the result was the same: I returned home
day after day without having made a single purchase. And I am
no ascetic: no man alive is freer than I am free from the fancy
that selfmortification will propitiate a spiteful deity or increase
my balance in a salvation bank in a world beyond the grave. I
would and could live the life of the idle rich if I liked it; and my
sole reason for not living it is that I dont like it. I have every
opportunity of observing it both in its daily practice and its remoter
results; and I know that a year of it would make me more unhappy
than anything else of an accepted kind that I can imagine. For,
just as the beanfeaster can live like a lord for an afternoon, and
the Lancashire factory operative have a gorgeous week at Blackpool
when the wakes are on, so I have had my afternoons as an idle
rich man, and know only too well what it is like. It makes me feel
suicidal. (P-TTTBG-9-10)

"Liberty: Thou Choicest Treasure." The only want that
money can satisfy without satiating for a few hours is the need for
food and drink and sleep. So from one serious meal a day and
two very minor ones you go on to three serious meals a day and two
minor ones. Then you work another minor one between breakfast and lunch "to sustain you"; and soon you find that you cannot tackle any meal without a cocktail, and that you cannot sleep.
That obliges you to resort to the latest soporific drug, guaranteed
in the advertisements to have none of the ruinous effects of its
equally guaranteed forerunner. Then comes the doctor, with his
tonics, which are simply additional cocktails, and his sure knowledge that if he tells you the truth about yourself and refuses to

prescribe the tonics and the drugs, his children will starve. If you indulge in such a luxury as a clerical spiritual adviser it is his duty to tell you that what is the matter with you is that you are an idle useless glutton and drunkard and that you are going to hell; but alas! he, like the doctor, cannot afford this, as he may have to ask you for a subscription tomorrow to keep his church going. And that is "Liberty: thou choicest treasure." (P-TTTBG-13-14)

More Money & Still More Money. When America got rid of monarchs and prelates and popes and British cabinets and the like, and plunged into the grand republican experiment which has become the rule instead of the exception in Europe since the war swept all the emperors into the dustbin of history, she raised the middle classes to the top of the social structure and thus delivered civilization into their hands without ennobling their traditions. Naturally they raced for more money, for more money, and still more money, and damned the public when they were not doping it with advertisements which were by tacit agreement exempted from the law against obtaining money by false pretenses or practicing medicine without qualifications. It is true that they were forced to govern as well by the impossibility of maintaining civilization without government; but their government was limited and corrupted by their principle of letting nothing stand in the way of their getting rich quickly. And the ablest of them at that game (which has no attraction for the ability that plays the higher games by which finally civilization must live) soon became rich at a rate that made the European middle classes envious. In my youth I heard little of great men arising in America—not that America did not produce them, but that her money masters were more apt to persecute than to advertise them—but I heard much of the great fortunes that were being made there. Vanderbilt, Jay Gould, Carnegie, Rockefeller became famous by bringing our civilization to the point to which Crassus and the other millionaire contemporaries of Sulla and Julius Caesar brought the civilization of ancient republican Rome just before it set up Emperor Idolatry as a resting place on the road to ruin. (IWGSC-x-xi)

Sacrifice? . . . Some of the rich do very well out of the taxes. By far the heaviest single item of Government expenditure is the annual payment for the hire of the money we borrowed for the war. It is all spent and gone; but we must go on paying for the hire until we replace and repay it. Most of it was borrowed from the rich, because they alone had any spare money to lend. . . .

It is sometimes said that the capitalists who lent the Government the money for the war deserve the hire of it because they made sacrifices. As I was one of them myself I can tell you without malice that this is sentimental nonsense. They were the only people who were not called upon to make any sacrifice: on the contrary, they were offered a gilt-edged investment at five percent when they would have taken four. The people who were blinded, maimed, or killed by the war were those really sacrificed; and those who worked and fought were the real saviors of the country; whilst the people who did nothing but seize the national loaf that others had made, and take a big bite out of it (they and their servants) before passing on what they left of it to the soldiers, did no personal service at all: they only made the food shortage still shorter. The reason for pampering them in this absurd fashion was not for any service or merit on their part: it was the special consideration we have to shew to spare money as such because we are afraid there would not be any available if we did not pamper a class by giving it more than it can spend. (IWGSC-114-115)

The Rich & Their Employment. It is no excuse for such a state of things that the rich give employment. There is no merit in giving employment: a murderer gives employment to the hangman; and a motorist who runs over a child gives employment to an ambulance porter, a doctor, an undertaker, a clergyman, a mourning-dressmaker, a hearse driver, a gravedigger: in short, to so many worthy people that when he ends by killing himself it seems ungrateful not to erect a statue to him as a public benefactor. The money with which the rich give the wrong sort of employment would give the right sort of employment if it were equally distributed; for then there would be no money offered for motor cars and diamonds until everyone was fed, clothed, and lodged, nor any wages offered to men and women to leave useful employments and become servants to idlers. There would be less ostentation, less idleness, less wastefulness, less uselessness; but there would be more food, more clothing, better houses, more security, more health, more virtue: in a word, more real prosperity. (IWGSC-52)

Obligation-Free Slavemasters. When every possible qualification of the words Idle Rich has been made, and it is fully understood that idle does not mean doing nothing (which is impossible), but doing nothing useful, and continually consuming without producing, the term applies to the class, numbering at the extreme outside one-tenth of the population, to maintain whom in their idleness the other nine-tenths are kept in a condition of slavery so complete that their slavery is not even legalized as such: hunger keeps them sufficiently in order without imposing on their masters any of those obligations which make slaves so expensive to their owners. What is more, any attempt on the part of a rich woman to do a stroke of ordinary work for the sake of her health would be bitterly resented by the poor because, from their point of view, she would be a rich woman meanly doing a poor woman out of a job. (IWGSC-62)

Why We Put up with It. The rich are very charitable: they understand that they have to pay ransom for their riches. The simple and decent village woman whose husband is a woodman or gardener or gamekeeper, and whose daughters are being taught manners as domestic servants in the country house, sees in the lord of the manor only a kind gentleman who gives employment, and whose wife gives clothes and blankets and little comforts for the sick, and presides over the Cottage Hospital and all the little shows and sports and well-meant activities that relieve the monotony of toil, and rob illness of some of its terrors. Even in the towns, where the rich and poor do not know oneanother, the lavish expenditure of the rich is always popular. It provides much that people enjoy looking at and gossiping about. The tradesman is proud of having rich customers, and the servant of serving in a rich house. At the public entertainments of the rich there are cheap seats for the poor. Ordinary thoughtless people like all this finery. They will read eagerly about it, and look with interest at the pictures of it in the illustrated papers, whereas when they read that the percentage of children dying under the age of five years has risen or fallen, it means nothing to them but dry statistics which make the paper dull. It is only when people learn to ask "Is this good for all of us all the time as well as amusing to me for five minutes?" that they are on the way to understand how one fashionably dressed woman may cost the life of ten babies. (IWGSC-65-66)

THE INEVITABLE COLLAPSE

The Fat's in the Fire. Old Dr. Marx—Karl Marx they call him now—my father knew him well—thought that when he'd explained the Capitalist System to the working classes of Europe theyd unite and overthrow it. Fifty years after he founded his Red International the working classes of Europe rose up and shot one another down and blew one another to bits, and turned millions and millions of their infant children out to starve in the snow or steal and beg in the sunshine, as if Dr Marx had never been born. And theyd do it again tomorrow if they was set on to do it. Why did you set them on? All they wanted was to be given their job, and fed and made comfortable according to their notion of comfort. If youd done that for them you wouldnt be having all this trouble. But you werent equal to it; and now the fat's in the fire." (*Hipney,* OR-264)

Our Capitalist Destiny. Nothing more diabolical can be conceived than the destiny of a civilization in which the material resources of the people's subsistence are privately owned by a handful of persons taught from childhood that every penny they can extort from the propertyless is an addition to the prosperity of their country and an enrichment of the world at large. (P-TM-123-124)

Big Business Prosperity: A Volcano. "The more I see of the sort of prosperity that comes of your leaving our vital industries to big business men as long as they keep your constituents quiet with high wages, the more I feel as if I were sitting on a volcano." (*Magnus,* AC-63)

Burning the Candle at Both Ends. Distribution, it must be remembered, is not only distribution of material product, but of work and leisure. If modern methods of production enable a single machine tender to turn out more product in a day than an eighteenth-century worker in the same trade, without a machine, turned out in a year, there is a gain in leisure, realizable by a reduction in working hours, of 300 per cent or thereabouts. If this and all cognate gains in leisure were equally distributed the result would be a steady reduction in the hours of labor and a steady increase in the hours of individual liberty. But there is an alternative to this. It is just as possible to keep the workers working as long as before, or longer, and to increase the number or the luxury, or both, of the leisured rich. Now this is precisely what the Capitalist system does, and even aims at doing. And in its present stage, when it is adding an army of unemployed to the leisured rich, and thus burning the candle at both ends, the reform of distribution has become a matter of life and death to civilization. (P-FE-viii)

Laisser-Faire. Have you noticed, . . . that we no longer speak of letting things alone in the old-fashioned way? We speak of letting them slide; and this is a great advance in good sense; for it shews that we at last see that they slide instead of staying put; and it implies that letting them slide is a feckless sort of conduct. So you must rule out once for all the notion of leaving things as they are in the expectation that they will stay where they are. They wont. All we can do in that line is to sit idly and wonder what will happen next. And this is not like sitting on the bank of the stream waiting for the water to go by. It is like sitting idly in a carriage when the horse is running away. You can excuse it by saying "What else can I do?"; but your impotence will not avert a smash. People in that predicament must all think hard of some way of getting control of the horse, and meanwhile do all they can to keep the carriage right side up and out of the ditch.

The policy of letting things alone, in the practical sense that the Government should never interfere with business or go into business itself, is called Laisser-faire by economists and politicians. It has broken down so completely in practice that it is now discredited; but it was all the fashion in politics a hundred years ago, and is still influentially advocated by men of business and their backers who naturally would like to be allowed to make money as they please without regard to the interests of the public. (IWGSC-40-41)

Possibilities of Private Enterprise Transcended. When, as at present, the work of organizing civilization outgrows the scope and financial capacity of private adventurers and personal interests, the first symptom of excessive strain is an abnormal increase of unemployment accompanied by reconstructions and amalgamations of commercial businesses, and appeals by them for State help: all of them desperate efforts to make private enterprise meet social needs which are more and more transcending its possibilities. When the number of unemployed runs into millions, and they consist to a considerable extent of demobilized soldiers who have learned in a war of unprecedented frightfulness to hold human life cheap, the unemployed become, in fact, an army living on the country. (P-FE-vi)

Unemployment a Means of Livelihood. . . . Capitalism always tries to buy off those whom it cannot employ and no longer dares leave to starve. Unemployment thus becomes a recognized means of livelihood for the proletariat. As I write, there are young men in the prime of early manhood who have never worked, and proletarian children who have never seen their parents work. If two or three unemployed share the same house they can live "on the dole" quite comfortably according to their own standards of comfort by blackmailing Capitalism until it consents to share its social plunder with them. If the combinations of two or three become combinations of two or three hundreds or even thousands, as they will if the dole system attains a reputation for permanence, the Ritz Hostels of the unemployed will put to shame the humble dwellings of those for whom the Labor Exchanges can still find jobs. Members of seasonal trades now draw the dole through the off-season for which the on-season formerly provided. This state of things is clearly the "bread and circuses" of the ancient Roman proletariat over again; and the parallel will soon be more exact; for since our police have urged the opening of the cinemas on Sunday because they keep the streets empty and orderly, State-provided cinemas are quite likely to be instituted as a means of preventing riots of the unemployed. That must end as the Roman Empire ended, in bankruptcy. (P-FE-vi-vii)

Chains: The Gold as Bad as the Iron. When I propose the abolition of our capitalistic system to redeem mankind from the double curse of poverty and riches, loud wailings arise. The most articulate sounds in the hubbub are to the effect that the wretched slaves of the curse will lose their liberty if they are forced to earn their living honorably. The retort that they have nothing to lose but their chains, with the addition that the gold chains are as bad as the iron ones, cannot silence them, because they think they are free, and have been brought up to believe that unless the country remains the private property of irresponsible owners maintaining a parliament to make any change impossible, with churches schools and universities to inculcate the sacredness of private property and party government disguised as religion education and democracy, civilization must perish. I am accused of every sort of reactionary extravagance by the people who think themselves advanced, and of every sort of destructive madness by people who thank God they are no wiser than their fathers. (P-TTTBG-14-15)

The Reserve Army of Unemployed. Some time ago I mentioned the subject of Universal Old Age Pensions to my fellow Socialist Mr. Cobden-Sanderson, famous as an artist-craftsman in bookbinding and printing. "Why not Universal Pensions for Life?" said Cobden-Sanderson. In saying this, he solved the industrial problem at a stroke. At present we say callously to each citizen: "If you want money, earn it," as if his having or not having it were a matter that concerned himself alone. We do not even secure for him the opportunity of earning it: on the contrary, we allow our industry to be organized in open dependence on the maintenance of "a reserve army of unemployed" for the sake of "elasticity." (P-MB-211-212)

Right To Exterminite Conferred by Private Property. . . . When a tract of land becomes the private property of an individual who has to depend on it for his substance, the relation between him and the inhabitants of that tract becomes an economic one; and if they become economically superfluous or wasteful, he must exterminate them. This is continually happening where private property in land exists. If I possess land and find it profitable to grow wheat on it, I need many agricultural laborers to enable me to do it; and I tolerate their existence accordingly. If I presently find that it is more profitable to cover my land with sheep and sell their wool, I have to tolerate the existence of the sheep; but I no longer need tolerate the existence of the laborers; so I drive them off my land, which is my legal method of extermination, retaining only a few to act as shepherds. Later on I find that it is more profitable to cover my land with wild deer, and collect money from ladies and gentlemen who enjoy shooting them. I then exterminate my shepherds and keep only a few gamekeepers. But I may do much better by letting my land to industrialists for the erection of factories. They exterminate the sheep and the deer; but they need far more men than I needed even when I grew wheat. The driven-offs crowd into the factories and multiply like rabbits; and for the moment population grows instead of diminishing. But soon machines come along and make millions of proletarians superfluous. The factory owner accordingly sacks them, which is his legal method of extermination. During these developments the exterminated, or, as we call them, the evicted and sacked, try to avoid starvation partly by emigration, but mostly by offering themselves for all sorts of employment as soldiers, servants, prostitutes, police officers, scavengers, and operators of the immense machinery of amusement and protection for the idle rich classes created by the private property system. By organization in trade unions, municipal and parliamentary Labor Parties, and the like, and maintaining a sort of continual civil war consisting of strikes and riots, they extort from the proprietors enough to reduce the rate of extermination (shewn by the actuarial expectation of life of the unpropertied) for periods described as progressive, until the proprietors, by engaging in suicidal wars, are forced to intensify their economies, and the rate of extermination rises again. (P-OR-183-184)

Financiers' Delusions.   If you read the money articles in the papers, you will notice that the prosperity of a country is always measured at present by the money it receives for its exports. "A favorable balance of trade" is what the financiers clamor for; and by a favorable balance of trade they mean an excess of exports over imports. Now this seems reasonable enough to people who think in terms of money. To people who think in terms of goods it is raving nonsense. Foreign trade is nothing but barter conducted with money; and to maintain that in barter the more you give and the less you get in exchange the more prosperous you are, is to qualify yourself for the asylum. Yet in America and England it qualifies you for the Cabinet. A financier cannot think in terms of bread and butter or bricks and mortar: he thinks in figures. He has never been inside a factory or down a mine or on a farm. Sending goods out of the country means to him nothing but attracting money into it. His ideal is a country which exports everything it produces, and gets nothing in return but title deeds to gold, of which you in America have too much already. (FPSA-27-28)

Foreign Markets & Empires in Collision. . . . Imagine yourself for a moment a German trader, with more goods than you can sell in Germany, having either to shut your factory and be ruined, or find a foreign market in Africa. Imagine yourself looking at the map of Africa. The entire Mediterranean coast, the pick of the basket, is English, Italian, French, and Spanish. The Hinterland, as you call it, is English and French. You cannot get anywhere without going through the English Suez canal or round the cape to some remote place down south. Do you now understand what the German Kaiser meant when he complained that Germany had not been left "a place in the sun"? That hideous war of 1914-18 was at bottom a fight between the capitalists of England, France, and Italy on the one side, and those of Germany on the other, for command of the African markets. On top, of course, it was about other things: about Austria making the murder of the Archduke a pretext for subjugating Serbia; about Russia mobilizing against Austria to prevent this; about Germany being dragged into the Austro-Russian quarrel by her alliance with Austria; about France being dragged in on the other side by her alliance with Russia; about the German army having to make a desperate attempt to conquer the French army before the Russian troops could reach her; about England having to attack Germany because she was allied to France and Russia; and about the German army having taken the shortest cut through Belgium, not knowing that Belgium had a secret arrangement with England to have a British expedition sent to defend her if Germany invaded her. Of course the moment the first shot was fired all the Britons and Belgians and Germans and French and Austrians and Russians became enraged sheep, and imagined all sorts of romantic reasons for fighting, in addition to the solid reasons that if Tommy and the Poilu and Ivan did not kill Hans and Fritz, Hans and Fritz would kill Tommy and the Poilu and Ivan. Before the killing had gone on very long, the Turks, the Bulgarians, the Japanese, the Americans, and other states that had no more to do with the first quarrel than you had, were in it and at it hammer and tongs. The whole world went mad, and never alluded to markets except when they ridiculed the Kaiser for his demand for a place in the sun.

Yet there would have been no war without the alliances; and the alliances could not have fought if they had not set up great armaments, especially the new German navy, to protect their foreign markets and frontiers. These armaments, created to produce a sense of security, had produced a sense of terror in which no nation dared go unarmed unless it was too small to have any chance against the great Powers, and could depend on their jealousy of oneanother to stave off a conquest by any one of them. Soon the nations that dared not go unarmed became more terrified still, and dared not go alone: they had to form alliances and go in twos and threes, like policemen in thieves' quarters, Germany and Austria in one group and England, France, and Russia in another, both trying to induce Italy and Turkey and America to join them. Their differences were not about their own countries: the German navy was not built to bombard Portsmouth nor the British navy to bombard Bremerhaven. But when the German navy interfered in the north of Africa, which was just what it was built for, and the French and British navies frightened it off from that market in the sun, the capitalist diplomats of these nations saw that the first thing to concentrate on was not the markets but the sinking of the German navy by the combined French and British navies (or vice versa) on any available pretext. And as you cannot have fleets fighting on the sea without armies fighting on the land to help them, the armies grew like the fleets; the Race of Armaments became as familiar as the Derby; all the natural and kindly sentiments of white civilizations towards oneanother were changed into blustering terror, the parent of hatred, malice, and all uncharitableness: and after all, when the explosive mixture blew up at last, and blew millions of us with it, it was not about the African markets, but about a comparatively trumpery quarrel between Austria and Serbia which the other Powers could have settled with the greatest ease, without the shedding of one drop of blood, if they had been on decent human terms with oneanother instead of on competitive capitalistic terms. (IWGSC-152-154)

Slaughterhouse Heroism. And please do not fail to note that whereas in the early days of Capitalism our capitalists did not compel us to fight for their markets with our own hands, but hired German serfs and British voluntary professional soldiers for the job, their wars have now become so colossal that every woman's husband, father, son, brother, or sweetheart, if young and strong enough to carry a rifle, must go to the trenches as helplessly as cattle go to the slaughterhouse, abandoning wife and children, home and business, and renouncing normal morality and humanity, pretending all the time that such conduct is splendid and heroic and that his name will live forever, though he may have the greatest horror of war, and be perfectly aware that the enemy's soldiers, against whom he is defending his hearth, are in exactly the same predicament as himself, and would never dream of injuring him or his if the pressure of the drive for markets were removed from both. (IWGSC-154-155)

The Original Sin behind War. It is absurd to pretend that the young men of Europe ever wanted to hunt each other into holes in the ground and throw bombs into the holes to disembowel oneanother, or to have to hide in those holes themselves, eaten with lice and sickened by the decay of the unburied, in unutterable discomfort, boredom, and occasionally acute terror, or that any woman ever wanted to put on her best Sunday clothes and be gratified at the honor done to her son for killing some other woman's babies. The capitalists and their papers try to persuade themselves and us that we are like that and always will be, in spite of all the Christmas cards and Leagues of Nations. It is not a bit true. The staggering fact about all these horrors was that we found ourselves compelled to do them in spite of the fact that they were so unintended by us, and so repugnant and dreadful to us that, when at last the war suddenly stopped, our heroic pretences dropped from us like blown-off hats, and we danced in the streets for weeks, mad with joy, until the police had to stop us to restore the necessary traffic. We still celebrate, by two minutes' national silence, not the day on which the glorious war broke out, but the day on which the horrible thing came to an end. Not

the victory, which we have thrown away by abusing it as helplessly
as we fought for it, but the Armistice, the Cessation, the stoppage
of the Red Cross vans from the terminuses of the Channel railways with their heartbreaking loads of mutilated men, was what
we danced for so wildly and pitifully. If ever there was anything
made clear in the world it was that we were no more directly
guilty of the war than we were guilty of the earthquake of Tokio.
We and the French and the Germans and the Turks and the rest
found ourselves conscripted for an appalling slaughtering match,
ruinous to ourselves, ruinous to civilization, and so dreaded by the
capitalists themselves that it was only by an extraordinary legal
suspension of all financial obligations (called the Moratorium)
that the City was induced to face it. The attempt to fight out the
war with volunteers failed: there were not enough. The rest went
because they were forced to go, and fought because they were
forced to fight. The women let them go partly because they could
not help themselves, partly because they were just as pugnacious
as the men, partly because they read the papers (which were not
allowed to tell them the truth), and partly because most of them
were so poor that they grasped at the allowances which left most
of them better off with their husbands in the trenches than they
had ever been with their husbands at home.

How had they got into this position? Simply by the original
sin of allowing their countries to be moved and governed and fed
and clothed by the pursuit of profit for capitalists instead of by
the pursuit of righteous prosperity for "all people that on earth
do dwell." (IWGSC-155-157)

Capitalism: Eternal Enmity. True, we no longer exploit
colonies capitalistically: we allow them to do it for themselves,
and to call the process self-government. Whilst we persisted in
governing them they blamed us for all the evils Capitalism brought
upon them; and they finally refused to endure our government.
When we left them to govern themselves they became less and
less hostile to us. But the change always impoverishes them, and
leaves them in comparative disorder. The capitalistic evils for which

they blamed us still oppress them. Their self-government is more tyrannical than our alien government ever dared to be. Their new relation to the Imperial State becomes more dangerously strained than the old relation, precisely as the relation of England to Germany was more dangerously strained in 1913 than the relation of England to Ireland. The most liberal allowance of self-government cannot reconcile people as long as their capitalists are competing for markets. Nationalism may make Frenchmen and Englishmen, Englishmen and Irishmen, savage enemies when it is infringed. Frenchmen and Irishmen laid their own countries waste to get rid of English rule. But Capitalism makes all men enemies all the time without distinction of race, color, or creed. When all the nations have freed themselves Capitalism will make them fight more furiously than ever, if we are fools enough to let it. (IWGSC-159-160)

The Runaway Car of Capitalism. Fancy yourself in a car which you do not know how to steer and cannot stop, with an inexhaustible supply of petrol in the tank, rushing along at fifty miles an hour on an island strewn with rocks and bounded by cliff precipices! That is what living under Capitalism feels like when you come to understand it. Capital is running away with us; and we know that it has always ended in the past by taking its passengers over the brink of the precipice at the foot of which are strewn the ruins of empires. The desperately pressing present problem for all governments is how to get control of this motion; make safe highways for it; and steer it along those highways. If only we could stop it whilst we sit down and think! But no: the car will not stop: on the contrary it goes faster and faster as capital accumulates in greater and greater quantities, and as we multiply our numbers. One statesman after another snatches at the wheel and tries his hand. Kings try their hands; dictators try their hands; democratic prime ministers try their hands; committees and Soviets try their hands; and we look hopefully to them for a moment, imagining that they have got control because they do it with an air of authority, and assure us that it will be all right if only we will sit quiet. But Capital runs away with them all; and we palpitate between relief when our ungovernable vehicle blunders into a happy valley, and despair when we hear the growl of the waves at the foot of the cliffs grow louder and louder instead of dying away in the distance. Blessed then are those who do not know and cannot think: to them life seems a joyride with a few disagreeable incidents that must be put up with. They sometimes make the best rulers, just as the best railway signalman is he who does not feel his responsibility enough to be frightened out of his wits by it. But in the long run civilization depends on our governments gaining an intelligent control of the forces that are running away with Capitalism; and for that an understanding of them is necessary. Mere character and energy, much as we admire them, are positively mischievous without intellect and knowledge. (IWGSC-315-316)

Capitalist Mankind Detestable. We have to confess it: Capitalist mankind in the lump is detestable. Class hatred is not a mere matter of envy on the part of the poor and contempt and dread on the part of the rich. Both rich and poor are really hateful in themselves. For my part I hate the poor and look forward eagerly to their extermination. I pity the rich a little, but am equally bent on their extermination. The working classes, the business classes, the professional classes, the propertied classes, the ruling classes, are each more odious than the other: they have no right to live: I should despair if I did not know that they will all die presently, and that there is no need on earth why they should be replaced by people like themselves. I do not want any human child to be brought up as I was brought up, nor as any child I have known was brought up. (IWGSC-456)

Capitalism in Summary. And yet I am not in the least a misanthrope. I am a person of normal affections, as you probably are; but for that very reason I hate to be surrounded, not by people whose interests are the same as my own, whom I cannot injure without injuring myself, and who cannot injure me without injuring themselves, but by people whose interest it is to get as much out of me as they possibly can, and give me as little for it as possible (if anything). If I were poor, my relatives, now that I am old, would have to support me to keep me out of the workhouse, which means that they would have a strong interest in my death. As I am rich enough to leave some property, my children, if I had any, would be looking forward impatiently to my funeral and the reading of my will. The whole propertied class is waiting for dead men's shoes all the time. If I become ill and send for a doctor I know that if he does not prolong my illness to the utmost, and send me to expensive nursing homes to submit to still more expensive operations, he will be taking bread out of his children's mouths. My lawyer is bound by all his affections to encourage me in litigation, and to make it as protracted and costly as he can. Even my clergyman, partly State supported as he is, dare not if I belong to the Church of England rebuke me for oppressing the poor any more than he dare champion me against the oppression of the rich if I were poor. The teacher in the school where my neighbors' children have their morals formed would find herself in the gutter if she taught any child that to live on what is called an independent income without working is to live the life of a thief without the risks and enterprise that make the pirate and the burglar seem heroic to boys. My tradesmen's business is to overcharge me as much as they can without running too great a risk of being undersold by trade rivals. My landlord's business is to screw out of me the uttermost extractable farthing of my earnings for his permission to occupy a place on earth. Were I unmarried I should be pursued by hordes of women so desperately in need of a husband's income and position that their utmost efforts to marry me would be no evidence of their having the smallest personal regard for me. I cannot afford the friendship of people much richer than myself: those much poorer cannot afford mine. Between those who do the daily work of my house, and are therefore necessary partners in my work, and me there is a gulf of class which is nothing but a gulf of unequal distribution of wealth. Life is made lonely and difficult for me in a hundred unnecessary ways; and so few people are clever and tactful and sen-

sible and self-controlled enough to pick their way through the
world without giving or taking offense that the first quality of
capitalistic mankind is quarrelsomeness. Our streets are fuller of
feuds than the Highlands or the Arabian desert. The social friction set up by inequality of income is intense: society is like a
machine designed to work smoothly with the oil of equality, into
the bearings of which some malignant demon keeps pouring the
sand of inequality. If it were not for the big pools of equality
that exist at different levels, the machine would not work at all.
As it is, the seizings-up, the smashings, the stoppages, the explosions, never cease. They vary in magnitude from a railway worker
crushed in the shunting-yard to a world war in which millions of
men with the strongest reasons for saving each other's lives destroy them instead in the cruellest manner, and from a squabble
over a penny in a one-room tenement to a lawsuit lasting twenty
years and reducing all the parties to it to destitution. And to
outface this miserable condition we bleat once a year about peace
on earth and good-will to men: that is, among persons to whom we
have distributed incomes ranging from a starvation dole to several
thousands a day, piously exhorting the recipients to love oneanother. Have you any patience with it? I have none. (IWGSC-456-
458)

Socialism

You will find constitutional changes specially bothersome because of the continual clashing between the tightening-up of social discipline demanded by Socialism and the jealousy of official power and desire to do what we like which we call Democracy. (IWGSC-450-451)

The Class War. "The Class War is a fact. We face it. What we want we shall have to take; and we know it. The good of the community is nothing to you: you care only for surplus value. You will never give up your privileges voluntarily. History teaches us that: the history you never read." (*Aloysia*, OR-307)

Fundamental Natural Conditions of Human Society.

1. Government is necessary wherever two or three are gathered together—or two or three billions—for keeps.

2. Government is neither automatic nor abstract: it must be performed by human rulers and agents as best they can.

3. The business of the rulers is to check disastrously selfish or unexpected behavior on the part of individuals in social affairs.

4. This business can be done only by devising and enforcing rules of social conduct codifying the greatest common measure of agreement as to the necessary sacrifice of individual liberty to the good of the community.

5. The paradox of government is that as the good of the community involves a maximum of individual liberty for all its mem-

bers the rulers have at the same time to enslave everyone ruthlessly
and to secure for everyone the utmost possible freedom.

6. In primitive communities people feed and lodge themselves
without bothering the Government. In big civilizations this is impossible; so the first business of the government is to provide for
the production and distribution of wealth from day to day and
the just sharing of the labor and leisure involved. Thus the individual citizen has to be compelled not only to behave himself
properly, but to work productively.

7. The moral slavery of the compulsion to behave properly is a
whole-time compulsion admitting of no liberty; but the personal
slavery of the compulsion to work lasts only as many hours daily
as suffice to discharge the economic duties of the citizen, the re-
maining hours (over and above those needed for feeding, sleeping,
locomotion, etc.) being his leisure.

8. Leisure is the sphere of individual liberty: labor is the sphere
of slavery.

9. People who think they can be honestly free all the time are
idiots: people who seek whole-time freedom by putting their share
of productive work on others are thieves.

10. The use of the word slavery to denote subjection to public
government has grown up among the idiots and thieves, and is
resorted to here only because it is expedient to explain things to
fools according to their folly. (P-TTTBG-16-17)

Nature's Indifference. Nature makes short work of our aspirations toward utter impunity. She leaves communities in no wise
"free" to choose whether they will labor and govern themselves.
It is either that or starvation and chaos. Her tasks are inexorably
set: her penalties are inevitable: her payment is strictly "payment
by results." All the individual can do is to shift and dodge his
share of the task on to the shoulders of others, or filch some of
their "natural wage" to add to his own. If they are fools enough
to suffer it, that is their own affair as far as Nature is concerned.
But it is the aim of Social Democracy to relieve these fools by
throwing on all an equal share in the inevitable labor imposed by

the eternal tyranny of Nature, and so secure to every individual no less than his equal quota of the nation's product in return for no more than his equal quota of the nation's labor. These are the best terms humanity can make with its tyrant. (IOA-93-94)

Socialism in Short. It cannot be too thoroughly understood that Socialism is not charity nor loving-kindness, nor sympathy with the poor, nor popular philanthropy with its something-for-nothing almsgiving and mendacity, but the economist's hatred of waste and disorder, the aesthete's hatred of ugliness and dirt, the lawyer's hatred of injustice, the doctor's hatred of disease, the saint's hatred of the seven deadly sins: in short, a combination of the most intense hatreds against institutions which give economists a strong pecuniary interest in wasteful and anarchic capitalism, artists in venality and pornography, lawyers in injustice, doctors in disease, and saints in catering for the seven deadly sins or flattering them instead of denouncing them. (EPWW-78)

The Economic Object of Socialism. What the achievement of Socialism involves economically, is the transfer of rent from the class which now appropriates it to the whole people. Rent being that part of the produce which is individually unearned, this is the only equitable method of disposing of it. There is no means of getting rid of economic rent. So long as the fertility of land varies from acre to acre, and the number of persons passing by a shop window per hour varies from street to street, with the result that two farmers or two shopkeepers of exactly equal intelligence and industry will reap unequal returns from their year's work, so long will it be equitable to take from the richer farmer or shopkeeper the excess over his fellow's gain which he owes to the bounty of Nature or the advantage of situation, and divide that excess or rent equally between the two. If the pair of farms or shops be left in the hands of a private landlord, he will take the excess, and, instead of dividing it between his two tenants, live on it himself idly at their expense. The economic object of Socialism is not, of course, to equalize farmers and shopkeepers in couples, but to carry out the principle over the whole community by collecting all rents and throwing them into the national treasury. As the private proprietor has no reason for clinging to his property except the legal power to take the rent and spend it on himself—this legal power being in fact what really constitutes him a proprietor—its abrogation would mean his expropriation. The socialization of rent would mean the socialization of the sources of production by the expropriation of the present private proprietors, and the transfer of their property to the entire nation. (TSD-39-40)

Henry Georgism Checkmated. Ever since Mr. Henry George's book reached the English Radicals, there has been a growing disposition to impose a tax of twenty shillings in the pound* on obviously unearned incomes: that is, to dump four hundred and fifty millions a year down on the Exchequer counter; and then retire with three cheers for the restoration of the land to the people.

The results of such a proceeding, if it actually came off, would considerably take its advocates aback. The streets would presently be filled with starving workers of all grades, domestic servants, coach builders, decorators, jewellers, lacemakers, fashionable professional men, and numberless others whose livelihood is at present gained by ministering to the wants of these and of the proprietary class. "This," they would cry, "is what your theories have brought us to! Back with the good old times, when we received our wages, which were at least better than nothing." Evidently the Chancellor of the Exchequer would have three courses open to him. (1) He could give the money back again to the landlords and capitalists with an apology. (2) He could attempt to start State industries with it for the employment of the people. (3) Or he could simply distribute it among the unemployed. The last is not to be thought of: anything is better than *panem et circenses.* The second (starting State industries) would be far too vast an undertaking to get on foot soon enough to meet the urgent

* Amounting to 100-per-cent taxation.

difficulty. The first (the return with an apology) would be a *re-ductio ad absurdum* of the whole affair—a confession that the private proprietor, for all his idleness and his voracity, is indeed performing an indispensable economic function—the function of capitalizing, however wastefully and viciously, the wealth which surpasses his necessarily limited power of immediate personal consumption. And here we have checkmate to mere Henry Georgism, or State appropriation of rent without Socialism. It is easy to shew that the State is entitled to the whole income of the Duke of Westminster, and to argue therefrom that he should straightway be taxed twenty shillings in the pound. But in practical earnest the State has no right to take five farthings of capital from the Duke or anybody else until it is ready to invest them in productive enterprise. The consequences of withdrawing capital from private hands merely to lock it up unproductively in the treasury would be so swift and ruinous, that no statesman, however fortified with the destructive resources of abstract economics, could persist in it. It will be found in the future as in the past that governments will raise money only because they want it for specific purposes, and not on *a priori* demonstrations that they have a right to it. But it must be added that when they *do* want it for a specific purpose, then, also in the future as in the past, they will raise it without the slightest regard to *a priori* demonstrations that they have no right to it. (TSD-49-50)

The Sunday School Prize. We are bewildered by an absurdly unpractical notion that in some way a man's income should be given to him, not to enable him to live, but as a sort of Sunday School prize for good behavior. And this folly is complicated by a less ridiculous but quite as unpractical belief that it is possible to assign to each person the exact portion of the national income that he or she has produced. To a child it seems that the blacksmith has made a horseshoe, and that therefore the horseshoe is his. But the blacksmith knows that the horseshoe does not belong solely to him, but to his landlord, to the rate-collector and tax-gatherer, to the men from whom he bought the iron and anvil and the coals,

leaving only a scrap of its value for himself; and this scrap he has
to exchange with the butcher and baker and the clothier for the
things he really appropriates as living tissue or its wrappings, paying for all of them more than their cost; for these fellow traders
of his have also their landlords and moneylenders to satisfy. If,
then, such simple and direct village examples of apparent individual production turn out on a moment's examination to be the
products of an elaborate social organization, what is to be said
of such products as dreadnoughts, factory-made pins and needles,
and steel pens? If God takes the dreadnought in one hand and a
steel pen in the other, and asks Job who made them, and to whom
they should belong by maker's right, Job must scratch his puzzled
head with a potsherd and be dumb, unless indeed it strikes him
that God is the ultimate maker, and that all we have a right to
do with the product is to feed his lambs. (P-AL-54-55)

Distribution According to Merit?   Many people, especially
those who are comfortably off, think that . . . the industrious and
sober and thrifty are never in want, and that poverty is due to
idleness, improvidence, drink, betting, dishonesty, and bad character generally. They can point to the fact that a laborer whose
character is bad finds it more difficult to find employment than
one whose character is good; that a farmer or country gentleman
who gambles and bets heavily, and mortgages his land to live
wastefully and extravagantly, is soon reduced to poverty; and that
a man of business who is lazy and does not attend to it becomes
bankrupt. But this proves nothing but that you cannot eat your
cake and have it too: it does not prove that your share of the
cake was a fair one. It shews that certain vices and weaknesses make
us poor; but it forgets that certain other vices make us rich. People
who are hard, grasping, selfish, cruel, and always ready to take advantage of their neighbors, become very rich if they are clever
enough not to overreach themselves. On the other hand, people who
are generous, public-spirited, friendly, and not always thinking of
the main chance, stay poor when they are born poor unless they
have extraordinary talents. Also, as things are today, some are born

poor and others are born with silver spoons in their mouths: that is to say, they are divided into rich and poor before they are old enough to have any character at all. The notion that our present system distributes wealth according to merit, even roughly, may be dismissed at once as ridiculous. Every one can see that it generally has the contrary effect: it makes a few idle people very rich, and a great many hardworking people very poor. (IWGSC-26-27)

The Worth of Human Souls. You can find out how many candles are worth a pound of butter in the market on any particular day; but when you try to estimate the worth of human souls the utmost you can say is that they are all of equal value before the throne of God. And that will not help you in the least to settle how much money they should have. You must simply give it up, and admit that distributing money according to merit is beyond mortal measurement and judgement. (IWGSC-29)

Equal Incomes. When reading what follows it must not be forgotten that though we differ widely in practical ability and mental scope, the same basic income, or ration, or minimum wage, or national dividend, or whatever the newspapers call it for the moment, will suffice for mayor and scavenger, for admiral and cabin boy, for judge and executioner, for field marshal and drummer boy, for sexton and archbishop, bank manager and bank porter, sister of charity and prison wardress, and who not. What is more, they are all equally indispensable. An industrial magnate once wrote asking me did I realize that his army of laborers would be destitute and helpless without him. I replied that if he did not realize that without them he would be a nobody he was no gentleman. This closed the correspondence.

Equality of income is an obvious corollary. Yes; but how much income? A national dividend of, say, thirteen shillings a week per family, which was the share agricultural laborers got in the nineteenth century, kept them alive for thirty years or so, but left no surplus for education and culture: in short, for civilization. Now without cultured homes civilization is impossible. Without culture possible in every home democratic civilization is impossible, because equality of opportunity is impossible. The present combination of class culture and general savagery produces civil war, called class war, until strikes, lock-outs, and police batons are succeeded by shot and shell. Then the final destruction of civilization is threatened. (FF-65)

The Parrot's Repetition. When some inconsiderate person repeats like a parrot that if you gave everybody the same money, before the year was out you would have rich and poor again just as before, all you have to do is to tell him to look around him and see millions of people who get the same money and remain in the same position all their lives without any such change taking place. The cases in which poor men become rich are most exceptional; and though the cases in which rich men become poor are commoner, they also are accidents and not ordinary everyday circumstances. The rule is that workers of the same rank and calling are paid alike, and that they neither sink below their condition nor rise above it. No matter how unlike they are to oneanother, you can pay one of them two and sixpence* and the other half a crown* with the assurance that as they are put so they will stay, though here and there a great rogue or a great genius may surprise you by becoming much richer or much poorer than the rest. Jesus complained that he was poorer than the foxes and birds, as they had their holes and nests whilst he had not a house to shelter him; and Napoleon became an Emperor; but we need take no more account of such extraordinary persons in forming our general plan than a maker of readymade clothes takes of giants and dwarfs in his price list. You may with the utmost confidence take it as settled by practical experience that if we could succeed in distributing income equally to all the inhabitants of the country, there would be no more tendency on their part to divide into rich and poor than there is at present for postmen to divide into beggars and millionaires. The only novelty proposed is that the postmen should get as much as the postmasters, and the postmasters no less than anybody else. If we find, as we do, that it answers to give all

* The same.

judges the same income, and all navy captains the same income, why should we go on giving judges five times as much as navy captains? That is what the navy captain would like to know; and if you tell him that if he were given as much as the judge he would be just as poor as before at the end of the year he will use language unfit for the ears of anyone but a pirate. So be careful how you say such things.

Equal distribution is then quite possible and practicable, not only momentarily but permanently. It is also simple and intelligible. It gets rid of all squabbling as to how much each person should have. It is already in operation and familiar over great masses of human beings. And it has the tremendous advantage of securing promotion by merit for the more capable. (IWGSC-69-70)

Equal Distribution of Leisure. Modern methods of production enable each person in the nation to produce much more than they need consume to keep themselves alive and reproduce themselves. That means that modern methods produce not only a national fund of wealth but a national fund of leisure or liberty. Now just as you can distribute the wealth so as to make a few people monstrously rich whilst leaving all the rest as poor as before, you can distribute the leisure in such a way as to make a few people free for fifteen hours a day whilst the rest remain as they were, with barely four hours to dispose of as they please. And this is exactly what the institution of private property has done, and why a demand for its abolition and for the equal distribution of the national leisure or liberty among the whole population has arisen under the banner of Socialism. (IWGSC-325)

The Abolition of Property. To the mass of men, the intelligent abolition of property would mean nothing except an increase in the quantity of food, clothing, housing and comfort at their personal disposal, as well as a greater control over their time and circumstances. Very few persons now make any distinction between virtually complete property and property held on such highly developed public conditions as to place its income on the same footing as that of a propertyless clergyman, officer, or civil servant. A landed proprietor may still drive men and women off his land, demolish their dwellings, and replace them with sheep or deer; and in the unregulated trades the private trader may still spunge on the regulated trades and sacrifice the life and health of the nation as lawlessly as the Manchester cotton manufacturers did at the beginning of last century. But though the Factory Code on the one hand, and Trade Union organization on the other, have, within the lifetime of men still living, converted the old unrestricted property of the cotton manufacturer in his mill and the cotton spinner in his labor into a mere permission to trade or work on stringent public or collective conditions, imposed in the interest of the general welfare without any regard for individual hard cases, people in Lancashire still speak of their "property" in the old terms, meaning nothing more by it than the things a thief can be punished for stealing. The total abolition of property, and the conversion of every citizen into a salaried functionary in the public service, would leave much more than 99 per cent of the nation quite unconscious of any greater change than now takes place when the son of a shipowner goes into the navy. They would still call their watches and umbrellas and back gardens their property. (RHPC-187-188)

Socialism's First & Last Commandment. The first and last commandment of Socialism is "Thou shalt not have a greater or less income than thy neighbor"; but before such a commandment can be even approximately obeyed we shall have not only to pass hundreds of new Acts of Parliament and repeal hundreds of old ones, but to invent and organize new Government departments; train and employ no end of women and men as public servants; educate children to look at their country's affairs in a new way; and struggle at every step with the opposition of ignorance, stupidity, custom, prejudice, and the vested interests of the rich. (IWGSC-97)

Modern Capitalist Communism. Modern Capitalism has made short work of the primitive pleas for inequality. The Pharisees themselves have organized communism in capital. Joint stock is the order of the day. An attempt to return to individual properties as the basis of our production would smash civilization more completely than ten revolutions. You cannot get the fields tilled today until the farmer becomes a co-operator. Take the shareholder to his railway, and ask him to point out to you the particular length of rail, the particular seat in the railway carriage, the particular lever in the engine that is his very own and nobody else's; and he will shun you as a madman, very wisely. And if, like Ananias and Sapphira, you try to hold back your little shop or whatnot from the common stock, represented by the Trust, or Combine, or Cartel, the Trust will presently freeze you out and rope you in and finally strike you dead industrially as thoroughly as St. Peter himself. There is no longer any practical question open as to Communism in production: the struggle today is over the distribution of the product: that is, over the daily dividing-up which is the first necessity of organized society. (P-AL-53-54)

Communism in Our Midst. All the time we are denouncing Communism as a crime, every street lamp and pavement and water tap and police constable is testifying that we could not exist for a week without it. Whilst we are shouting that Socialistic confiscation of the incomes of the rich is robbery and must end in red revolution, we are actually carrying it so much further than any other fully settled country that many of our capitalists have gone to live in the south of France for seven months in the year to avoid it, though they affirm their undying devotion to their native country by insisting that our national anthem shall be sung every Sunday on the Riviera as part of the English divine service, whilst the Chancellor of the Exchequer at home implores heaven to "frustrate their knavish tricks" until he can devise some legal means of defeating their evasions of his tax collectors. (IWGSC-287)

Communism through Taxes. By taxation rich people have a quarter or a third of their incomes, and very rich people more than half, taken from them by the Government, not for any specified public service, but as pure nationalization (communization) of their income to that extent without compensation, and by simple coercion. This is now taken so completely as a matter of course that the rich never dream of asking for compensation, or refusing to pay until their goods are forcibly seized, or even of calling it Bolshevik Confiscation; and so we are apt to talk as if such things never happened except in the imaginations of wicked Communists; but they happen in Great Britain regularly every January; and the Act authorizing them is brought in every April by the Chancellor of the Exchequer. Though reassuringly called the Appropriation Act it is really an Expropriation Act.

There is nothing in the law or the Constitution, or in any custom or tradition or parliamentary usage or any other part of our established morality, to prevent this confiscated third or half being raised to three-quarters, nine-tenths, or the whole. Besides this, when a very rich person dies, the Government confiscates the entire income of the property for the next eight years. The smallest taxable properties have to give up their incomes to the Government for ten months, and the rest for different periods between these extremes, in proportion to their amount.

In addition, there are certain taxes paid by rich and poor alike, called indirect taxes. Some of them are taxes on certain articles of food, and on tobacco and spirits, which you pay in the shop when you buy them, as part of the price. Others are stamp duties: twopence if you give a receipt for £2 or more, sixpence if you make a simple written agreement, hundreds of pounds on certain other documents which propertyless people never use. None of these taxes are levied for a named service like the police rate or the water rate: they are simple transfers of income from private pockets to the national pocket, and, as such, acts of pure Communism. It may surprise you to learn that even without counting the taxes on food, which fall on all classes, the private property thus communized already amounts to nearly a million a day.

The rich may well gasp at the figure, and ask what does the Government do with it all? What value do they get for this contribution which appears so prodigious to most of us who have to count our incomes in hundreds a year and not in millions a day? Well, the Government provides an army and a navy, a civil service, courts of law and so forth, and, as we have seen, it provides them either at cost price or more nearly at cost price than any commercial concern would. But over a hundred million solid pounds of it are handed over every year in hard cash in pensions and doles to the unfortunate people who have small incomes or none.

This is purely redistribution of income: that is, pure Socialism. (IWGSC-113-114)

The More Communism, the More Civilization. Would you ever have supposed from reading the newspapers that Communism, instead of being a wicked invention of Russian revolutionaries and British and American desperadoes, is a highly respectable way of sharing our wealth, sanctioned and practised by the apostles, and an indispensable part of our own daily life and civilization? We could not get on without it, and are continually extending it. We could give up some of it if we liked. We could put turnpike gates on the roads and make everybody pay for passing along them: indeed we may still see the little toll houses where the old turnpike gates used to be. We could abolish the street lamps, and hire men with torches to light us through the streets at night: are not the extinguishers formerly used by hired linkmen still to be seen on old-fashioned railings? We could even hire policemen and soldiers by the job to protect us, and then disband the police force and the army. But we take good care to do nothing of the sort. In spite of the way people grumble about their rates and taxes they get better value for them than for all the other money they spend. To find a bridge built for us to cross the river without having to think about it or pay anyone for it is such a matter of course to us that some of us come to think, like the children, that bridges are provided by nature, and cost nothing. But if the bridges were allowed to fall down, and we had to find out for ourselves how to cross the river by fording it or swimming it or hiring a boat, we should soon realize what a blessed thing Communism is, and not grudge the few shillings that each of us has to pay the rate collector for the upkeep of the bridge. In fact we might come to think Communism such a splendid thing that everything ought to be communized. (IWGSC-14)

Scientific & Unscientific Hoggishness. Even under the most perfect Social Democracy we should, without Communism, still be living like hogs, except that each hog would get his fair share of grub. High as that ideal must seem to anyone who complacently accepts the present social order, it is hardly high enough to satisfy a man in whom the social instinct is well developed. So long as vast quantities of labor have to be expended in weighing and measuring each man's earned share of this and that commodity—in watching, spying, policing, and punishing in order to prevent Tom getting a crumb of bread more or Dick a spoonful of milk less than he has a voucher for, so long will the difference between Unsocialism and Socialism be only the difference between unscientific and scientific hoggishness. I do not desire to underrate the vastness of that difference. Whilst we are hogs, let us at least be well-fed, healthy, reciprocally useful hogs, instead of—well, instead of the sort we are at present. But we shall not have any great reason to stand on the dignity of our humanity until a just distribution of the loaves and fishes becomes perfectly spontaneous, and the great effort and expense of a legal distribution, however just, is saved. For my part, I seek the establishment of a state of society in which I shall not be bothered with a ridiculous pocketful of coppers, nor have to waste my time in perplexing arithmetical exchanges of them with booking clerks, bus conductors, shopmen, and other superfluous persons before I can get what I need. I aspire to live in a community which shall be at least capable of averaging the transactions between us well enough to ascertain how much work I am to do for it in return for the right to take what I want of the commoner necessaries and conveniences of life. The saving of friction by such an arrangement may be guessed from the curious fact that only specialists in sociology are conscious of the numerous instances in which we are today forced to adopt it by the very absurdity of the alternative. Most people will tell you that Communism is known only in this country as a visionary project advocated by a handful of amiable cranks. Then they will stroll off across the common bridge, along the common embankment, by the light of the common gas lamp shining alike on the just and the unjust, up the common street, and into the common Trafalgar Square, where, on the smallest hint on their part that Communism is to be tolerated for an instant in a civilized country, they will be handily bludgeoned by the common policeman, and haled off to the common gaol.* When you suggest to these people that the application of Communism to the bread supply is only an extension, involving no new principle, of its application to street lighting, they are bewildered. Instead of picturing the Communist man going to the common store, and thence taking his bread home with him, they instinctively imagine him bursting obstreperously into his neighbor's house and snatching the bread off his table on the "as much mine as yours" principle—which, however, has an equally sharp edge for the thief's throat in the form "as much yours as mine." In fact, the average Englishman is only capable of understanding Communism when it is explained as a state of things under which everything is paid for out of the taxes, and taxes are paid in labor. And even then he will sometimes say, "How about the brainwork?" and begin the usual novice's criticism of Socialism in general. (IOA-78-79)

Weary Willie's Protest. Weary Willie may say that he hates work, and is quite willing to take less, and be poor and dirty and ragged or even naked for the sake of getting off with less work. But that, as we have seen, cannot be allowed: voluntary poverty is just as mischievous socially as involuntary poverty: decent nations must insist on their citizens leading decent lives, doing their full share of the nation's work, and taking their full share of its income. When Weary Willie has done his bit he can be as lazy as he likes. He will have plenty of leisure to lie on his back and listen to the birds, or watch his more impetuous neighbors working furiously at their hobbies, which may be sport, exploration, literature, the arts, the sciences, or any of the activities

* Written in the 1887-92 period, during which Trafalgar Square was forcibly closed against public meetings by the Salisbury administration.

we pursue for their own sakes when our material needs are satisfied. But poverty and social irresponsibility will be forbidden luxuries. Poor Willie will have to submit, not to compulsory poverty as at present, but to the compulsory well-being which he dreads still more. (IWGSC-72-73)

Unanswerable Rightness of Compulsory Social Service. If everybody refused to work, nine-tenths of the inhabitants of these islands would be dead within a month; and the rest would be too weak to bury them before sharing their fate. It is useless for a lady to plead that she has enough to live on without work: if she is not producing her own food and clothing and lodging other people must be producing them for her; and if she does not perform some equivalent service for them she is robbing them. It is absurd for her to pretend that she is living on the savings of her industrious grandmother; for not only is she alleging a natural impossibility, but there is no reason on earth why she should be allowed to undo by idleness the good that her grandmother did by industry. Compulsory social service is so unanswerably right that the very first duty of a government is to see that everybody works enough to pay her way and leave something over for the profit of the country and the improvement of the world. Yet it is the last duty that any government will face. What governments do at present is to reduce the mass of the people by armed force to a condition in which they must work for the capitalists or starve, leaving the capitalists free from any such obligation, so that capitalists can not only be idle but produce artificial overpopulation by withdrawing labor from productive industry and waste it in coddling their idleness or ministering to their vanity. This our Capitalist Governments call protecting property and maintaining personal liberty; but Socialists believe that property, in that sense, is theft, and that allowable personal liberty no more includes the right to idle than the right to murder. (IWGSC-357-358)

The Illusion about Dirty Work. . . . What about the dirty work? We are so accustomed to see dirty work done by dirty and poorly paid people that we have come to think that it is disgraceful to do it, and that unless a dirty and disgraced class existed it would not be done at all. This is nonsense. Some of the dirtiest work in the world is done by titled surgeons and physicians who are highly educated, highly paid, and move in the best society. The nurses who assist them are often their equals in general education, and sometimes their superiors in rank. Nobody dreams of paying nurses less or respecting them less than typists in city offices, whose work is much cleaner. Laboratory work and anatomical work, which involves dissecting dead bodies, and analysing the secretions and excretions of live ones, is sometimes revoltingly dirty from the point of view of a tidy housekeeper; yet it has to be done by gentlemen and ladies of the professional class. And every tidy housekeeper knows that houses cannot be kept clean without dirty work. The bearing and nursing of children are by no means elegant drawingroom amusements; but nobody dares suggest that they are not in the highest degree honorable, nor do the most fastidiously refined women shirk their turn when it comes. (IWGSC-74-75)

Dirty Work & Degradation.   It must be remembered too that a great deal of work which is now dirty because it is done in a crude way by dirty people can be done in a clean way by clean people. Ladies and gentlemen who attend to their own motor cars, as many of them do, manage to do it with less mess and personal soiling than a slovenly general servant will get herself into when laying a fire. On the whole, the necessary work of the world can be done with no more dirt than healthy people of all classes can stand. The truth of the matter is that it is not really the work that is objected to so much as its association with poverty and degradation. Thus a country gentleman does not object to drive his car; but he would object very strongly to wear the livery of his chauffeur; and a lady will tidy up a room without turning a hair, though she would die rather than be seen in a parlormaid's cap and apron, neat and becoming as they are. These are as honorable as any other uniform, and much more honorable than the finery of an idle woman: the parlormaids are beginning to object to them only because they have been associated in the past with a servile condition and a lack of respect to which parlormaids are no longer disposed to submit. But they have no objection to the work. Both the parlormaid and her employer (I dare not say her mistress), if they are fond of flowers and animals, will grub in a garden all day, or wash dogs or rid them of vermin with the greatest solicitude, without considering the dirt involved in these jobs in the least derogatory to their dignity. If all dustmen were dukes nobody would object to the dust: the dustmen would put little pictures on their notepaper of their hats with flaps down the backs just as now dukes put little pictures of their coronets; and everyone would be proud to have a dustman to dinner if he would condescend to come. We may take it that nobody objects to necessary work of any kind because of the work itself; what everybody objects to is being seen doing something that is usually done only by persons of lower rank or by colored slaves. (IWGSC-75-76)

MUNICIPAL TRADING OR PUBLIC VERSUS PRIVATE ENTERPRISE

Anarchic Licence of Private Enterprise. . . . Private enterprise enjoys a degree of licence which may be described as almost anarchic. It has for its area the heaven above, the earth beneath, and the minerals under the earth. National frontiers and local boundaries do not exist for it. In the matter of advertising it is exempt from all moral obligations: the most respectable newspapers give up the greater part of their space every day to statements which every well-instructed person knows to be false, and dangerously false, since they lead people to trust in imaginary cures in serious illness, and to ride bicycles through greasy mud in heavy traffic on tires advertised as "non-slipping": in short, to purchase all sorts of articles and invest in all sorts of enterprises on the strength of shameless lies, perfectly well known to be lies by the newspaper proprietor, who would at once dismiss the editor if a falsehood of the same character appeared in a leading article. Its operations are practically untrammelled by restrictive legislation; the accepted principle of the State towards it is *laisser-faire;* it has an overwhelming direct representation in Parliament; and in private life there are ten thousand people engaged in it for every one who knows anything of the municipality of which he is a constituent except that it periodically extorts money from him by the hands of the detested rate collector. Political ignorance, individual selfishness, the habit of regarding every piece of public work as a job for somebody, the narrowness that makes the Englishman's house a castle to be defended *contra mundum,* the poverty and long hours of work that leave the toiler no energy to spare for public work or public interest, the vague association of public aid with pauperism and of private enterprise with independence, the intense sense of caste which resents municipal activity as the meddling of pretentious tradesmen and seditious labor agitators: all these symptoms of the appalling poverty of public spirit, and the virulence and prevalence of private spirit in our commercial civilization, are on the side of private enterprise, and have hitherto secured for it a monopoly, as far as a monopoly was practicable, of the national industry: a monopoly that is only slowly giving way before the manifest private advantages of municipal employment to the employee class, and of municipal gas and water to the employer class. (CSMT-207-208)

Public Bankruptcy?—Private Prosperity? . . . Let us imagine a city in which the poor rates, police rates, and sanitary rates are very low, and the children in the schools flourishing and of full weight, whilst all the public services of the city are municipalized and conducted without a farthing of profit, or even with occasional deficits made up out of the rates. Suppose another city in which all the public services are in the hands of flourishing joint stock companies paying from 7 to 12 per cent, and in which the workhouses, the prisons, the hospitals, the sanitary inspectors, the disinfectors and strippers and cleansers, are all as busy as the joint stock companies, whilst the schools are full of rickety children. According to the commercial test, the second town would be a triumphant proof of the prosperity brought by private enterprise, and the first a dreadful example of the bankruptcy of municipal trade. But which town would a wise man rather pay rates in? The very shareholders of the companies in the second town would take care to live in the first. And what chance would a European State consisting of towns of the second type have in a struggle for survival with a State of the first? (CSMT-196)

Mythical Profit & Loss. Take the most popular branch of commercial enterprise: the drink traffic. It yields high profits. Take the most obvious and unchallenged branch of public enterprise: the making of roads. It is not commercially profitable at all. But suppose the drink trade were debited with what it costs in disablement, inefficiency, illness, and crime, with all their depressing effects on industrial productivity, and with their direct cost in doctors, policemen, prisons, &c. &c. &c.! Suppose at the same time the municipal highways and bridges account were credited with the value of the time and wear and tear saved by them! It would at once appear that the roads and bridges pay for themselves many times over, whilst the pleasures of drunkenness are costly beyond all reason. Consequently a municipalized drink traffic which should check drinking at the point of excess would be a much better bargain for the ratepayers than our present system, even if the profits made at present by brewers and publicans were changed to losses made up by subsidies from the rates. (CSMT-183-184)

The Main Factor. But the drink traffic is not the best illustration of the fallacy of the commercial test. The main factor to be taken into account in comparing private with public enterprise is neither the Drink Question nor any of the other Questions which occupy so many sectional bodies of reformers, but the Poverty Question, of which all the others are only facets. Give a man a comfortable income and you solve all the Questions for him, except perhaps the Servant Question. Now the all-important difference between the position of the commercial investor and the ratepayer is that whilst the commercial investor has no responsibility for the laborers whom he employs beyond paying them their wages whilst they are working for him, the ratepayer is responsible for their subsistence from the cradle to the grave. Consequently private companies can and do make large profits out of sweated and demoralized labor at the expense of the ratepayers; and these very profits are often cited as proofs of the superior efficiency of private enterprise, especially when they are set in sensational contrast to the inability of municipalities to make any commercial profits at all in the same business. (CSMT-184)

Advantage of Public Enterprise. Now it is the chief and overwhelming advantage of public enterprise that it can and does reap the total benefit of its operations when there is a benefit, just as it suffers and is warned by the total damage of them when there is damage. In the technical language of the political economists, public enterprise goes into business to gain the value in use or total utility of industrial activity, whilst commercial enterprise can count only the value in exchange or marginal utility. (CSMT-193-194)

Commercial Enterprise Limited. It is commonly enough understood that there are certain highly beneficial industrial operations which cannot be left to commercial enterprise, because their profits are necessarily communized from the beginning; so that a company undertaking the work could not get paid for it. The provision of thoroughfares in a city is a case in point. It has never been possible to put a toll-bar at the end of every city street and compel each passenger to pay for using it. Commercially, therefore, city street-making "does not pay"; so it is left to the municipality, with the result that the ratepayers gain enormously by their expenditure. What is not so generally recognized is that this power of the ratepayers to realize profits inaccessible to private speculators, applies to a greater or less extent over the whole field of public industry. (CSMT-194)

Municipal Loss: Public Profit. When a joint stock company spends more than it takes, it is carrying on business at a loss. When a public authority does so, it may be carrying on business at a huge profit. And there is no question here of the shopkeeper's trick of selling canary seed under cost price in order to induce bird fanciers to buy their flour and fodder from him. A municipality might trade in this manner too, if it saw fit: for instance, it might wire houses for electric light under cost price in order to stimulate a commercially profitable consumption of current. But it is quite possible that a municipality might engage in a hundred departments of trade; it might shew a commercial loss on every one of them at the end of every half year; and yet continue in that course with the full approval and congratulation of the ratepayers who would have to make up the loss. Its total gains are immeasurable; and its success can only be estimated by constant reference to the statistics of public welfare. For instance, if the statistics of health, and of crime, had been applied a century ago to test the alleged prosperity of Manchester under unrestricted private enterprise, nobody would have boasted of a factory system that "used up nine generations of men in one generation" as profitable because it produced a commercial peerage of cotton lords. (CSMT-195-196)

Commercial Auditing Absurd in Municipal Business. Experience soon reduces commercial auditing to absurdity when it is applied to municipal business, quite as much because it is too tolerant in some directions as because it is too exacting in others. Municipal auditing is technically a distinct branch not only of accountancy but of law; and it is no more the business of the ordinary accountant or barrister than pleading points of international law before the judicial committee of the Privy Council is the business of the Old Bailey practitioner. It will finally develop as a practically separate profession; and it is only in the meantime that we need be on our guard against the vulgar cry for treating a municipal enterprise like any other business, on sound business lines, etc., etc., etc. (CSMT-225)

Incentive: Commercial & Municipal. The commercial incentive stops where its profit stops. The municipal incentive extends to the total social utility, direct and indirect, of the enterprise. What is more, the incentive of commercial profit is often actually

stronger on the side of socially harmful enterprises than of beneficial ones. Vicious entertainments and exhibitions, unscrupulous
newspapers and books, liquor licences in neighborhoods already
overstocked with drink-shops, are only the obvious instances, just
as our commercially unprofitable cathedrals, national galleries,
and blue books* are conspicuous at the opposite extreme. (CSMT-
196-197)

Public Need & Purchasing Power. The public need is greatest where the purchasing power is least: the commercial incentive
is strongest where purchasing power is heaped up in ridiculous
superfluity. Private enterprise begins with 100 horsepower racing
automobiles, and reluctantly filters down to cheap and useful locomotion: public enterprise begins at the other end and helps those
who cannot individually help themselves. Thus, even if we grant
that the desire to make money is a stronger incentive than public
spirit and public need, we must admit that it is strongest at the
wrong end, and dwindles to nothing at the right end, whereas
public spirit and public need are strongest at the right end and are
not wanted at the other except for repressive purposes. It may be
said that the remedy is a redistribution of purchasing power and
not more municipal trading. This proposition is quite unquestion-
able from the extreme Socialist point of view; but as the present
opponents of municipal trading would certainly reject this remedy
as far more fatal to their hopes than the disease, it need not be
dealt with here further than by an emphatic reminder that poverty
is at the root of most of our social difficulties; that it is incompatible with liberty and variety; and that it has put the opponents
of municipal trading so far in a cleft stick that they cannot abolish
poverty except by public enterprise, and cannot escape public
enterprise except by the abolition of poverty. (CSMT-206)

Private Enterprise Not Enterprising Enough. The truth
about private enterprise is that it is not enterprising enough for
modern public needs. It will not start a new system until it is

* Municipal reports.

forced to scrap the old one. And the reason—one that no profusion of technical education will wholly remove—is that only a fraction of the public benefit of industrial enterprise is commercially appropriable by it. It will not risk colossal capitals with the certainty that it must do enormous service to the public, and create a prodigious unearned increment for the ground landlords, before it can touch a farthing of dividend; and therefore, however crying the public need may be, if the municipalities will not move in the matter nothing is done until millionaires begin to loathe their superfluity and become reckless as to its investment; until railways are promoted merely to buy tubes from Steel Trusts, and monster hotels floated, after the usual three liquidations, to buy tables and carpets from furniture companies. And even then what is done is only enough to shew that it should have been done fifty years sooner, and might even have been done commercially but for the fatal, though inevitable, commercial habit of mind which must consider only the dividend which it can grasp and not the social benefit that it must share with its neighbors. (CSMT-197-198)

Commercial Man's Grievance. One of the keenest grievances of the commercial man who sees profitable branches of his own trade undertaken by the municipality is that it is competing against him "with his own money," meaning that it forces him to pay rates, and then uses the rates to ruin him in his business. The effective platform reply to this is that the profitable municipal trades, far from costing the ratepayers anything, actually lighten their burden. The commercially unprofitable trades are left to the municipality without demur. The trades by which private contractors make profit and the municipality none are, as we have seen, mostly sweated or parasitic trades which in the long run add heavily to the ratepayer's public and private burdens. (CSMT-228)

The Ordinary Citizen: His Sense of Property. Nothing shews the economic superficiality and political ignorance of the ordinary citizen more than the fact that he submits without a word to the private appropriation of large portions of the proceeds of his business as rent by private landlords, whilst he protests furiously against every penny in the pound collected from him by the municipality for his own benefit. The explanation probably is that in signing his lease he has explicitly accepted the rent as inevitable, and at least has his house or shop to shew for it; whereas the rate collector strikes him as a predatory person who makes him pay for streets and lamps, schools and police stations, in which he has no sense of property. (CSMT-228-229)

Unfair Competition? In comparing municipal with commercial enterprise, the power of the munipicality to make apparently unlimited calls on the ratepayers' pockets is generally classed with those advantages on the municipal side which are so overwhelming as to be called unfair, meaning only that they are advantages beyond the reach of commerce. In the same sense the competition of the mammoth universal provider with the petty shopkeeper is unfair; the competition of the electric light with gas or of the railway with the stage coach was unfair; and the use of rifles by civilized armies against Zulus armed with assegais is unfair. But it is easy to exaggerate the advantage of the municipality in this respect. Every additional penny in the pound is so fiercely contested by the ratepayer, who is also an elector, that far more mischief is done and money wasted by municipal impecuniosity than by municipal extravagance. In spite of the fact that our citizens get better value for their rates than for any other portion of their expenditure, they voluntarily give thousands to company promoters to make ducks and drakes of with a better grace than they give shillings to the rate collector for the most indispensable requirements of civilization. (CSMT-236)

Municipal Enterprise Struggles. Municipal enterprise . . . is handicapped . . . by the national presumption against State action of all kinds inherited from the long struggle for individual liberty which followed the break-up of the medieval system. That struggle led men to assume that corruption is inherent in public offices; that a trading municipality is the same thing as a seventeenth century monopoly; and that the remedy for all such evils is free competition between private enterprisers rigidly protected from public competition. Nominally this view is obsolete; but in practice it is still assumed that whereas private men and private companies may do anything they are not expressly forbidden to do, a municipality may do nothing that it is not expressly authorized to do; and as every authorization has to come from a parliament in which private enterprise is powerfully represented, the municipalities so far can get little more than the refuse of private enterprise. The municipality, in fact, does not enjoy freedom of trade, and the private capitalist does, the natural result being that whilst municipal trade is struggling to get trading Bills through hostile parliaments, and agitating for larger powers, private enterprise is forming gigantic industrial conspiracies which ruthlessly stamp out the old-fashioned huckstering competition on which the nation foolishly relied for protection against monopoly, and establishing a predatory capitalistic collectivism which has knocked more anti-Socialist nonsense out of the English people in the last five years than the arguments and pamphlets of the Socialists have done in the last fifty. Nevertheless the race between municipal and national Collectivism, and the frankly plutocratic Collectivism of the Trusts, is one in which, under existing circumstances, the municipalities have no chance except in the industries which the Trusts will not touch because they do not pay in the commercial sense. (CSMT-208-209)

Human Relations

"When two people live together—it don't matter whether they're father and son, husband and wife, brother and sister— they can't keep up the polite humbug which comes so easy for ten minutes on an afternoon call." (Frank Gardner, MWP-211)

SEX

A Special Occasion Difference. "I am a woman; and you are a man, with a slight difference that doesnt matter except on special occasions." (A, VW-222)

The Question We Never Tire of. "The great question. The question that men and women will spend hours over without complaining. The question that occupies all the novel readers and all the playgoers. The question they never get tired of. . . .
The question which particular young man some young woman will mate with." (*Lord Summerhays,* M-187)

Sex Relation Impersonal. "In the sex relation the universal creative energy, of which the parties are both the helpless agents, over-rides and sweeps away all personal considerations and dispenses with all personal relations. The pair may be utter strangers to one another, speaking different languages, differing in race and color, in age and disposition, with no bond between them but a possibility of that fecundity for the sake of which the Life Force

throws them into one another's arms at the exchange of a glance."
(*Don Juan*, MS-125)

Two Storeys to Men & Women. "But when men and women
pick one another up just for a bit of fun, they find theyve picked
up more than they bargained for, because men and women have a
top storey as well as a ground floor; and you cant have the one without the other. Theyre always trying to; but it doesnt work. Youve
picked up my mind as well as my body; and youve got to explore
it. You thought you could have a face and a figure like mine with
the limitations of a gorilla. Youre finding out your mistake: thats
all." (*The Sergeant*, TTTBG-100)

Majority Ignorance. The modern notion that democracy
means governing a country according to the ignorance of its
majorities is never more disastrous than when there is some question of sexual morals to be dealt with. (P-GM-143)

Secrecy No Solution. When people were ashamed of sanitary problems, and refused to face them, leaving them to solve
themselves clandestinely in dirt and secrecy, the solution arrived
at was the Black Death; and the remedy for that is not salvarsan,
but sound moral hygiene, the first foundation of which is the dis-
continuance of our habit of telling not only the comparatively
harmless lies that we know we ought not to tell, but the ruinous
lies that we foolishly think we ought to tell. (P-O-149)

Sexual Instruction: Nasty Stories & Whispered Traditions.
Whilst the subject is considered shameful and sinful we shall
have no systematic instruction in sexual hygiene, because such
lectures as are given in Germany, France, and even prudish
America (where the great Miltonic tradition in this matter still
lives) will be considered a corruption of that youthful innocence
which now subsists on nasty stories and whispered traditions
handed down from generation to generation of school-children:
stories and traditions which conceal nothing of sex but its dignity,

its honor, its sacredness, its rank as the first necessity of society and the deepest concern of the nation. (P-GM-197-198)

Sex Candor Curiously Disconcerting. Writers of belles lettres who are rash enough to admit that their whole life is not one constant preoccupation with adored members of the opposite sex, and who even countenance La Rochefoucauld's remark that very few people would ever imagine themselves in love if they had never read anything about it, are gravely declared to be abnormal or physically defective by critics of crushing unadventurousness and domestication. French authors of saintly temperament are forced to include in their retinue countesses of ardent complexion with whom they are supposed to live in sin. Sentimental controversies on the subject are endless; but they are useless, because nobody tells the truth. Rousseau did it by an extraordinary effort, aided by a superhuman faculty for human natural history; but the result was curiously disconcerting because, though the facts were so conventionally shocking that people felt that they ought to matter a great deal, they actually mattered very little. And even at that everybody pretends not to believe him. (P-O-139)

The Duel of Sex. "During this whole century, my dear Mrs. Clandon, the progress of artillery has been a duel between the maker of cannons and the maker of armor plates to keep the cannon balls out. You build a ship proof against the best gun known: somebody makes a better gun and sinks your ship. You build a heavier ship, proof against that gun: somebody makes a heavier gun and sinks you again. And so on. Well, the duel of sex is just like that." (*Valentine,* YNCT-83)

Jealousy Independent of Sex. That jealousy is independent of sex is shewn by its intensity in children, and by the fact that very jealous people are jealous of everybody without regard to relationship or sex, and cannot bear to hear the person they "love" speak favorably of anyone under any circumstances (many women, for instance, are much more jealous of their husbands' mothers and sisters than of unrelated women whom they suspect him of fancying); but it is seldom possible to disentangle the two passions in practice. (P-O-137)

Honorable Advances: An Extraordinary Irrelevance. "When I was on earth, and made those proposals to ladies which, though universally condemned, have made me so interesting a hero of legend, I was not infrequently met in some such way as this. The lady would say that she would countenance my advances, provided they were honorable. On inquiring what that proviso meant, I found that it meant that I proposed to get possession of her property if she had any, or to undertake her support for life if she had not; that I desired her continual companionship, counsel and conversation to the end of my days, and would bind myself under penalties to be always enraptured by them; and, above all, that I would turn my back on all other women for ever for her sake. I did not object to these conditions because they were exorbitant and inhuman: it was their extraordinary irrelevance that prostrated me. I invariably replied with perfect frankness that I had never dreamt of any of these things; that unless the lady's character and intellect were equal or superior to my own, her conversation must degrade and her counsel mislead me; that her constant companionship might, for all I knew, become intolerably tedious to me; that I could not answer for my feelings for a week in advance, much less to the end of my life; that to cut me off from all natural and unconstrained relations with the rest of my fellow creatures would narrow and warp me if I submitted to it, and, if not, would bring me under the curse of clandestinity; that, finally, my proposals to her were wholly unconnected with any of these matters, and were the outcome of a perfectly simple impulse of my manhood towards her womanhood." (*Don Juan*, MS-126)

Scientific Natural History Needed. Of one thing I am persuaded: we shall never attain to a reasonably healthy public opinion on sex questions until we offer, as the data for that opinion, our actual conduct and our real thoughts instead of a moral fiction which we agree to call virtuous conduct, and which we then—and here comes in the mischief—pretend is our conduct and our thoughts. (P-O-138)

Sexual Attraction Misused. It is no doubt necessary under existing circumstances for a woman without property to be sexually attractive, because she must get married to secure a livelihood; and the illusions of sexual attraction will cause the imagination of young men to endow her with every accomplishment and virtue that can make a wife a treasure. The attraction being thus constantly and ruthlessly used as a bait, both by individuals and by society, any discussion tending to strip it of its illusions and get at its real natural history is nervously discouraged. But nothing can well be more unwholesome for everybody than the exaggeration and glorification of an instinctive function which clouds the reason and upsets the judgment more than all the other instincts put together. The process may be pleasant and romantic; but the consequences are not. It would be far better for everyone, as well as far honester, if young people were taught that what they call love is an appetite which, like all other appetites, is destroyed for the moment by its gratification; that no profession, promise, or proposal made under its great natural purpose so completely transcends the personal interests of any individual or even of any ten generations of individuals that it should be held to be an act of prostitution, whether by process of law or not. By all means let it be the subject of contracts with society as to its consequences; but to make marriage an open trade in it as at present, with money, board and lodging, personal slavery, vows of eternal exclusive personal sentimentalities and the rest of it as the price, is neither virtuous, dignified, nor decent. (P-GM-161)

Absolute Right to Sexual Experience. No political constitution will ever succeed or deserve to succeed unless it includes the recognition of an absolute right to sexual experience, and is untainted by the Pauline or romantic view of such experience as sinful in itself. (P-GM-148)

The Woman of Fifty. "They talk of the wickedness and vanity of women painting their faces and wearing auburn wigs at fifty. But why shouldnt they? Why should a woman allow Nature to put a false mask of age on her when she knows that she's as young as ever? Why should she look in the glass and see a wrinkled lie when a touch of fine art will shew her a glorious truth? The wrinkles are a dodge to repel young men. Suppose she doesnt want to repel young men! Suppose she likes them!" (*John Tarleton*, M-125)

"Oh, these sex episodes! Why can I not resist them? Disgraceful!" (*Burge-Lubin*, BM-114)

Daydreams about Women. Just as I cannot remember any time when I could not read and write, I cannot remember any time when I did not exercise my imagination in daydreams about women. (SSS-176)

Sexual Intercourse Not Delinquency. I never associated sexual intercourse with delinquency, nor had any scruples or remorses or misgivings of conscience about it. Of course I had scruples, and effectively inhibitive ones too, about getting women "into trouble" or cuckolding my friends; and I held chastity to be a passion just as I hold intellect to be a passion; but St Paul's case was to me always pathological. Sexual experience seemed a natural appetite, and its satisfaction a completion of human experience necessary for fully qualified authorship. I was not attracted by virgins as such. I preferred fully matured women who knew what they were doing. (SSS-175-176)

Sex: A Prelude to Intellectual Ecstasy. I was never duped by sex as a basis for permanent relations, nor dreamt of marriage in connection with it. I put everything else before it, and never refused or broke an engagement to speak on Socialism to pass a gallant evening. I valued sexual experience because of its power of producing a celestial flood of emotion and exaltation which, however momentary, gave me a sample of the ecstasy that may one day be the normal condition of conscious intellectual activity. (SSS-178)

The Promiscuity Legend. There is, too, a really appalling prevalence of the superstition that the sexual instinct in men is utterly promiscuous, and that the least relaxation of law and custom must produce a wild outbreak of licentiousness. As far as our moralists can grasp the proposition that we should deal with the sexual relation as impersonal, it seems to them to mean that we should encourage it to be promiscuous: hence their recoil from it. But promiscuity and impersonality are not the same thing. No man ever fell in love with the entire female sex. We often do not fall in love at all; and when we do we fall in love with one person and remain indifferent to thousands of others who pass before our eyes every day. Selection, carried even to such fastidiousness as to induce people to say quite commonly that there is only one man or woman in the world for them, is the rule in nature. If anyone doubts this, let him open a shop for the sale of picture postcards, and, when an enamoured lady customer demands a portrait of her favorite actor or a gentleman of his favorite actress, try to substitute some other portrait on the ground that since the sexual instinct is promiscuous, onc portrait is as pleasing as another. I suppose no shopkeeper has ever been foolish enough to do such a thing; and yet all our shopkeepers, the moment a discussion arises on marriage, will passionately argue against all reform on the ground that nothing but the most severe coercion can save their wives and daughters from quite indiscriminate rapine. (P-GM-165-166)

Disproportionately Savage Punishments. Few people have any knowledge of the savage punishments that are legally inflicted for aberrations and absurdities to which no sanely instructed community would call any attention. We create an artificial morality, and consequently an artificial conscience, by manufacturing disastrous consequences for events which, left to themselves, would do very little harm (sometimes not any) and be forgotten in a few days. (P-O-139)

Lopsided Sex Laws. At present a ridiculous distinction is made between vice and crime, in order that men may be vicious with impunity. Adultery, for instance, though it is sometimes fiercely punished by giving an injured husband crushing damages in a divorce suit (injured wives are not considered in this way), is not now directly prosecuted; and this impunity extends to illicit relations between unmarried persons who have reached what is called the age of consent. There are other matters, such as notification of contagious disease and solicitation, in which the hand of the law has been brought down on one sex only. Outrages which were capital offences within the memory of persons still living when committed on women outside marriage, can still be inflicted by men on their wives without legal remedy. (P-GM-172)

Monogamy Will Take Care of Itself. Monogamy has a sentimental basis which is quite distinct from the political one of equal numbers of the sexes. Equal numbers in the sexes are quite compatible with a change of partners every day or every hour. Physically there is nothing to distinguish human society from the farm-yard except that children are more troublesome and costly than chickens and calves, and that men and women are not so completely enslaved as farm stock. Accordingly, the people whose conception of marriage is a farm-yard or slave-quarter conception are always more or less in a panic lest the slightest relaxation of the marriage laws should utterly demoralize society; whilst those to whom marriage is a matter of more highly evolved sentiments and needs (sometimes said to be distinctively human, though birds and animals in a state of freedom evince them quite as touchingly as we) are much more liberal, knowing as they do that monogamy will take care of itself provided the parties are free enough, and that promiscuity is a product of slavery and not of liberty. (P-GM-173-174)

Sedulously Inculcated False Notion. When we hear of young women being led astray and the like, we find that what has led them astray is a sedulously inculcated false notion that the relation they are tempted to contract is so intensely personal, and the vows made under the influence of its transient infatuation so sacred and enduring, that only an atrociously wicked man could make light of or forget them. What is more, as the same fantastic errors are inculcated in men, and the conscientious ones therefore feel bound in honor to stand by what they have promised, one of the surest methods to obtain a husband is to practise on his susceptibilities until he is either carried away into a promise of marriage to which he can be legally held, or else into an indiscretion which he must repair by marriage on pain of having to regard himself as a scoundrel and a seducer, besides facing the utmost damage the lady's relatives can do him. (P-GM-162)

"Dont Tell Me: I Dont Want To Know." As to the evils of disease and contagion, our consciences are sound enough: what is wrong with us is ignorance of the facts. No doubt this is a very formidable ignorance in a country where the first cry of the soul is "Dont tell me: I dont want to know," and where frantic denials and furious suppressions indicate everywhere the cowardice and want of faith which conceives life as something too terrible to be faced. In this particular case "I dont want to know" takes a righteous air, and becomes "I dont want to know anything about the diseases which are the just punishment of wretches who should not be mentioned in my presence or in any book that is intended for family reading." Wicked and foolish as the spirit of this attitude is, the practice of it is so easy and lazy and uppish that it is very common. But its cry is drowned by a louder and more sincere one. We who do not want to know also do not want to go blind, to go mad, to be disfigured, to be barren, to become pestiferous, or to see such things happen to our children. We learn, at last, that the majority of the victims are not the people of whom we so glibly say "Serve them right," but quite innocent children and innocent parents, smitten by a contagion which, no matter in what vice it

may or may not have originated, contaminates the innocent and
the guilty alike once it is launched exactly as any other contagious disease does; that indeed it often hits the innocent and
misses the guilty because the guilty know the danger and take
elaborate precautions against it, whilst the innocent, who have
been either carefully kept from any knowledge of their danger,
or erroneously led to believe that contagion is possible through mis-
conduct only, run into danger blindfold. Once knock this fact into
people's minds, and their self-righteous indifference and intolerance soon change into lively concern for themselves and their
families. (P-GM-189-190)

LOVE

Love the First Need. "We all go about longing for love: it is the first need of our natures, the first prayer of our hearts; but we dare not utter our longing: we are too shy." (*Marchbanks*, C-35)

"Ah, if we were only good enough for Love! There is nothing like Love: there is nothing else but Love: without it the world would be a dream of sordid horror." (*Octavius*, MS-54)

"Love gets people into difficulties, not out of them." (*The Patient*, TTTBG-117)

"How is a man to look dignified when he's infatuated?" (*Valentine*, YNCT-98)

A Queer Thing. "It's a queer thing, isnt it, that though there is a point at which I'd rather kiss a woman than do anything else in the world, yet I'd rather be shot than let anyone see me doing it?" (*The Sergeant*, TTTBG-104)

Love: Three Quarters Curiosity. "Take this tip from me: one man at a time. I am advising you for your good, because youre only a beginner; and what you think is love, and interest, and all that, is not real love at all: three quarters of it is only unsatisfied curiosity. Ive lived at that address myself; and I know." (*The Countess,* TTTBG-81)

A Man Cant Keep It Up. "The real secret of it is that though men are awfully nice for the first few days, it doesnt last. You get the best out of men by having them always new. What I say is that a love affair should always be a honeymoon. And the only way to make sure of that is to keep changing the man; for the same man can never keep it up." (*The Countess,* TTTBG-78)

Love: Slavery. "What complicates the affair is that I am in love with this man. And I dare not marry a man I love. I should be his slave." (*She,* BB-41)

Love the Inexplicable. "Love means many different things: love of parents and children, love of pet animals, love of whisky or strawberry ices, love of cricket or lawn tennis, also love of money. My case is a specific one of animal magnetism, as inexplicable as the terrestrial magnetism that drags a steel ship to a north or south pole that is not the astronomical pole. The ship can be demagnetized: who can demagnetize me?" (*He,* BB-41)

Love in Imagination. "Oh, love! Have you no imagination? Do you think I have never been in love with wonderful men? heroes! archangels! princes! sages! even fascinating rascals! and had the strangest adventures with them? Do you know what it is to look at a mere real man after that? a man with his boots in every corner, and the smell of his tobacco in every curtain? (*Lesbia,* GM-219)

Love: A Tiresome Subject. "Men do fall in love with me. They all seem to think me a creature with volcanic passions: I'm sure I dont know why; for all the volcanic women I know are plain little creatures with sandy hair. I don't consider human volcanoes respectable. And I'm so tired of the subject. Our house is always full of women who are in love with my husband and men who are in love with me. We encourage it because it's pleasant to have company." (*Mrs Lunn*, O-162)

Love: Illusions, Infatuations, Impulses. "I had illusions, infatuations, impulses that were utterly unreasonable and irresistible. Desires in which my body was taking command of my soul. And all for a man of whom I knew nothing: a passing vagabond who had begged a meal from me. He came to me next day and said he had fallen in love with me at first sight, and that he was going quite mad about me. He warned me to run away and leave no address, as he would follow me to the ends of the earth if he knew where I was; and we should both make fools of ourselves by getting married. So I fled; and here I am. He does not know my name, nor I his. But when I think of him everything is transfigured and I am magically happy. Unreadable poems like the Song of Solomon delight me: bagatelles by Beethoven deepen into great sonatas: every walk through the country is an exploration of the plains of heaven. My reason tells me that this cannot possibly be real; that the day will come when it will vanish and leave me face to face with reality; perhaps tied to a husband who may be anything from a criminal to an intolerable bore. So I have run away and put the seas between me and this figure that looks like a beautiful and wonderful celestial messenger—a Lohengrin—but really does not exist at all except in my imagination." (*She*, BB-34-35)

The Brain Says No, Life Says Yes. "Do you not understand that when I stood face to face with Woman, every fibre in my clear critical brain warned me to spare her and save myself? My morals said No. My conscience said No. My chivalry and pity for her said No. My prudent regard for myself said No. My ear, practised on a thousand songs and symphonies; my eye, exercised on a thousand paintings, tore her voice, her features, her color to shreds. I caught all those tell-tale resemblances to her father and mother by which I knew what she would be like in thirty years time. I noted the gleam of gold from a dead tooth in the laughing mouth: I made curious observations of the strange odors of the chemistry of the nerves. The visions of my romantic reveries, in which I had trod the plains of heaven with a deathless, ageless creature of coral and ivory, deserted me in that supreme hour. I remembered them and desperately strove to recover their illusion; but they now seemed the emptiest of inventions: my judgment was not to be corrupted: my brain still said no on every issue. And whilst I was in the act of framing my excuse to the lady, Life seized me and threw me into her arms as a sailor throws a scrap of fish into the mouth of a sea-bird." (*Don Juan*, MS-119)

The Test of Domestic Familiarity. "Petrarch didn't see half as much of Laura, nor Dante of Beatrice, as you see of Ann now; and yet they wrote first-rate poetry—at least so I'm told. They never exposed their idolatry to the test of domestic familiarity; and it lasted them to their graves." (*Tanner*, MS-53-54)

A Man's Heart. "Look here, Mrs Lunn: do you think a man's heart is a potato? or a turnip? or a ball of knitting wool? that you can throw it away like this?" (*Juno*, O-163)

"Remember: a man's power of love and admiration is like any other of his powers: he has to throw it away many times before he learns what is really worthy of it." (*Valentine*, YNCT-88)

An Unregretted Deficiency. "My case is a very common one, Mr. Valentine. I married before I was old enough to know what I was doing. As you have seen for yourself, the result was a bitter disappointment for both my husband and myself. So you see, though I am a married woman, I have never been in love; I have never had a love affair; and to be quite frank with you, Mr. Valentine, what I have seen of the love affairs of other people has not led me to regret that deficiency in my experience. (*Mrs. Clandon,* YNCT-81)

Love's Growing Pains. "The process of growing from romantic boyhood into cynical maturity usually takes fifteen years. When it is compressed into fifteen minutes, the pace is too fast; and growing pains are the result." (*He,* HHLHH-192)

Love: Tedious & Terrifying. "What am I to do? I can't fall in love; and I can't hurt a woman's feelings by telling her so when she falls in love with me. And as women are always falling in love with my moustache I get landed in all sorts of tedious and terrifying flirtations in which I'm not a bit in earnest." (*Hector,* HH-40)

"Yes, my dear, it's very wearing to be in love with you. If it lasts, I think I shall die young." (*Cusins,* MB-282)

A Common Mistake. "I made a very common mistake. I thought that this irresistible athlete would be an ardent lover. He was nothing of the kind. All his ardor was in his fists." (*Epifania,* TM-139)

"The fickleness of women I love is only equaled by the infernal constancy of the women who love me." (*Charteris,* TP-121)

Passion: Mathematics or Concupiscence? "And who dares say that mathematics and reasoning are not passions? Mathematic perception is the noblest of all the faculties! This cant about their being soulless, dead, inhuman mechanisms is contrary to the plainest facts of life and history. What has carried our minds farther than mathematical foresight? Who has done more for enlightenment and civilization than Giordano Bruno, Copernicus, Galileo, Newton, Descartes, Rutherford, Einstein, all of them far seeing guessers carried away by the passion for measuring truth and knowledge that possessed and drove them? Will you set above this great passion the vulgar concupiscences of Don Juan and Casanova, and the romance of Beatrice and Francesca, of Irish Deirdre, the greatest bores in literature, mere names and incidentally immortalized by a few lines in a great poem?" (*Secondborn*, BB-57)

Love Guarantees Nothing. "Come, come, Flopper! You know as well as I do that people who marry for money are happy together as often as other people. It is the love matches that break down because Providence wants sound children and does not care a snap of its fingers whether the parents are happy or not. It makes them mad about one another until the children are born, and then drops them like hot potatoes. Money guarantees comfort and what you call culture. Love guarantees nothing. I know this. You know it. My daughter knows it. The young man knows it. Are we mad because we act and speak accordingly? Are you sane because you pretend to be shocked by it? It is you who should go to the mental hospital." (*Old Bill*, BB-53)

Our Private Alsatia: Chronic Life-long Love. In our anxiety to provide for ourselves a little private Alsatia in which we can indulge ourselves as we please without reproach or interference from law, religion, or even conscience (and this is what marriage has come to mean to many of us), we have forgotten that we cannot escape restraints without foregoing rights; that all the laws that are needed to compel strangers to respect us are equally if not more necessary to compel our husbands and wives to respect us; and that society without law, whether between two or two million persons, means tyranny and slavery.

If the incorrigible sentimentalists here raise their little pipe of "Not if they love one another," I tell them, with such patience as is possible, that if they had ever had five minutes experience of love they would know that love is itself a tyranny requiring special safeguards; that people will perpetrate "for the sake of" those they love, exactions and submissions that they would never dream of proposing to or suffering from those they dislike or regard with indifference; that healthy marriages are partnerships of companionable and affectionate friendship; that cases of chronic life-long love, whether sentimental or sensual, ought to be sent to the doctor if not to the executioner; and that honorable men and women, when their circumstances permit it, are so far from desiring to be placed helplessly at one another's mercy that they employ every device the law now admits of, from the most stringent marriage settlements to the employment of separate legal advisers, to neutralize the Alsatian evils of the marriage law. (P-GM-191)

MARRIAGE

There is no subject on which more dangerous nonsense is talked and thought than marriage. (P-GM-119)

Marriage as a fact is not in the least like marriage as an ideal. (P-GM-157)

Selecting a Wife. "If you can tell me of any trustworthy method of selecting a wife, I shall be happy to make use of it. I await your suggestions." (*Percival*, M-190)

Considering Does Not Prevent Marriage. "All marriages are very anxiously considered; but considering has never yet prevented a marriage. If you are her man she will have you, consideration or no consideration." (*Old Bill*, BB-49)

Marriage: Heart Tearing Adventure. "You must learn to take chances in this world. This disappointed philanderer tries to frighten you with my unfaithfulness. He has never been married: I have. And I tell you that in the very happiest marriages not a day passes without a thousand moments of unfaithfulness. You begin by thinking you have only one husband: you find you have a dozen. There is a creature you hate and despise and are tied to for life; and before breakfast is over the fool says something nice and becomes a man whom you admire and love; and between these extremes there are a thousand degrees with a different man and woman at each of them. A wife is all women to one man: she is everything that is devilish: the thorn in his flesh, the jealous termagant, the detective dogging all his movements, the nagger, the scolder, the worrier. He has only to tell her an affectionate lie and she is his comfort, his helper, at best his greatest treasure, at worst his troublesome but beloved child. All wives are all these women in one, all husbands all these men in one. What do the unmarried know of this infinitely dangerous heart tearing everchanging life of adventure that we call marriage?" (*Epifania*, TM-198-199)

Impossible Partners. "There are two sorts of people in the world: the people anyone can live with and the people that no one can live with. The people that no one can live with may be very goodlooking and vital and splendid and temperamental and romantic and all that; and they can make a man or woman happy for half an hour when they are pleased with themselves and disposed to be agreeable; but if you try to live with them they just eat up your whole life running after them or quarreling or attending to them one way or another: you cant call your soul your own. As Sunday husbands or wives, just to have a good tearing bit of lovemaking with, or a blazing row, or mostly one on top of the other, once a month or so, theyre all right. But as everyday partners theyre just impossible." (*Patricia*, TM-144-145)

The Comfortable Despot. "I heartily despise a woman who marries a fool in order that she may be comfortably despotic in her own house." (*Mary Sutherland*, LAA-236)

Childish Temper Makes a Terrible Husband. "It must be terrible to live in constant dread of childish explosions of temper from one's husband, or to fear, at every crisis, that he will not act like a man of sense and honor." (*Mary Sutherland*, LAA-236)

You Never Can Tell. "Cheer up, sir, cheer up: every man is frightened of marriage when it comes to the point; but it often turns out very comfortable, very enjoyable and happy indeed, sir —from time to time. *I* never was master in my own house, sir: my wife was like your young lady: she was of a commanding and masterful disposition, which my son has inherited. But if I had my life to live twice over, I'd do it again, I'd do it again, I assure you. You never can tell, sir: you never can tell." (*Waiter*, YNCT-124)

Marriage Totalizator Needed. "Regret is essentially mathematical. What are the mathematical probabilities? How many marriages are regretted? How much are they regretted? How long are they regretted? What is the proportion of divorces? The registrar of marriages should have a totalizator balancing these quantities. There should be one in every church. People would then know what chances they are taking. Should first cousins marry? Should Catholics and Protestants marry? Should lepers marry? At what ages should they marry? Without these statistics you cannot give scientific answers to these questions: you have only notions and guesswork to go on." (*Secondborn*, BB-42)

The Bachelor Class. It must not be forgotten that the refusal to accept the indignities, risks, hardships, softships, and divided duties of marriage is not confined to our voluntary old maids. There are men of the mould of Beethoven and Samuel Butler, whom one can hardly conceive as married men. There are the great ecclesiastics, who will not own two loyalties: one to the Church and one to the hearth. There are men like Goethe, who marry late and reluctantly solely because they feel that they cannot in honest friendship refuse the status of marriage to any woman of whose attachment to them they have taken any compromising advantage, either in fact or in appearance. No sensible man can, under existing circumstances, advise a woman to keep house with a man without insisting on his marrying her, unless she is independent of conventional society (a state of things which can occur only very exceptionally); and a man of honor cannot advise a woman to do for his sake what he would not advise her to do for anyone else's. The result is that our Beethovens and Butlers—of whom, in their ordinary human aspect, there are a good many—become barren old bachelors, and rather savage ones at that. (P-GM-186)

The Respectable Voluptuary. As to the respectable voluptuary, who joins Omar Khayyam clubs and vibrates to Swinburne's invocation of Dolores to "come down and redeem us from virtue," he is to be found in every suburb. (P-GM-133-134)

Marriage: Ignominious Capitulation. "Marriage is to me apostasy, profanation of the sanctuary of my soul, violation of my manhood, sale of my birthright, shameful surrender, ignominious capitulation, acceptance of defeat. I shall decay like a thing that has served its purpose and is done with; I shall change from a man with a future to a man with a past; I shall see in the greasy eyes of all the other husbands their relief at the arrival of a new prisoner to share their ignominy. The young men will scorn me as one who has sold out: to the young women I, who have always been an enigma and a possibility, shall be merely somebody else's property —and damaged goods at that: a secondhand man at best." (*Tanner*, MS-169)

"A man who is complete in himself needs no wife." (*Conolly*, LAA-237)

Love Extinguished by Marriage? "Of all the lies invented by people who never felt love, the lie of marriage extinguishing love is the falsest, as it is the most worldly and cynical." (*Adrian Herbert*, LAA-261)

The Heavier Burden. "At present I have exchanged the burden of disliking my mother for the heavier one of loving my wife." (*Adrian Herbert,* LAA-262)

Who'll Marry the Plain Fellows? "Ha! The old complaint. You all want geniuses to marry. This demand for clever men is ridiculous. Somebody must marry the plain, honest, stupid fellows. Have you thought of that?" (*The General,* GM-231)

The Weak Have No Trouble Marrying. No doubt there are slavish women as well as slavish men; and women, like men, admire those that are stronger than themselves. But to admire a strong person and to live under that strong person's thumb are two different things. The weak may not be admired and hero-worshipped; but they are by no means disliked or shunned; and they never seem to have the least difficulty in marrying people who are too good for them. They may fail in emergencies; but life is not one long emergency: it is mostly a string of situations for which no exceptional strength is needed, and with which even rather weak people can cope if they have a stronger partner to help them out. Accordingly, it is a truth everywhere in evidence that strong people, masculine or feminine, not only do not marry stronger people, but do not shew any preference for them in selecting their friends. When a lion meets another with a louder roar "the first lion thinks the last a bore." The man or woman who feels strong enough for two, seeks for every other quality in a partner than strength. (P-P-115)

Man or Woman: They All Taste Alike. "A man is like a phonograph with half-a-dozen records. You soon get tired of them all; and yet you have to sit at table whilst he reels them off to every new visitor. In the end you have to be content with his common humanity; and when you come down to that, you find out about men what a great English poet of my acquaintance used to say about women: that they all taste alike." (*The Bishop,* GM-236)

Marriage Tolerable Enough. "Marriage is tolerable enough in its way if youre easygoing and dont expect too much from it. But it doesnt bear thinking about. The great thing is to get the young people tied up before they know what theyre letting themselves in for." (*Collins*, GM-262)

If the Prisoner Is Happy, Why Lock Him In? "Send me to the galleys and chain me to the felon whose number happens to be next before mine; and I must accept the inevitable and make the best of the companionship. Many such companionships, they tell me, are touchingly affectionate; and most are at least tolerably friendly. But that does not make a chain a desirable ornament nor the galleys an abode of bliss. Those who talk most about the blessings of marriage and the constancy of its vows are the very people who declare that if the chain were broken and the prisoners left free to choose, the whole social fabric would fly asunder. You cannot have the argument both ways. If the prisoner is happy, why lock him in? If he is not, why pretend that he is?" (*Don Juan*, MS-122)

Marriages Differ as People Differ. "Well, my lord, you see people do persist in talking as if marriages was all of one sort. But theres almost as many different sorts of marriages as theres different sorts of people. Theres the young things that marry for love, not knowing what theyre doing, and the old things that marry for money and comfort and companionship. Theres the people that marry for children. Theres the people that dont intend to have children and that arnt fit to have them. Theres the people that marry because theyre so much run after by the other sex that they have to put a stop to it somehow. Theres the people that want to try a new experience, and the people that want to have done with experiences. How are you to please them all? Why, youll want half a dozen different sorts of contract." (*Collins*, GM-270)

"Larochefoucauld said that there are convenient marriages but no delightful ones. You dont know the comfort of seeing through

and through a thundering liar and rotten cynic like that fellow."
(*Morell*, C-26)

Marriage Not Easily Evaded. Now most laws are, and all
laws ought to be, stronger than the strongest individual. Certainly
the marriage law is. The only people who successfully evade it are
those who actually avail themselves of its shelter by pretending to
be married when they are not, and by Bohemians who have no
position to lose and no career to be closed. In every other case
open violation of the marriage laws means either downright ruin
or such inconvenience and disablement as a prudent man or
woman would get married ten times over rather than face. (P-GM-
120)

Home Life Naturally Monogamous. It must be repeated
here that no law, however stringent, can prevent polygamy among
groups of people who choose to live loosely and be monogamous
only in appearance. But such cases are not now under consideration. Also, affectionate husbands like Samuel Pepys, and affectionate wives of the corresponding temperament, may, it appears,
engage in transient casual adventures out of doors without breaking
up their home life. But within doors that home life may be regarded as naturally monogamous. It does not need to be protected against polygamy: it protects itself. (P-GM-177)

Keeping a Wife in Good Humor. "My late wife and I were
so indispensable to oneanother that a separation would have been
for us a desolating calamity. Yet I repeatedly found myself irresistibly attracted biologically by females with whom I could not
converse seriously for five minutes. My wife needed some romance
in her life when I ceased to be romantic to her and became only her
matter-of-fact husband. To keep her in good humor and health I
had to invite and entertain a succession of interesting young men
to keep her supplied with what I call Sunday husbands." (*The
Widower*, BB-35)

"Every married woman requires a holiday from her husband
occasionally, even when he suits her perfectly." (*Conolly*, IK-304)

When Is a Wife Well Off? If we take a document like
Pepys' Diary, we learn that a woman may have an incorrigibly un-
faithful husband, and yet be much better off than if she had an
ill-tempered, peevish, maliciously sarcastic one, or was chained for
life to a criminal, a drunkard, a lunatic, an idle vagrant, or a person
whose religious faith was contrary to her own. Imagine being married to a liar, a borrower, a mischief maker, a teaser or tormentor
of children and animals, or even simply to a bore! Conceive yourself tied for life to one of the perfectly "faithful" husbands who
are sentenced to a month's imprisonment occasionally for idly leaving their wives in childbirth without food, fire, or attendance!
What woman would not rather marry ten Pepyses? what man a
dozen Nell Gwynnes? Adultery, far from being the first and only
ground for divorce, might more reasonably be made the last, or
wholly excluded. (P-GM-178)

Adultery: A Sentimental Grievance. The present law is perfectly logical only if you once admit (as no decent person ever
does) its fundamental assumption that there can be no companionship between men and women because the woman has a
"sphere" of her own, that of housekeeping, in which the man must
not meddle, whilst he has all the rest of human activity for his
sphere: the only point at which the two spheres touch being that
of replenishing the population. On this assumption the man naturally asks for a guarantee that the children shall be his because he
has to find the money to support them. The power of divorcing a
woman for adultery is this guarantee, a guarantee that she does
not need to guarantee her against a similar imposture on his part,
because he cannot bear children. No doubt he can spend the money
that ought to be spent on her children on another woman and her
children; but this is desertion, which is a separate matter. The
fact for us to seize is that in the eye of the law, adultery without
consequences is merely a sentimental grievance, whereas the plant-
ing on one man of another man's offspring is a substantial one.
(P-GM-178-179)

We Must Make the Best of It. We may take it then that

when a joint domestic establishment, involving questions of children or property, is contemplated, marriage is in effect compulsory upon all normal people; and until the law is altered there is nothing for us but to make the best of it as it stands. (P-GM-120)

What Does the Word Marriage Mean? However much we may all suffer through marriage, most of us think so little about it that we regard it as a fixed part of the order of nature, like gravitation. Except for this error, which may be regarded as constant, we use the word with reckless looseness, meaning a dozen different things by it, and yet always assuming that to a respectable man it can have only one meaning. The pious citizen, suspecting the Socialist (for example) of unmentionable things, and asking him heatedly whether he wishes to abolish marriage, is infuriated by a sense of unanswerable quibbling when the Socialist asks him what particular variety of marriage he means: English civil marriage, sacramental marriage, indissoluble Roman Catholic marriage, marriage of divorced persons, Scotch marriage, Irish marriage, French, German, Turkish, or South Dakotan marriage. (P-GM-121)

Marriage Intimacy. It is remarkable that the very people who romance most absurdly about the closeness and sacredness of the marriage tie are also those who are most convinced that the man's sphere and the woman's sphere are so entirely separate that only in their leisure moments can they ever be together. A man as intimate with his own wife as a magistrate is with his clerk, or a Prime Minister with the leader of the Opposition, is a man in ten thousand. The majority of married couples never get to know one another at all: they only get accustomed to having the same house, the same children, and the same income, which is quite a different matter. The comparatively few men who work at home—writers, artists, and to some extent clergymen—have to effect some sort of segregation within the house or else run a heavy risk of overstraining their domestic relations. When the pair is so poor that it can afford only a single room, the strain is intolerable: violent quarrelling is the result. Very few couples can live in a single-roomed tenement without exchanging blows quite frequently. In the leisured classes there is often no real family life at all. The boys are at a public school; the girls are in the schoolroom in charge of a governess; the husband is at his club or in a set which is not his wife's; and the institution of marriage enjoys the credit of a domestic peace which is hardly more intimate than the relations of prisoners in the same gaol or guests at the same garden party. (P-GM-140-141)

Too Much of a Good Thing. We must be reasonable in our domestic ideals. I do not think that life at a public school is altogether good for a boy any more than barrack life is altogether good for a soldier. But neither is home life altogether good. Such good as it does, I should say, is due to its freedom from the very atmosphere it professes to supply. That atmosphere is usually described as an atmosphere of love; and this definition should be sufficient to put any sane person on guard against it. The people who talk and write as if the highest attainable state is that of a family stewing in love continuously from the cradle to the grave, can hardly have given five minutes serious consideration to so outrageous a proposition. They cannot have even made up their minds as to what they mean by love; for when they expatiate on their thesis they are sometimes talking about kindness, and sometimes about mere appetite. In either sense they are equally far from the realities of life. No healthy man or animal is occupied with love in any sense for more than a very small fraction indeed of the time he devotes to business and to recreations wholly unconnected with love. A wife entirely preoccupied with her affection for her husband, a mother entirely preoccupied with her affection for her children, may be all very well in a book (for people who like that kind of book); but in actual life she is a nuisance. Husbands may escape from her when their business compels them to be away from home all day; but young children may be, and quite often are, killed by her cuddling and coddling and doctoring and preaching: above all, by her continuous attempts to excite precocious sentimentality, a practice as objectionable, and possibly as mischievous, as the worst tricks of the worst nursemaids. (P-GM-134-135)

No Magic in Marriage. To impose marriage on two unmarried people who do not deire to marry one another would be admittedly an act of enslavement. But it is no worse than to impose a continuation of marriage on people who have ceased to desire to be married. It will be said that the parties may not agree on that; that one may desire to maintain the marriage the other wishes to dissolve. But the same hardship arises whenever a man in love proposes marriage to a woman and is refused. The refusal is so painful to him that he often threatens to kill himself and sometimes even does it. Yet we expect him to face his ill luck, and never dream of forcing the woman to accept him. His case is the same as that of the husband whose wife tells him she no longer cares for him, and desires the marriage to be dissolved. You will say, perhaps, if you are superstitious, that it is not the same—that marriage makes a difference. You are wrong: there is no magic in marriage. If there were, married couples would never desire to separate. But they do. And when they do, it is simple slavery to compel them to remain together. (P-GM-181-182)

The Invaded Marriage. What an honorable and sensible man does when his household is invaded is what the Reverend James Mavor Morell does in my play [*Candida*]. He recognizes that just as there is not room for two women in that sacredly intimate relation of sentimental domesticity which is what marriage means to him, so there is no room for two men in that relation with his wife; and he accordingly tells her firmly that she must choose which man will occupy the place that is large enough for one only. He is so far shrewdly unconventional as to recognize that if she chooses the other man, he must give way, legal tie or no legal tie; but he knows that either one or the other must go. And a sensible wife would act in the same way. If a romantic young lady came into her house and proposed to adore her husband on a tolerated footing, she would say "My husband has not room in his life for two wives: either you go out of the house or I go out of it." The situation is not at all unlikely: I had almost said not at all unusual. Young ladies and gentlemen in the greensickly condition which is called calf-love, associating with married couples at dangerous periods of mature life, quite often find themselves in it; and the extreme reluctance of proud and sensitive people to avoid any assertion of matrimonial rights, or to condescend to jealousy, sometimes makes the threatened husband or wife hesitate to take prompt steps and do the apparently conventional thing. But whether they hesitate or act the result is always the same. In a real marriage of sentiment the wife or husband cannot be supplanted by halves; and such a marriage will break very soon under the strain of polygyny or or polyandry. What we want at present is a sufficiently clear teaching of this fact to ensure that prompt and decisive action shall always be taken in such cases without any false shame of seeming conventional (a shame to which people capable of such real marriage are specially susceptible), and a rational divorce law to enable the marriage to be dissolved and the parties honorably resorted and recoupled without disgrace and scandal if that should prove the proper solution. (P-GM-176-177)

We Must Mind Our Own Business. It is generally admitted that people should not be encouraged to petition for a divorce in a fit of petulance. What is not so clearly seen is that neither should they be encouraged to petition in a fit of jealousy, which is certainly the most detestable and mischievous of all the passions that enjoy public credit. Still less should people who are not jealous be urged to behave as if they were jealous, and to enter upon duels and divorce suits in which they have no desire to be successful. There should be no publication of the grounds on which a divorce is sought or granted; and as this would abolish the only means the public now has of ascertaining that every possible effort has been made to keep the couple united against their wills, such privacy will only be tolerated when we at last admit that the sole and sufficient reason why people should be granted a divorce is that they want one. Then there will be no more reports of divorce cases, no more letters read in court with an indelicacy that makes every sensitive person shudder and recoil as from a profanation, no more washing of household linen, dirty or clean, in public. We must learn in these matters to mind our own business and not impose our individual notions of propriety on one another, even if it carries us to the length of openly admitting what we are now compelled to assume silently, that every human being has a right to sexual experience, and that the law is concerned only with parentage, which is now a separate matter. (P-GM-179-180)

Economic Slavery the Root Difficulty. The husband, then, is to be allowed to discard his wife when he is tired of her, and the wife the husband when another man strikes her fancy? One must reply unhesitatingly in the affirmative; for if we are to deny every proposition that can be stated in offensive terms by its opponents, we shall never be able to affirm anything at all. But the question reminds us that until the economic independence of women is achieved, we shall have to remain impaled on the other horn of the dilemma and maintain marriage as a slavery. And here let me ask the Government of the day (1910) a question with regard to the Labor Exchanges it has very wisely established throughout the country. What do these Exchanges do when a woman enters and states that her occupation is that of a wife and mother; that she is out of a job; and that she wants an employer? If the Exchanges refuse to entertain her application, they are clearly excluding nearly the whole female sex from the benefit of the Act. If not, they must become matrimonial agencies, unless, indeed, they are prepared to become something worse by putting the woman down as a housekeeper and introducing her to an employer without making marriage a condition of the hiring. (P-GM-182)

Divorce No Destruction of Marriage. Divorce, in fact, is not the destruction of marriage, but the first condition of its maintenance. A thousand indissoluble marriages mean a thousand marriages and no more. A thousand divorces may mean two thousand marriages; for the couples may marry again. Divorce only re-assorts the couples: a very desirable thing when they are ill-assorted. (P-GM-184)

The Church Confused on Marriage Matters. The Church solemnized and sanctified marriage without ever giving up its original Pauline doctrine on the subject. And it soon fell into another confusion. At the point at which it took up marriage and endeavoured to make it holy, marriage was, as it still is, largely a survival of the custom of selling women to men. Now in all trades a marked difference is made in price between a new article and a second-hand one. The moment we meet with this difference in value between human beings, we may know that we are in the slave-market, where the conception of our relations to the persons sold is neither religious nor natural nor human nor superhuman, but simply commercial. The Church, when it finally gave its blessing to marriage, did not, in its innocence, fathom these commercial traditions. Consequently it tried to sanctify them too, with grotesque results. The slave-dealer having always asked more money for virginity, the Church, instead of detecting the money-changer and driving him out of the temple, took him for a sentimental and chivalrous lover, and, helped by its only half-discarded doctrine of celibacy, gave virginity a heavenly value to ennoble its commercial pretensions. In short, Mammon, always mighty, put the Church in its pocket, where he keeps it to this day, in spite of the occasional saints and martyrs who contrive from time to time to get their heads and souls free to testify against him. (P-GM-194)

Wanted: An Immoral Statesman. We now see that the statesman who undertakes to deal with marriage will have to face an amazingly complicated public opinion. In fact, he will have to leave opinion as far as possible out of the question, and deal with human nature instead. For even if there could be any real public opinion in a society like ours, which is a mere mob of classes, each with its own habits and prejudices, it would be at best a jumble of superstitions and interests, taboos and hypocrisies, which could not be reconciled in any coherent enactment. It would probably proclaim passionately that it does not matter in the least what sort of children we have, or how few or how many, provided the children are legitimate. Also that it does not matter in the least what sort of adults we have, provided they are married. No statesman worth the name can possibly act on these views. He is bound to prefer one healthy illegitimate child to ten rickety legitimate ones, and one energetic and capable unmarried couple to a dozen inferior apathetic husbands and wives. (P-GM-141-142)

Monogamy, Polygyny, and Polyandry. Experience shews that women do not object to polygyny when it is customary: on the contrary, they are its most ardent supporters. The reason is obvious. The question, as it presents itself in practice to a woman, is whether it is better to have, say, a whole share in a tenth-rate man or a tenth share in a first-rate man. Substitute the word Income for the word Man, and you will have the question as it presents itself economically to the dependent woman. The woman whose instincts are maternal, who desires superior children more than anything else, never hesitates. She would take a thousandth share, if necessary, in a husband who was a man in a thousand, rather than have some comparatively weedy weakling all to herself. It is the comparatively weedy weakling, left mateless by polygyny, who objects. Thus, it was not the women of Salt Lake City nor even of America who attacked Mormon polygyny. It was the men. And very naturally. On the other hand, women object to polyandry, because polyandry enables the best women to monopolize all the men, just as polygyny enables the best men to monopolize all the women. That is why all our ordinary men and women are unanimous in defence of monogamy, the men because it excludes polygyny, and the women because it excludes polyandry. The women, left to themselves, would tolerate polygyny. The men, left to themselves, would tolerate polyandry.

But polygyny would condemn a great many men, and polyandry a great many women, to the celibacy of neglect. Hence the resistance any attempt to establish unlimited polygny always provokes, not from the best people, but from the mediocrities and the inferiors. If we could get rid of our inferiors and screw up our average quality until mediocrity ceased to be a reproach, thus making every man reasonably eligible as a father and every woman reasonably desirable as a mother, polygyny and polyandry would immediately fall into sincere disrepute, because monogamy is so much more convenient and economical that nobody would want to share a husband or a wife if he (or she) could have a sufficiently good one all to himself (or herself). Thus it appears that it is the scarcity of husbands or wives of high quality that leads women to polygyny and men to polyandry, and that if this scarcity were cured, monogamy, in the sense of having only one husband or wife at a time (facilities for changing are another matter), would be found satisfactory. (P-GM-150-151)

Life Force Cares Not for Moral Figments. "Let us face the facts, dear Ana. The Life Force respects marriage only because marriage is a contrivance of its own to secure the greatest number of children and the closest care of them. For honor, chastity and all the rest of your moral figments it cares not a rap." (*Don Juan*, MS-121)

The Right To Bear a Child. The right to bear a child, perhaps the most sacred of all women's rights, is not one that should have any conditions attached to it except in the interest of race welfare. There are many women of admirable character, strong, capable, independent, who dislike the domestic habits of men; have no natural turn for mothering and coddling them; and find the concession of conjugal rights to any person under any conditions intolerable by their self-respect. Yet the general sense of the community recognizes in these very women the fittest people to have charge of children, and trusts them, as schoolmistresses and matrons of institutions, more than women of any other type when it is possible to procure them for such work. Why should the taking of a husband be imposed on these women as the price of their right to maternity? (P-GM-153)

To a woman without property or marketable talent a husband is more necessary than a master to a dog. (P-GM-163)

Independence for Women Mandatory.   It is in the general movement for the prevention of destitution that the means for making women independent of the compulsory sale of their persons, in marriage or otherwise, will be found; but meanwhile those who deal specifically with the marriage laws should never allow themselves for a moment to forget this abomination that "plucks the rose from the fair forehead of an innocent love, and sets a blister there," and then calmly calls itself purity, home, motherhood, respectability, honor, decency, and any other fine name that happens to be convenient, not to mention the foul epithets it hurls freely at those who are ashamed of it. (P-GM-164)

Personal Interests in Marriage.   We all have personal interests in marriage which we are not prepared to sink. It is not only the women who want to get married: the men do too, sometimes on sentimental grounds, sometimes on the more sordid calculation that bachelor life is less comfortable and more expensive, since a wife pays for her status with domestic service as well as with the other services expected of her. Now that children are avoidable, this calculation is becoming more common and conscious than it was: a result which is regarded as "a steady improvement in general morality." (P-GM-165)

Concubines Necessary.   "I hold that concubines are a necessary institution. In a nation wellbred biologically there should be concubines as well as wives and husbands. Some marriages are between couples who have no children because they have hereditary ailments which they fear to transmit to their offspring. Others are of shrews and bullies who produce excellent bastards, though domestic life between them is impossible. They should be concubines, not husbands and wives. All concubinages are exactly alike. No two marriages are alike." (*The Widower*, BB-36)

Fashionable Society: Unhappy Slaves. "Look at fashionable society as you know it. What does it pretend to be? An exquisite dance of nymphs. What is it? A horrible procession of wretched girls, each in the claws of a cynical, cunning, avaricious, disillusioned, ignorantly experienced, foul-minded old woman whom she calls mother, and whose duty it is to corrupt her mind and sell her to the highest bidder. Why do these unhappy slaves marry anybody, however old and vile, sooner than not marry at all? Because marriage is their only means of escape from these decrepit fiends who hide their selfish ambitions, their jealous hatreds of the young rivals who have supplanted them, under the mask of maternal duty and family affection." (*Tanner*, MS-59)

"Well, sir, a man should have one woman to prevent him from thinking too much about women in general." (*The Sergeant*, TTTBG-124)

FAMILY LIFE

Dreary, Dreary! "Oh, I have heard it all a thousand times. They tell me too of their last-born: the clever thing the darling child said yesterday, and how much more wonderful or witty or quaint it is than any child that ever was born before. And I have to pretend to be surprised, delighted, interested; though the last child is like the first, and has said and done nothing that did not delight Adam and me when you and Abel said it. For you were the first children in the world, and filled us with such wonder and delight as no couple can ever again feel while the world lasts. When I can bear no more, I go to our old garden, that is now a mass of nettles and thistles, in the hope of finding the serpent to talk to. But you have made the serpent our enemy: she has left the garden, or is dead: I never see her now. So I have to come back and listen to Adam saying the same thing for the ten-thousandth time, or to receive a visit from the last great-great-grandson who has grown up and wants to impress me with his importance. Oh, it is dreary, dreary!" (*Eve*, BM-34)

A Woman's Lot. "That is the injustice of a woman's lot.

A woman has to bring up her children; and that means to restrain them, to deny them things they want, to set them tasks, to punish them when they do wrong, to do all the unpleasant things. And then the father, who has nothing to do but pet them and spoil them, comes in when all her work is done and steals their affection from her." (*Lady Britomart*, MB-265)

The Clingers. "No woman can shake off her mother. There should be no mothers: there should be only women, strong women able to stand by themselves, not clingers. I would kill all the clingers. Mothers cling: daughters cling: we are all like drunken women clinging to lamp posts: none of us stands upright." (*The Patient*, TTTBG-114)

This Unending Talk. "You see, I'm young; and I do so want something to happen. My mother tells me that when I'm her age, I shall be only too glad that nothing's happened; but I'm not her age; so what good is that to me? Theres my father in the garden, meditating on his destiny. All very well for him: he's had a destiny to meditate on; but I havnt had any destiny yet. Everything's happened to him: nothing's happened to me. Thats why this unending talk is so maddeningly uninteresting to me." (*Hypatia*, M-134-135)

Two Sorts of Family Life. "There are two sorts of family life, Phil; and your experience of human nature only extends, so far, to one of them. The sort you know is based on mutual respect, on recognition of the right of every member of the household to independence and privacy in their personal concerns. And because you have always enjoyed that, it seems such a matter of course to you that you don't value it. But there is another sort of family life: a life in which husbands open their wives' letters, and call on them to account for every farthing of their expenditure and every moment of their time; in which women do the same to their children; in which no room is private and no hour sacred; in which duty, obedience, affection, home, morality and religion are detestable tyrannies, and life is a vulgar round of punishments and lies, coercion and rebellion, jealousy, suspicion, recrimination —Oh! I cannot describe it to you: fortunately for you, you know nothing about it." (*Mrs. Clandon*, YNCT-20)

What Is a Child? An experiment. A fresh attempt to produce the just man made perfect: that is, to make humanity divine. And you will vitiate the experiment if you make the slightest attempt to abort it into some fancy figure of your own: for example, your notion of a good man or a womanly woman. If you treat it as a little wild beast to be tamed, or as a pet to be played with, or even as a means to save you trouble and to make money for you (and these are our commonest ways), it may fight its way through in spite of you and save its soul alive; for all its instincts will resist you, and possibly be strengthened in the resistance; but if you begin with its own holiest aspirations, and suborn them for your own purposes, then there is hardly any limit to the mischief you may do. Swear at a child, throw your books at it, send it flying from the room with a cuff or a kick; and the experience will be as instructive to the child as a difficulty with a short-tempered dog or a bull. Francis Place tells us that his father always struck his children when he found one within his reach. The effect on the young Places seems to have been simply to make them keep out of their father's way, which was no doubt what he desired, as far as he desired anything at all. Francis records the habit without bitterness, having reason to thank his stars that his father respected the inside of his head whilst cuffing the outside of it; and this made it easy for Francis to do yeoman's service to his country as that rare and admirable thing, a Freethinker: the only sort of thinker, I may remark, whose thoughts, and consequently whose religious convictions, command any respect. (P-M-7)

The Child Must Learn To Be Considerate. There is a point at which every person with human nerves has to say to a child "Stop that noise." But suppose the child asks why! There are various answers in use. The simplest: "Because it irritates me," may fail; for it may strike the child as being rather amusing to irritate you; also the child, having comparatively no nerves, may be unable to conceive your meaning vividly enough. In any case it may want to make a noise more than to spare your feelings. You may therefore have to explain that the effect of the irritation will be that you will do something unpleasant if the noise continues. The something unpleasant may be only a look of suffering to rouse the child's affectionate sympathy (if it has any), or it may run to forcible expulsion from the room with plenty of unnecessary violence; but the principle is the same: there are no false pretences involved: the child learns in a straightforward way that it does not pay to be inconsiderate. (P-M-8)

A Burden Beyond Bearing. The really natural feeling of adults for children in the long prosaic intervals between the moments of affectionate impulse is just that feeling that leads them to avoid their care and constant company as a burden beyond bearing, and to pretend that the places they send them to are well conducted, beneficial, and indispensable to the success of the children in after life. The true cry of the kind mother after her little rosary of kisses is "Run away, darling." It is nicer than "Hold your noise, you young devil; or it will be the worse for you"; but fundamentally it means the same thing: that if you compel an adult and a child to live in one another's company either the adult or the child will be miserable. There is nothing whatever unnatural or wrong or shocking in this fact; and there is no harm in it if only it be sensibly faced and provided for. The mischief that it does at present is produced by our efforts to ignore it, or to smother it under a heap of sentimental lies and false pretences. (P-M-17-18)

"Parents and children! No man should know his own child. No child should know its own father. Let the family be rooted out of civilization! Let the human race be brought up in institutions!" (*Tarleton*, M-194)

The Professional Child Fanciers. Parents and guardians are so worried by children and so anxious to get rid of them that anyone who is willing to take them off their hands is welcomed and whitewashed. The very people who read with indignation of Squeers and Creakle in the novels of Dickens are quite ready to hand over their own children to Squeers and Creakle, and to pretend that Squeers and Creakle are monsters of the past. But read the autobiography of Stanley the traveller, or sit in the company of men talking about their schooldays, and you will soon find that fiction, which must, if it is to be sold and read, stop short of being positively sickening, dare not tell the whole truth about the people to whom children are handed over on educational pretexts. Not very long ago a schoolmaster in Ireland was murdered by his boys; and for reasons which were never made public it was at first decided not to prosecute the murderers. Yet all these flogging schoolmasters and orphanage fiends and baby farmers are "lovers of children." They are really child fanciers (like bird fanciers or dog fanciers) by irresistible natural predilection, never happy unless they are surrounded by their victims, and always certain to make their living by accepting the custody of children, no matter how many alternative occupations may be available. And bear in mind that they are only the extreme instances of what is commonly called natural affection, apparently because it is obviously unnatural. (P-M-17)

Children as Nuisances. Here we have come to the central fact of the question: a fact nobody avows, which is yet the true explanation of the monstrous system of child imprisonment and torture which we disguise under such hypocrisies as education, training, formation of character and the rest of it. This fact is simply that a child is a nuisance to a grown-up person. What is more, the nuisance becomes more and more intolerable as the grown-up person becomes more cultivated, more sensitive, and more deeply engaged in the highest methods of adult work. The child at play is noisy and ought to be noisy: Sir Isaac Newton at work is quiet and ought to be quiet. And the child should spend most of its time at play, whilst the adult should spend most of his time at work. I am not now writing on behalf of persons who coddle themselves into a ridiculous condition of nervous feebleness, and at last imagine themselves unable to work under conditions of bustle which to healthy people are cheerful and stimulating. I am sure that if people had to choose between living where the noise of children never stopped and where it was never heard all the goodnatured and sound people would prefer the incessant noise to the incessant silence. But that choice is not thrust upon us by the nature of things. There is no reason why children and adults should not see just as much of one another as is good for them, no more and no less. (P-M-14)

Bringing Up a Child. I remember a servant who used to tell me that if I were not good, by which she meant if I did not behave with a single eye to her personal convenience, the cock would come down the chimney. Less imaginative but equally dishonest people told me I should go to hell if I did not make myself agreeable to them. Bodily violence, provided it be the hasty expression of normal provoked resentment and not vicious cruelty, cannot harm a child as this sort of pious fraud harms it. There is a legal limit to physical cruelty; and there are also human limits to it. There is an active Society which brings to book a good many parents who starve and torture and overwork their children, and intimidates a good many more. When parents of this type are caught, they are treated as criminals; and not infrequently the police have some trouble to save them from being lynched. The people against whom children are wholly unprotected are those who devote themselves to the very mischievous and cruel sort of abortion which is called bringing up a child in the way it should go. Now nobody knows the way a child should go. All the ways discovered so far lead to the horrors of our existing civilizations, described quite justifiably by Ruskin as heaps of agonizing human maggots, struggling with one another for scraps of food. Pious fraud is an attempt to pervert that divine mystery called the child's conscience into an instrument of our own convenience, and to use that wonderful and terrible power called Shame to grind our own axe. (P-M-9)

Divine Wrath or Detestable Lust?   Any parent or school teacher who takes a secret and abominable delight in torture is allowed to lay traps into which every child must fall, and then beat it to his or her heart's content. A gentleman once wrote to me and said, with an obvious conviction that he was being most reasonable and high-minded, that the only thing he beat his children for was failure in perfect obedience and perfect truthfulness. On these virtues, he said, he must insist. As one of them is not a virtue at all, and the other is the attribute of a god, one can imagine what the lives of this gentleman's children would have been if it had been possible for him to live down to his monstrous and foolish pretensions. And yet he might have written his letter to The Times (he very nearly did, by the way) without incurring any danger of being removed to an asylum, or even losing his reputation for taking a very proper view of his parental duties. And at least it was not a trivial view, nor an ill meant one. It was much more respectable than the general consensus of opinion that if a school teacher can devise a question a child cannot answer, or overhear it calling omega omeega, he or she may beat the child viciously. Only, the cruelty must be whitewashed by a moral excuse, and a pretence of reluctance. It must be for the child's good. The assailant must say "This hurts me more than it hurts you." There must be hypocrisy as well as cruelty. The injury to the child would be far less if the voluptuary said frankly "I beat you because I like beating you; and I shall do it whenever I can contrive an excuse for it." But to represent this detestable lust to the child as Divine wrath, and the cruelty as the beneficent act of God, which is exactly what all our floggers do, is to add to the torture of the body, out of which the flogger at least gets some pleasure, the maiming and blinding of the child's soul, which can bring nothing but horror to anyone. (P-M-10)

Childhood as a Prison.   In many families it is still the custom to treat childhood frankly as a state of sin, and impudently

proclaim the monstrous principle that little children should be
seen and not heard, and to enforce a set of prison rules designed
solely to make cohabitation with children as convenient as possible
for adults without the smallest regard for the interests, either remote or immediate, of the children. This system tends to produce
a tough, rather brutal, stupid, unscrupulous class, with a fixed
idea that all enjoyment consists in undetected sinning; and in
certain phases of civilization people of this kind are apt to get the
upper hand of more amiable and conscientious races and classes.
They have the ferocity of a chained dog, and are proud of it.
But the end of it is that they are always in chains, even at the
height of their military or political success; they win everything
on condition that they are afraid to enjoy it. Their civilizations
rest on intimidation, which is so necessary to them that when
they cannot find anybody brave enough to intimidate them they
intimidate themselves and live in a continual moral and political
panic. In the end they get found out and bullied. But that is
not the point that concerns us here, which is, that they are in
some respects better brought up than the children of sentimental
people who are always anxious and miserable about their duty
to their children, and who end by neither making their children
happy nor having a tolerable life for themselves. (P-M-18)

Ignorance: Waster and Warper of Children. The most
excusable parents are those who try to correct their own faults in
their offspring. The parent who says to his child: "I am one of
the successes of the Almighty: therefore imitate me in every particular or I will have the skin off your back" (a quite common
attitude) is a much more absurd figure than the man who, with
a pipe in his mouth, thrashes his boy for smoking. If you must
hold yourself up to your children as an object lesson (which is
not at all necessary), hold yourself up as a warning and not as
an example. But you had much better let the child's character
alone. If you once allow yourself to regard a child as so much
material for you to manufacture into any shape that happens to
suit your fancy you are defeating the experiment of the Life
Force. You are assuming that the child does not know its own

business, and that you do. In this you are sure to be wrong: the child feels the drive of the Life Force (often called the Will of God); and you cannot feel it for him. Handel's parents no doubt thought they knew better than their child when they tried to prevent his becoming a musician. They would have been equally wrong and equally unsuccessful if they had tried to prevent the child becoming a great rascal had its genius lain in that direction. Handel would have been Handel, and Napoleon and Peter of Russia *them*selves in spite of all the parents in creation, because, as often happens, they were stronger than their parents. But this does not happen always. Most children can be, and many are, hopelessly warped and wasted by parents who are ignorant and silly enough to suppose that they know what a human being ought to be, and who stick at nothing in their determination to force their children into their moulds. Every child has a right to its own bent. It has a right to be a Plymouth Brother though its parents be convinced atheists. It has a right to dislike its mother or father or sister or brother or uncle or aunt if they are antipathetic to it. It has a right to find its own way and go its own way, whether that way seems wise or foolish to others, exactly as an adult has. It has a right to privacy as to its own doings and its own affairs as much as if it were its own father. (P-M-11-12)

Interference with Child's Rights. Two adult parents, in spite of a house to keep and an income to earn, can still interfere to a disastrous extent with the rights and liberties of one child. But by the time a fourth child has arrived, they are not only outnumbered two to one, but are getting tired of the thankless and mischievous job of bringing up their children in the way they think they should go. The old observation that members of large families get on in the world holds good because in large families it is impossible for each child to receive what schoolmasters call "individual attention." The children may receive a good deal of individual attention from one another in the shape of outspoken reproach, ruthless ridicule, and violent resistance to their attempts at aggression; but the parental despots are compelled by the multitude of their subjects to resort to political rather than personal rule, and to spread their attempts at moral monster-making over so many children, that each child has enough freedom, and enough sport in the prophylactic process of laughing at its elders behind their backs, to escape with much less damage than the single child. In a large school the system may be bad; but the personal influence of the head master has to be exerted, when it is exerted at all, in a public way, because he has little more power of working on the affections of the individual scholar in the intimate way that, for example, the mother of a single child can, than the prime minister has of working on the affections of any individual voter. (P-M-12)

Our Relatives. "When our relatives are at home, we have to think of all their good points or it would be impossible to endure them. But when they are away, we console ourselves for their absence by dwelling on their vices." (*The Captain*, HH-9-10)

"I have always said that the great advantage of a hotel is that it's a refuge from home life, sir." (*The Waiter*, YNCT-64)

Eternal Grumblers. There are women who, through total disuse, have lost the power of kindly human speech and can only scold and complain: there are men who grumble and nag from inveterate habit even when they are comfortable. But their unfortunate spouses and children cannot escape from them. (P-GM-168)

Comforting Phrases versus Reality. Most working folk today either send their children to day schools or turn them out of doors. This solves the problem for the parents. It does not solve it for the children, any more than the tethering of a goat in a field or the chasing of an unlicensed dog into the streets solves it for the goat or the dog; but it shews that in no class are people willing to endure the society of their children, and consequently that it is an error to believe that the family provides children with edifying adult society, or that the family is a social unit. The family is in that, as in so many other respects, a humbug. Old people and young people cannot walk at the same pace without distress and final loss of health to one of the parties. When they are sitting indoors they cannot endure the same degrees of temperature and the same supplies of fresh air. Even if the main factors of noise, restlessness, and inquisitiveness are left out of account, children can stand with indifference sights, sounds, smells, and disorders that would make an adult of fifty utterly miserable; whilst on the other hand such adults find a tranquil happiness in conditions which to children mean unspeakable boredom. And since our system is to pack them all into the same house and pretend that they are happy, and that this particular sort of happiness is the foundation of virtue, it is found that in discussing family life we never speak of actual adults or actual children, or of realities of any sort, but always of ideals such as The Home, a Mother's Influence, a Father's Care, Filial Piety, Duty, Affection, Family Life, etc. etc., which are no doubt very comforting phrases, but which beg the question of what a home and a mother's influence and a father's care and so forth really come to in practice. (P-M-14-15)

The Wall Between Parents & Children.   "Read any man's letters to his children. Theyre not human. Theyre not about himself or themselves. Theyre about hotels, scenery, about the weather, about getting wet and losing the train and what he saw on the road and all that. Not a word about himself. Forced. Shy. Duty letters. All fit to be published: that says everything. I tell you theres a wall ten feet thick and ten miles high between parent and child." *(John Tarleton, M-143)*

A Dog Better Company than a Child?   How many hours a week of the time when his children are out of bed does the ordinary bread-winning father spend in the company of his children or even in the same building with them? The home may be a thieves' kitchen, the mother a procuress, the father a violent drunkard; or the mother and father may be fashionable people who see their children three or four times a year during the holidays, and then not oftener than they can help, living meanwhile in daily and intimate contact with their valets and lady's-maids, whose influence and care are often dominant in the household. Affection, as distinguished from simple kindliness, may or may not exist: when it does it either depends on qualities in the parties that would produce it equally if they were of no kin to one another, or it is a more or less morbid survival of the nursing passion; for affection between adults (if they are really adult in mind and not merely grown-up children) and creatures so relatively selfish and cruel as children necessarily are without knowing it or meaning it, cannot be called natural: in fact the evidence shews that it is easier to love the company of a dog than of a commonplace child between the ages of six and the beginnings of controlled maturity; for women who cannot bear to be separated from their pet dogs send their children to boarding schools cheerfully. They may say and even believe that in allowing their children to leave home they are sacrificing themselves for their children's good; but there are very few pet dogs that would not be the better for a month or two spent elsewhere than in a lady's lap or roasting on a drawing-room hearthrug. Besides, to allege that children are better continually away from home is to give up the whole popular sentimental theory of the family; yet the dogs are kept and the children are banished. (P-M-15-16)

Mother Is Like a Broomstick. The relation between parent and child has cruel moments for the parent even when money is no object, and the material worries are delegated to servants and school teachers. The child and the parent are strangers to one another necessarily, because their ages must differ widely. Read Goethe's autobiography; and note that though he was happy in his parents and had exceptional powers of observation, divination, and story-telling, he knew less about his father and mother than about most of the other people he mentions. I myself was never on bad terms with my mother: we lived together until I was forty-two years old, absolutely without the smallest friction of any kind; yet when her death set me thinking curiously about our relations, I realized that I knew very little about her. Introduce me to a strange woman who was a child when I was a child, a girl when I was a boy, an adolescent when I was an adolescent; and if we take naturally to one another I will know more of her and she of me at the end of forty days (I had almost said of forty minutes) than I knew of my mother at the end of forty years. A contemporary stranger is a novelty and an enigma, also a possibility; but a mother is like a broomstick or like the sun in the heavens, it does not matter which as far as one's knowledge of her is concerned: the broomstick is there and the sun is there; and whether the child is beaten by it or warmed and enlightened by it, it accepts it as a fact in nature, and does not conceive it as having had youth, passions, and weaknesses, or as still growing, yearning, suffering, and learning. (P-M-79)

"If parents would only realize how they bore their children." (*Hypatia*, M-134)

A Very Common Stage. "Lord Summerhays, youll join me, I'm sure, in pointing out to both father and daughter that they have now reached that very common stage in family life at which anything but a blow would be an anti-climax." (*Percival*, M-193)

Spurious Family Sentiment. If we could choose our relatives, we might, by selecting congenial ones, mitigate the repulsive effect of the obligation to like them and to admit them to our intimacy. But to have a person imposed on us as a brother merely because he happens to have the same parents is unbearable when, as may easily happen, he is the sort of person we should carefully avoid if he were anyone else's brother. All Europe (except Scotland, which has clans instead of families) draws the line at second cousins. Protestantism draws it still closer by making the first cousin a marriageable stranger; and the only reason for not drawing it at sisters and brothers is that the institution of the family compels us to spend our childhood with them, and thus imposes on us a curious relation in which familiarity destroys romantic charm, and is yet expected to create a specially warm affection. Such a relation is dangerously factitious and unnatural; and the practical moral is that the less said at home about specific family affection the better. Children, like grown-up people, get on well enough together if they are not pushed down one another's throats; and grown-up relatives will get on together in proportion to their separation and their care not to presume on their blood relationship. We should let children's feelings take their natural course without prompting. I have seen a child scolded and called unfeeling because it did not occur to it to make a theatrical demonstration of affectionate delight when its mother returned after an absence: a typical example of the way in which spurious family sentiment is stoked up. We are, after all, sociable animals; and if we are let alone in the matter of our affections, and well brought up otherwise, we shall not get on any the worse with particular people because they happen to be our brothers and sisters and cousins. The danger lies in assuming that we shall get on any better. (P-M-82-83)

Inhuman Domestic Laws. As long as the masses of our people are too poor to be good parents or good anything else except beasts of burden, it is no use requiring much more from them but hewing of wood and drawing of water: whatever is to be done must be done *for* them, mostly, alas! by people whose superiority is merely technical. Until we abolish poverty it is impossible to push rational measures of any kind very far: the wolf at the door will compel us to live in a state of siege and to do everything by a bureaucratic martial law that would be quite unnecessary and indeed intolerable in a prosperous community. But however we settle the question, we must make the parent justify his custody of the child exactly as we should make a stranger justify it. If a family is not achieving the purposes of a family it should be dissolved just as a marriage should when it, too, is not achieving the purposes of marriage. The notion that there is or ever can be anything magical and inviolable in the legal relations of domesticity, and the curious confusion of ideas which makes some of our bishops imagine that in the phrase "Whom God hath joined," the word God means the district registrar or the Reverend John Smith or William Jones, must be got rid of. Means of breaking up undesirable families are as necessary to the preservation of the family as means of dissolving undesirable marriages are to the preservation of marriage. If our domestic laws are kept so inhuman that they at last provoke a furious general insurrection against them as they already provoke many private ones, we shall in a very literal sense empty the baby out with the bath by abolishing an institution which needs nothing more than a little obvious and easy rationalizing to make it not only harmless but comfortable, honorable, and useful. (P-GM-202)

Education

I am still learning in my ninetysecond year. (SSS-117)

The Nation's Children Never Grow Up. Education is inextricably entangled in the problem of childhood. I have already pointed out that statesmen must not deal with the children of the nation as parents must deal with their own, because the children of the nation never grow up and the children of the parents do. Now the parents cannot learn their business as such until they have brought up more children than they will now consent to bring into the world, spoiling the first two or three in the process by either too much interference or too little. This gives the statesman an advantage over the parent. When dealing with children of any given age in the lump, he has the experience of all relevant human history to guide him, whereas the parents begin without any experience at all, and find their problems changing from year to year. (EPWW-147)

Some Children Older Mentally than Their Parents. Children are not childish all through any more than dotards are dotards all through. I have been a child and am a dotard; and I know. The wisdom and knowledge with which a child is born is not confined to digesting its food, changing its teeth, and substituting for mother's milk a diet richer in minerals. These are marvellous accomplishments; but there are mental inheritances no less remarkable. In some respects the wisdom of babes and sucklings, like their digestions, is more trustworthy than it will be when they are grown-up, and even when they have been Cabinet ministers in a half a dozen parliaments. And the very old, if the evolutionary process still persists, may be young in the first drawings of a new faculty. Consequently neither the infant school nor the estate in Surrey is a solution of the social problem for the very young and very old. Some children are older mentally than their parents, and some septuagenarians younger than their grandchildren. (EPWW-72)

Extricating Ourselves from Our Grossest Stupidities. Education is a word that in our mouths covers a good many things. At present we are only extricating ourselves slowly and, as usual, reluctantly and illhumoredly, from our grossest stupidities about it. One of them is that it means learning lessons, and that learning lessons is for children, and ceases when they come of age. I, being a septuagenarian, can assure you confidently that we never cease learning to the extent of our capacity for learning until our faculties fail us. As to what we have been taught in school and college, I should say roughly that as it takes us all our lives to find out the meaning of the small part of it that is true and the error of the large part that is false, it is not surprising that those who have been "educated" least know most. (IWGSC-413)

Our Lamed and Intimidated Children. We pay a frightful and inevitable penalty for our inhuman treatment of children, because of the fact, which we invariably forget, that the world is peopled, not by two distinct races called children and adults, but by human beings of various ages, from a second to a century. The ruthless repression which we practise on our fellow-creatures whilst they are too small to defend themselves, ends in their reaching their full bodily growth in a hopelessly lamed and intimidated condition, unable to conceive of any forces in the world except physically coercive and socially conventional ones. (SE-342)

Worse Tortures than the Cane. I need hardly add that the fact that at this moment the majority of schoolmasters are schoolmistresses does not affect my argument. They are quite as handy with the cane as the men. What is more important is that as it is possible to make a case for the statement that "corporal punishment is disappearing," we should bear jealously in mind that corporal punishment is only one of many available methods of intimidation and coercion, and by no means the most cruel and injurious. There are worse tortures, both physical and moral, in actual use (I shall not propagate them by giving particulars) in schools where "corporal punishment is not permitted." (SE-300-301)

Organizing Child Life. Child life should be so organized in its successive age groups as to create a strong collective opinion among children that there are certain things everyone must learn and know. Public opinion, far from being nonexistent among children, is so tyrannical that it needs restraint rather than release. Learning should bring, not book prizes and medals, but privileges and liberties, status and earnings; for in this way only can children be educated as citizens. Competitive examinations should be abolished, as they give the competitors an interest in oneanother's ignorance and failure, and associate success with the notion of doing the other fellow down. Competition should be between teams, as this incites members to share their knowledge and help oneanother.

I have included earnings among the incentives; for the habit of earning money and providing for needs by earning should begin early. Children should have regular pocket-money, and not be thrown on the world with no practice in fending for themselves out of an earned income. All this means that children should live in an organized society with rights and constitutions, and be brought up neither as household pets nor as chattel slaves. They must be policed as adults are. Some of them should be liquidated as congenital and incurable idiots or criminals; and they should all respect the police and be taught that unless they fit themselves to live in civilized society they cannot be allowed to live at all; but they should not regard their parents and teachers as police officers, judges, and executioners. Homes, families, and schools should not be workhouses and prisons as well. Children should be educated to live more abundantly, not apprenticed to a life sentence of penal servitude. (EPWW-177)

A Nation of Undesirable Acquaintances. Obstructing the way of the proper organization of childhood, as of everything else, lies our ridiculous misdistribution of the national income, with its accompanying class distinctions and imposition of snobbery on children as a necessary part of their social training. The result of our economic folly is that we are a nation of undesirable acquaintances; and the first object of all our institutions for children is segregation. (P-M-31)

Accumulated Rubbish Threatens Us. It is not the ignorance of the uneducated that threatens us most, though it has become very dangerous now that Votes for Everybody, masquerading as Democracy, has been established on the assumption that everybody is politically omniscient. Ignorance can be instructed: it is easy to write on a clean slate. But the slates in our schools are not clean: they are scrawled all over not only with sham Latin verses, but with fabulous history, barbarous superstitions, obsolete codes and slogans, and the accumulated nonsense and rubbish of centuries; for these slates are never cleaned; and anyone attempting to clean them is punished, or, if out of reach, is denounced as an enemy of God and Man. (EPWW-147)

The Most Erudite Graduates May Be Nitwits. Academic educational tests are better than none. Whoever has studied the steps from Aristotle to Lucretius, from Plato-cum-Socrates to Plotinus, Thucydides to Gibbon, Ptolemy to Copernicus, Saint

Peter to Robert Owen, Aquinas to Hus and Luther, Erasmus to Voltaire, can at least find out what was done last time and give certificates to those who can do it again. But without living experiences no person is educated. With nothing but academic degrees, even when overloaded by a smattering of dead languages and twopennorth of algebra, the most erudite graduates may be noodles and ignoramuses. The vital difference between reading and experience is not measurable by examination marks. On the strength of that difference I claim arrogantly to be one of the best educated men in the world, and on occasion have dismissed 95 per cent. of the academic celebrities, with all due respect for the specific talents enjoyed by a few of them, as nitwits. (SSS-115-116)

Dangerous Ignorances. Under rulers misguided enough to believe that the highest good on earth or in heaven is a life of opulent leisure people are not taught what their rulers do not want them to know, and do not themselves know. But there are ignorances which, being against all interests, plutocratic and proletarian alike, are purely stupid. Our children are taught how to put on their clothes and button them without assistance, and how to use knives and forks; but they are never taught how to feed themselves. Adults who have been through all the schools and taken their degrees believe that they cannot live without eating flesh and drinking alcohol. They go into pharmacies and buy and swallow tablets of the most dangerous drugs with as little misgiving as they bought and swallowed sweets at the confectioners when they were children. They learn of the existence of these drugs from their doctors, who prescribe them as recklessly as they prescribe fish, flesh, fowl, wine, and champagne jelly. It is nearly fifty years since I was assured by a conclave of doctors that if I did not eat meat I should die of starvation; and doctors still take the same line professionally as if all the vegetarians, including myself, had died of starvation in the meantime. I recall a symposium of eminent physicians who gravely decided that alcohol in the form of distilled or fermented drinks is an indispensable factor in human diet. (EPWW-175-176)

Subversive Knowledge Kept from Us. To my mind, a glance at subjects now taught in schools ought to convince any reasonable person that the object of the lessons is to keep children out of mischief, and not to qualify them for their part in life as responsible citizens of a free State. It is not possible to maintain freedom in any State, no matter how perfect its original constitution, unless its publicly active citizens know a good deal of constitutional history, law, and political science, with its basis of economics. If as much pains had been taken a century ago to make us all understand Ricardo's law of rent as to learn our catechisms, the face of the world would have been changed for the better. But for that very reason the greatest care is taken to keep such beneficially subversive knowledge from us, with the result that in public life we are either place-hunters, anarchists, or sheep shepherded by wolves. (P-M-26)

Education as a Tool of the Dishonest. Honest government is impossible without honest schools; for honest schools are illegal under dishonest governments. Honest education is dangerous to tyranny and privilege; and systems like the Capitalist system, kept in vogue by popular ignorance, Churches which depend on it for priestly authority, privileged classes which identify civilization with the maintenance of their privileges, and ambitious conquerors and dictators who have to instil royalist idolatry and romantic hero-worship, all use both ignorance and education as underpinnings for general faith in themselves as rulers. (EPWW-169)

Education: Corrupt Propaganda. Schoolmasters who teach their pupils such vital elementary truths about their duty to their country as that they should despise and pursue as criminals all able-bodied adults who do not by personal service pull their weight in the social boat, are dismissed from their employment, and sometimes prosecuted for sedition. And from this elementary morality up to the most abstruse and philosophic teaching in the universities, the same corruption extends. Science becomes a propaganda of quack cures, manufactured by companies in which the rich hold shares, for the diseases of the poor who need only better food and sanitary houses, and of the rich who need only useful occupation, to keep them both in health. Political economy becomes an impudent demonstration that the wages of the poor cannot be raised; that without the idle rich we should perish for lack of capital and employment; and that if the poor would take care to have fewer children everything would be for the best in the worst of all possible worlds.

Thus the poor are kept poor by their ignorance; and those whose parents are too well-off to make it possible to keep them ignorant, and who receive what is called a complete education, are taught so many flat lies that their false knowledge is more dangerous than the untutored natural wit of savages. (IWGSC-63-64)

A New Scapegoat: "The Machine." For some time past a significant word has been coming into use as a substitute for Destiny, Fate, and Providence. It is: "The Machine": the machine that has no god in it. Why do governments do nothing in spite of reports of Royal Commissions that establish the most frightful urgency? Why do our philanthropic millionaires do nothing, though they are ready to throw bucketfuls of gold into the streets? The Machine will not let them. Always The Machine. In short, they dont know how. They try to reform Society as an old lady might try to restore a broken down locomotive by prodding it with a knitting needle. And this is not at all because they are born fools, but because they have been educated, not into manhood and freedom, but into blindness and slavery by their parents and schoolmasters, themselves the victims of a similar misdirection, and consequently of The Machine. They do not want liberty. They have not been educated to want it. They choose slavery and inequality; and all the other evils are automatically added to them. (P-M-100-101)

Good Schools Intolerable in Bad Civilizations. The good school is now, unfortunately, the crank school: the problem is to

make the common school a good school. And good schools are
not easily tolerated by bad civilizations. The parent may wish in
his soul that his son could be taught that honesty is the best
policy; but he has to consider that if he is led to take that precept
seriously as a practical rule of life in competitive commerce he
may starve for it. All our conventional schools at present teach
false ethics, false science, false history, and even false hygiene.
And if there were sufficient vested interests in false geography and
false arithmetic they would teach these too. Truth is a guilty
secret, heavily punishable on discovery; and the parent who allows
his child to be taught truth without also leaving him an independent income must be prepared to hear his child curse him.
This, I think, is the real reason why we dare not embark on controversial education. It would tear away the camouflage from commercial civilization. (SE-320-321)

Men Must Reform Society to Reform Themselves. The
child must be taught, in direct contradiction to the current cult
of salvation by personal righteousness, that in all public respects
men in society must reform society before they can reform themselves. The individual may see a better line for the main road; but
he should be educated to understand that his business is to
persuade the authorities to make the new road and plough up the
old, and not immediately to trample and trespass along his pet
line as if the business concerned himself alone. (SE-314-315)

The Old School Tie: A Curious Monster. Not until the
ninteenth century, when the feudal aristocracy finally handed
over its rulership to, and associated and intermarried with, the
purse-proud snob tradesmen enriched by the industrial revolution,
were the children of the rich sent to school, not to get scholarship,
culture, and such knowledge as they were capable of, but solely
to be hallmarked as members of "the upper class." It was the fifty
years following the Reform Act of 1832 that produced the curious
monster we know now as the Old School Tie, who excels at cricket,
tennis, and golf; has class manners and a class accent; knows

nothing of the world he is living in or knows it all wrong; and is equipped mentally with the ideas of a seventeenth-century squire. (EPWW-77)

Rich & Poor Must Be Exterminated. When I describe the Old School Tie as a nineteenth-century monster, which he literally is, I must not be taken to imply that the opposite product of the industrial revolution, the proletarian, is not, in his way, also a monster. It is true that as he works for his living he may be a productive and serviceable monster, not a predatory and parasitical one. But he is a perverted and distorted creature all the same. I am not a friend of the poor and an enemy of the rich as ignorant people expect a Socialist to be. When I was a child the nursemaid who took me out to exercise me just as she might have taken a dog, took me into the slums where she had friends instead of into handsomer and more salubrious places. Naturally I hated the slums and the dwellers therein. I still want to have the slums demolished and the dwellers exterminated, and am writing this book with this end in view in my second childhood. And I have in my time elicited thunders of applause from slum audiences by expressing these sentiments. But as I grew out of the hands of the nursemaid and associated more with ladies and gentlemen, I did not find them more bearable morally. In their dreary snobbery and carefully guarded ignorance of the slum life on which they were battening and into which I had been clandestinely introduced I could find no comradeship: they also, I finally concluded, must be exterminated. (EPWW-77-78)

Ancient Beliefs versus Modern States. On the liberal side of education it is clear that a certain minimum of law, constitutional history, and economics is indispensable as a qualification for a voter even if ethics are left entirely to the inner light. In the case of young children, dogmatic commandments against murder, theft, and the more obvious possibilities of untutored social intercourse, are imperative; and it is here that we must expect fierce controversy. I need not repeat all that we have already been through as to the impossibility of ignoring this part of education and calling our neglect Secular Education. If on the ground that the subject is a controversial one you leave a child to find out for itself whether the earth is round or flat, it will find out that it is flat, and, after blundering into many mistakes and superstitions, be so angry with you for not teaching it that it is round, that when it becomes an adult voter it will insist on its own children having uncompromising positive guidance on the point.

What will not work in physics will not work in metaphysics either. No Government, Socialist or anti-Socialist or neutral, could possibly govern and administer a highly artificial modern State unless every citizen had a highly artificial modern conscience: that is, a creed or body of beliefs which would never occur to a primitive woman, and a body of disbeliefs, or negative creed, which would strike a primitive woman as fantastic blasphemies that must bring down on her tribe the wrath of the unseen powers. Modern governments must therefore inculcate these beliefs and disbeliefs, or at least see that they are inculcated somehow; or they cannot carry on. And the reason we are in such a mess at present is that our governments are trying to carry on with a set of beliefs and disbeliefs that belong to bygone phases of science and extinct civilizations. Imagine going to Moses or Mahomet for a code to regulate the modern money market! (IWGSC-422-423)

Social Creed Becomes Second Nature. The social creed must be imposed on us when we are children; for it is like riding, or reading music at sight: it can never become second nature to those who try to learn it as adults; and the social creed, to be really effective, must be a second nature to us. It is quite easy to give people a second nature, however unnatural, if you catch them early enough. There is no belief, however grotesque and even villainous, that cannot be made a part of human nature if it is inculcated in childhood and not contradicted in the child's hearing. Now that you are grown up, nothing could persuade you that it is right to lame every woman for life by binding her feet painfully in childhood on the ground that it is not lady-like to move about freely like an animal. If you are the wife of a general or admiral nothing could persuade you that when the King dies you and your husband are bound in honor to commit suicide so as to accompany your sovereign into the next world. Nothing could persuade you that it is every widow's duty to be cremated alive with the dead body of her husband. But if you had been caught early enough you could have been made to believe and do all these things exactly as Chinese, Japanese, and Indian women have believed and done them. You may say that these were heathen Eastern women, and that you are a Christian Western. But I can remember when your grandmother, also a Christian Western, believed that she would be disgraced for ever if she let anyone see her ankles in the street, or (if she was "a real lady") walk there alone. The spectacle she made of herself when, as a married woman, she put on a cap to announce to the world that she must no longer be attractive to men, and the amazing figure she cut as a widow in crape robes symbolic of her utter desolation and woe, would, if you could see or even conceive them, convince you that it was purely her luck and not any superiority of western to eastern womanhood that saved her from the bound feet, the suttee, and the hara-kiri. If you still doubt it, look at the way in which men go to war and commit frightful atrocities because they believe it is their duty, and also because the women would spit in their faces if they refused, all because this had been inculcated upon them from their childhood, thus creating the public opinion which enables the Government not only to raise enthusiastic volunteer armies, but to enforce military service by heavy penalties on the few people who, thinking for themselves, cannot accept wholesale murder and ruin as patriotic virtues. (IWGSC-427-428)

How Much Learning Shall Be Provided?   How much, then, should our future citizens be taught? That "A little learning is a dangerous thing" is true; but the proposed remedy "Therefore drink deeply at the Pierian spring" is not advisable in more than a percentage of the cases. A monarchy in which every citizen was trained for kingship, an army in which every infantry soldier had to be qualified to act as field-marshal, an observatory in which the porters and cleaners were required to be proficient in higher mathematics, or the like, would soon convince us that people who are too clever for their jobs are as troublesome and inefficient as people who are too stupid for them. By all means throw the extremes of learning open to everyone so that no talent or capacity shall be thrown away for lack of training and opportunity. Statesmen must know the importance of this, and see to it that whoever wills and can shall have ways open for them to the utmost instruction. (EPWW-164-165)

Should Everything Be Taught to Everybody? When changing we must be careful not to empty the baby out with the bath in mere reaction against the past. In Russia, for instance, the reaction against the illiteracy and tyranny of capitalist-dominated Tsardom was so intemperate that when it was placed in power by the revolution of 1917, it went too far. Education was decreed for all at the public expense; but authority and discipline in schools were regarded as treasonable. Middle class Bohemianism, mistaken for proletarian emancipation, was at first the order of the day. Teachers were strictly forbidden, as they still rightly are, to hurt children as a teaching method; yet the urgent need for a common doctrine in education, and a religious faith in the omniscience of its prophet, was such that the Soviet Government aimed at making every little Russian a complete Marxist philosopher as madly as Eton aims at making every English boy a complete Latin poet, theologian, and higher mathematician. This inhuman process, restricted at Eton to the plutocratic, professional, and baronial classes by its cost, was imposed in Russia on the entire population. It is not surprising to learn that for years past now discipline has been re-established in the Russian schools, and that though what we call secondary education is provided at the public expense for those proved capable of it, literary scholarship has to be paid for by those who think it worth the money. To teach either Latin versification or the Marxist dialectic to children who should be learning arts and crafts is as wasteful and mischievous as teaching trades or crafts to pupils who are keen on mathematics, history, or languages, but have hardly enough manual dexterity to sharpen their pencils or lace their shoes securely. The educationists who think that everything should be taught to everybody are as bad as the "practical" people at the opposite end who think it is sufficient to teach people the technical routine of the trades or professions by which they will have to earn their livings. Such education may produce efficient robots: it will not produce citizens. (EPWW-172-173)

Treat Every Child as a Potential Genius? Is there, then, an irreducible minimum of aesthetic education as there is of elementary education? Granted that it is waste of time to teach music to a deaf child or painting to a blind one, how far should we treat every child who can hear as a potential Handel, who can see as a potential Raphael, and who can speak and write as a potential Homer or Shakespear, in view of the fact that such prodigies occur in the world perhaps once in many generations? We are tempted to reply "Not at all" but are checked on considering that the value of the prodigies when they do occur is so enormous, and lasts for so many centuries, that everybody should at least be given a chance of attaining creative eminence. For poverty, ignorance, drudgery, hunger, and squalor will extinguish talent and hinder genius; and such extinction goes on all the time wherever ninetenths of the population are proletarians. "Owen Meredith" (the first Earl of Lytton) proclaimed that "Genius is master of Man: Genius does what it must; and talent does what it can"; and certainly, in spite of slavery, serfdom, and proletarianism, ancient Greece produced Phidias and Praxiteles, Eschylus and Sophocles, Aristophanes and Euripides; Italy produced Michael Angelo and Raphael, Titian and Tintoretto; England produced Shakespear, Germany Goethe, Norway Ibsen, and Ireland my astonishing self, to say nothing of the great composers who have carried music to heavenly summits. But none of them came from the illiterate poor. Get rid of the curse of poverty and the possibility of fruitful genius will be multiplied tenfold. (EPWW-173-174)

Leave Higher Cultivation to Individual Choice. When the
child has learnt its social creed and catechism, and can read, write,
reckon, and use its hand: in short, when it is qualified to make its
way about in modern cities and do ordinary useful work, it had
better be left to find out for itself what is good for it in the direction of higher cultivation. If it is a Newton or a Shakespear
it will learn the calculus or the art of the theatre without having
them shoved down its throat: all that is necessary is that it should
have access to books, teachers, and theatres. If its mind does not
want to be highly cultivated, its mind should be let alone on the
ground that its mind knows best what is good for it. Mentally,
fallow is as important as seedtime. Even bodies can be exhausted
by overcultivation. (IWGSC-428)

Secondary Self-Education. There is, fortunately, a great
deal of secondary self-education: indeed civilization would not
hold together if its culture depended on its schools instead of on
its bookshops and lectures and summer schools and general currency of intellectual intercourse. (SE-307)

Education by Discussion & Controversy. At last a superstition has arisen that popular ignorance has some mystic sanction
which makes it more trustworthy than science and knowledge.
This is pestilent nonsense: the truth is that the popular movements
are educated by open discussion and vehement controversy, and
know all the facts and have balanced all the considerations more
thoroughly than the professionals. It is not ignorance shaming
education: it is controversial education shaming dogmatic cram-
ming. (SE-310)

Controversial Education the Solution. The only solution
of the difficulty is controversial education. That is what all the
real education we have at present is. The student must be warned
that religion, science, and philosophy are all fiercely controversial
subjects, and that if he feels interested he must hear champions
of the opposed views fighting it out in debate and be permitted
to question them afterwards.

The result in many cases will be to leave the student in the very common case of a jury unable to agree on its verdict. But juries learn more from such cases than from the plain sailing ones. Controversy is education in itself: a controversially educated person with an open mind is better educated than a dogmatically educated one with a closed mind. The student should hear the case, but should never be asked for a verdict. It may take him forty years to arrive at one. (SE-314)

Persecution & Toleration Must Be Mixed. But if civilization is to be maintained by everybody doing what everybody else does, what is to become of progress, of change, of evolution, of invention, of free will, free thought, free speech, personal rights, and everything that distinguishes living men from automatic stick-in-the-muds? The question comes home to me because in many respects which seem to me of vital importance I want the world to stop doing what everybody is doing and do something else, even to the extent of making some present activities criminal. And history shews that if nobody is allowed to advocate and initiate such changes, civilization will fossilize and perish. So without law and order, convention and etiquet, there can be no civilization; yet when these are established there must be privilege for sedition, blasphemy, heresy, eccentricity, innovation, variety and change, or civilization will crash again by failing to adapt itself to scientific discovery and mental growth. Governments have to persecute and tolerate simultaneously: they have to determine continually what and when to persecute and what and when to tolerate. (EPWW-149)

Laws & Creeds Mutable. The practical conclusion is that though we must teach and enforce a code of morals, and make every child learn its catechism as well as the multiplication and pence tables, yet we must keep all our moral measures open to discussion. The devil's advocate must always be allowed to plead his case against the wisdom and spirit of our laws, though not to resist their execution until he has persuaded us to repeal them.

This is the correct academic attitude; but as opportunities for discussing laws are limited, and the desire for their repeal or alteration is often quite irrational, it may happen that the only way to change the law is for so many people to break it that it becomes a dead letter, in which case it repeals itself, and should be formally repealed by the government lest it should be revived later on for tyrannical purposes.

Under these puzzling circumstances the best we can do educationally is to let children know, as soon as they are capable of such knowledge, that laws and creeds are mutable and not eternal, and must change as our mental and spiritual powers evolve, but are meanwhile necessary instruments of civilized discipline, and indispensable factors in what we call gentlemen's agreements, without which social life is impossible. (EPWW-171-172)

CHRONOLOGICAL BIBLIOGRAPHY

IK   *The Irrational Knot* (1880), New York: Brentano's, 1926.

LAA   *Love Among the Artists* (1881), New York: The Viking Press, Compass Books Edition, 1962.

TSD   "The Transition to Social Democracy" (1888), in *Essays in Fabian Socialism*, London: Constable, 1932.

EBS   "The Economic Basis of Socialism" (1889), *ibid.*

IOA   "The Impossibilities of Anarchism" (1891), *ibid.*

WH   *Widower's Houses* (1892), in *Plays, Pleasant & Unpleasant, Volume I: The Three Unpleasant Plays: Widower's Houses, The Philanderer, and Mrs. Warren's Profession*, New York: Brentano's, 1912.

TP   *The Philanderer* (1893), *ibid.*

MWP   *Mrs. Warren's Profession* (1893), *ibid.*

C   *Candida* (1894), Baltimore: Penguin Books, 1961.

SSB   "Socialism & Superior Brains" (1894), in *Essays in Fabian Socialism*.

SFM   "Socialism for Millionaires" (1896), *ibid.*

YNCT   *You Never Can Tell* (1896), New York: Dodd, Mead, 1926.

MS   *Man and Superman* (1901-03), New York: Brentano's, 1905.

RHPC   *The Revolutionist's Handbook and Pocket Companion* (1903), (Appendix to *Man and Superman*).

HHLHH   *How He Lied to Her Husband* (1904), in *John Bull's Other Island, How He Lied to Her Husband, and Major Barbara*, London: Constable, 1931.

CSMT   "The Common Sense of Municipal Trading" (1904), in *Essays in Fabian Socialism.*

P-IK   Preface to *The Irrational Knot* (1905), New York: Brentano's, 1926.

MB   *Major Barbara* (1905), in *op. cit.*

P-MB   Preface to *Major Barbara, ibid.*

GM   *Getting Married* (1908), in *The Doctor's Dilemma, Getting Married, and The Shewing-Up of Blanco Posnet*, New York: Brentano's, 1918.

P-GM   Preface to *Getting Married, ibid.*

M   *Misalliance* (1910), in *Misalliance, The Dark Lady of the Sonnets, and Fanny's First Play*, London: Constable, 1932.

P-M   Preface to *Misalliance, ibid.*

AL   *Androcles and the Lion* (1911-12), in *Androcles and the Lion, Overruled, and Pygmalion*, London: Constable, 1939.

E-AL   Epilogue to *Androcles and the Lion, ibid.*

P-P   Postscript to *Pygmalion* (1912-13), Baltimore: Penguin Books, 1951.

O   *Overruled* (1912), in *Seven One-Act Plays*, Baltimore: Penguin Books, 1958.

P-O   Preface to *Overruled, ibid.*

HH   *Heartbreak House* (1913-16), in *Heartbreak House, Great Catherine, and Playlets of the War*, New York: Brentano's, 1919.

P-AL   Preface (1915) to *Androcles and the Lion*, in *op. cit.*

SE   *Sham Education* (1918), in *Doctors' Delusions, Crude Criminology, and Sham Education*, London: Constable, 1950.

PCH   *Peace Conference Hints*, London: Constable, 1919.

BM   *Back to Methuselah* (1921), New York: Brentano's, 1929.

CC   *Crude Criminology* (1921-22), in *op. cit.*

IWGSC   *The Intelligent Woman's Guide to Socialism and Capitalism* (1928), New York: Brentano's, 1928.

AC   *The Apple Cart* (1929), Baltimore: Penguin Books, 1956.

P-AC   Preface (1930) to *The Apple Cart, ibid.*

P-FE   Preface to *Fabian Essays* (1931 reprint, Jubilee Edition), London: George Allen & Unwin, 1948.

TTTBG   *Too True To Be Good* (1931), in *Too True To Be Good, Village Wooing, and On the Rocks*, New York: Dodd, Mead, 1934.

P-TTTBG   Preface (1933) to *Too True To Be Good, ibid.*

VW   *Village Wooing* (1933), in *Seven One-Act Plays, op. cit.*

OR   *On the Rocks* (1933), in *op. cit.*

P-OR   Preface to *On the Rocks, ibid.*

FPSA   *The Future of Political Science in America* (1933), New York: Dodd, Mead, 1933.

P-SUI   Preface to *The Simpleton of the Unexpected Isles* (1935), in *The Simpleton, The Six, and The Millionairess*, London: Constable, 1936.

P-TM   Preface to *The Millionairess* (1935), *ibid.*

TM   *The Millionairess* (1936), *ibid.*

EPWW   *Everybody's Political What's What?* (1944), London: Constable, 1944.

SSS   *Sixteen Self Sketches* (1947), New York: Dodd, Mead, 1949.

BB   *Buoyant Billions* (1947), in *Buoyant Billions, Farfetched Fables, and Shakes Versus Shav*, New York: Dodd, Mead, 1951.

FF   *Farfetched Fables* (1948), *ibid.*

P-FF   Preface (1948-49) to *Farfetched Fables, ibid.*

About the Editor

N. H. LEIGH-TAYLOR, who writes also under the name
N. H. Taylor, was born in Capetown, South Africa, in 1913,
and came to the United States with his family in 1927,
settling in Los Angeles, California, where he has lived
ever since. His Scots wife Janet, to whom he has been
married for twenty-nine years, is a harpist. Their daughter
Elizabeth, who is nineteen, is an artist. Leigh-Taylor has
been a Shavian for more than thirty years, having been
introduced to the works of Shaw by his own father. Like
Bernard Shaw, he began his professional journalistic career
in his twenties as a critic, writing music reviews for a
California fortnightly called *Pacific Coast Musician*. Later,
under several names, he wrote columns on art, books,
music, the theater and films for the California magazine of
opinion, *Frontier*. At age twenty-seven, inspired by Shaw's
The Perfect Wagnerite, he wrote a short book on the
modern composer Arnold Schoenberg, for whom he had
worked as literary adviser, and called it *The Astute Schoenbergian*. The work was printed in condensed form in 1944
in S. I. Hayakawa's *ETC., A Review of General Semantics*.
The author's dedication on *The Astute Schoenbergian*
was "To Bernard Shaw, who shakes hands with the future
without waiting for an introduction." A shorter version of
the *Ready-Reckoner* was compiled in 1939-1940, when
Leigh-Taylor was twenty-six. It was never published. The
present work is an enlargement of the book completed a
quarter century ago, and incorporates material written by
Shaw up to the time of his death in 1950.